DATE DUE

JE 1 0 '09			

Upward Dreams, Downward Mobility

Upward Dreams, Downward Mobility

The Economic Decline of the American Middle Class

Frederick R. Strobel

Rowman & Littlefield Publishers, Inc.

ROWMAN & LITTLEFIELD PUBLISHERS, INC.

Published in the United States of America
by Rowman & Littlefield Publishers, Inc.
4720 Boston Way, Lanham, Maryland 20706

British Cataloging in Publication Information Available

Library of Congress Cataloging-in-Publication Data
Strobel, Frederick R.
Upward dreams, downward mobility : the economic decline of the
American middle class / Frederick R. Strobel.
p.   cm.
Includes bibliographical references and index.
1. Middle classes—United States. 2. United States—Economic
policy—1981–. 3. United States—Economic conditions—1981–.
I. Title.
HT690.U6S77   1992   305.5'5'0973   92-28014   CIP

ISBN 0-8476-7756-7 (cloth : alk. paper)

Printed in the United States of America

The paper used in this publication meets the minimum requirements of American
National Standard for Information Sciences—Permanence of Paper for Printed
Library Materials, ANSI Z39.48–1984.

Contents

Chart and Tables   vii

Preface   ix

Introduction: Downward Mobility: The New American
Middle-class Reality   xi

PART I: THE RISE AND FALL OF THE NEW DEAL

1   Building the New Deal: The Foundation for an
Expanding Middle Class   3

2   Undoing the New Deal   21

PART II: THE ASCENT OF CAPITAL, THE DESCENT
OF THE MIDDLE CLASS

3   The Economic Facts: Middle-class Decline and the New
Super Rich   41

4   Washington's Failure at Home and Abroad: The Decline
Begins in the Early 1970s   55

5   Methods of Capital Ascent: The Frontal Assault by
Corporate America   73

6   Shifting the Tax Burden: "The Great Escape" of
    Corporate America   91

7   The Argument Summarized: Eleven Reasons for
    Middle-class Decline   103

**PART III: THE DECLINE ACCELERATES: AMERICA
             IN THE REAGAN–BUSH YEARS**

8   Reaganomics: A Wolf in Sheep's Clothing   123

9   Twilight in America: The Reagan–Bush Economic
    Legacy   133

PART IV: AT THE END OF THE DAY

10 Two Nations in America: The Consequences of a
    Two-class Society   165

11 What Happened? The Failure of Key Institutions   179

12 Rescuing the Middle Class: Some Modest Proposals   187

Epilogue: Middle-class Issues in the 1992 Presidential
             Campaign and Beyond   207

Index   227

About the Author   231

Chart and Tables

Chart

3-1   Average Weekly Earnings, United States, 1947–1991   49

Tables

2-1   Tax Share of Total Federal Receipts during Presidential
      Administrations, 1945–1992   29

2-2   Average Tax Share of Total Federal Receipts, 1934–1992   31

3-1   Distribution of U.S. Families by Income, 1973–1984   45

4-1   U.S. Foreign Trade and Gross National Product, Selected
      Years   57

4-2   Change in U.S. Average Weekly Earnings, Productivity,
      and Prices, 1950–1991   58

4-3   Employment Growth of Selected U.S. Nonagricultural
      Sectors, 1950–1989   59

4-4   "High" Estimate of Immigrant Component in U.S.
      Labor-force Growth, 1978–1986   63

4-5   "Low" Estimate of Immigrant Component in U.S.
      Labor-force Growth, 1978–1986   64

4-6   Government Employees on Nonagricultural Payrolls in
      the United States, 1950–1989   68

4-7   Goods-producing and Service-producing Employment,
      1946–1991   69

6-1   Percentage Contribution of Federal Receipts by Source,
      1949–1991 and Estimated 1992   93

6-2   State and Local Taxes with an Initial Impact on Business
      and on Individuals, by Type of Tax, 1957, 1962, 1967,
      1977   95

6-3   Percentage Contribution of State and Local Receipts by
      Source, Selected Years during 1977–1990   96

6-4   Real Personal and Business Savings per Employee in the
      United States, Selected Years during 1960–1990   99

6-5   Business Savings, Personal Savings, and U.S. Gross
      National Product, Selected Years during 1946–1990   100

9-1   Federal Fiscal Trends, 1961–1992   134

9-2   U.S. Investment Behavior Measures, 1961–1992   136

9-3   Selected U.S. Economic Performance Measures, Annual
      Average Percentages, 1961–1991   138

9-4   U.S. Productivity, Compensation, and Savings,
      1961–1988   140

9-5   Business Savings and Investment in the United States,
      1980–1988   142

Preface

Since the early years of the Reagan administration, when the massive business tax cuts were enacted and the prevalent economic philosophy swung to the right of Adam Smith, my thoughts turned to writing a book on the economic impact of what was dubbed "Reaganomics." This project I began as a visiting scholar in the hospitable Economics Department at Michigan State University in 1988, while on leave from Kalamazoo College.

Embarking on the project, I found that the numbers confirmed my suspicions of a general economic decline of the average American partly stemming from the policies of the Reagan administration. However, it also became evident that this decline had actually begun in the early 1970s, if not the late 1960s. And this was a change in the economic status of the American middle class, not for the better but for the worse, which meant an enlarged lower class. My focus then turned to the necessarily longer time period which encompasses the rise and demise of the American middle class in which Reaganomics was a part, but not the whole. The book nonetheless concludes that the decline certainly accelerated in the Reagan–Bush years, and continues to the date of this writing.

Not having completed a project of this type for a number of years, I had forgotten the loneliness of the nature of such research and writing. But I had also forgotten the satisfaction of new discovery, new conclusions, and equally, the personal enrichment from the help and encouragement of colleagues, friends and loved ones, new and old, one finds along the way.

At Michigan State I'm particularly indebted to the following for their insights, ideas, and time generously given: Walter Adams, Charles Ballard, Dan Hamermesh, Harry Holzer, Nancy Jianakopolis, Paul Menchik, Bob Rasche, Warren Samuels, and John Wolfe.

At Kalamazoo College my colleagues David Barclay, Jeanine Braithwaite, Hannah McKinney, and Blaine Gilles all spent considerable time reading the manuscript, making meaningful suggestions, and giving no small measure of encouragement. Other help came from colleagues David Strauss, Bob Stauffer, Gary Dorrien, Scotty Allen, Ahmed Hussen, Phil Thomas, Tom Breznau, Dick Means, and Kim Cummings. Kalamazoo College funding was also very helpful.

I'm particularly indebted to Kim McQuaid of Lake Erie College whose work on business influence in Washington contributed substantially to the book's historical content and analysis. Paul Zane Pilzer of Dallas, James Brock of Miami University of Ohio, and Kim McQuaid also all gave me some meaningful suggestions and encouragement. Also helpful were Michael Ames, David Broder, Tom Edsall, Ellen Hosmer, Ross LaRoe, Drake McFeely, Kit Ward, and Congressman Howard Wolpe.

At Rowman and Littlefield I'm thankful to Maureen Muncaster for her early and strong confidence in the book. Editor Jon Sisk gave me many good ideas, but allowed me maximum freedom in making this truly my book. Copyeditor Pat Merrill of Melbourne, Florida, pursued her craft with such thoroughness and understanding of the content that the book's readability, style, and message are greatly improved.

To Chris Snyder whose organizational and word-processing skills are superb, I am deeply grateful. Also assisting in a significant way in manuscript preparation were Marjorie Smith, Theresa Perry, Kari Foreback, Connie Haigh, and Stacy Panigay.

Nearly last but not least, I'm indebted to those close to me who have given me much and have tolerated my absences and preoccupations while completing this work: Kathleen Cashen, Gretchen, Heidi, and Marilyn Strobel.

Finally my thanks go out to Roger Van Tassel and the late James Maxwell of Clark University, my professors, mentors, friends.

Frederick R. Strobel
Lake Park, Michigan
August 1992

Introduction
Downward Mobility:
The New Middle-class Reality

The American middle class in the 1990s is under tremendous financial and emotional pressure. The financial pressure is from higher taxes at all levels, lower pay increases, and higher medical costs with less insurance coverage. Along with this is a genuine fear of job loss as more and more American manufacturers shut their doors due to foreign competition while still others "downsize" their companies to avoid the same. In many cases, the fear of job loss becomes reality not only from competitive factors, but from mergers, acquisitions, and takeovers, much of which has been fueled by dishonest financial practices.

With all of this, the middle class is confused and dispirited. Yet it doesn't understand what is really happening. What it does understand, however—and is perfectly justified in its understanding—is that it and its children, for the first time in the "American experience," are downwardly mobile.

So why doesn't it stand up and fight? Because it has been lulled by a slow, steady erosion of its economic benefits. As the erosion began, wives began to work part-time and then full-time. But that only kept the wolf at bay. What has happened since 1973 is that the two-earner middle-class family has been eroded in numbers and in economic vitality. Yet, the middle class plugs on, working harder, thinking somehow it can hang on.

The middle class is bombarded by politicians and economists who claim that America doesn't save enough, that Americans import too much, and that Americans are not hardworking and productive. Yet most two-earner family adults work from eight to six every day and longer hours thereafter, looking after kids. Very little time remains for political or intellectual pursuits. They buy imports because they're cheap and they don't save because there's no money left over.

The American middle class is the hardest working in the world. It works the longest hours, with the shortest vacations, and is provided less in the way of government services than any of the major industrial giants such as Canada, England, France, Germany, Australia, Japan, or the Scandinavian nations. But the enormous demands placed on the middle class leave little time nor energy to figure out why the economic system is failing them. So more political activity is concentrated into simple, single-issue politics such as prayer in the schools, abortion or freedom of choice, or flag burning. The real financial and economic issues are just too complicated.

Without an economically sound middle class—one that comprises the majority of the population—the American democratic and capitalist systems cannot survive. This is a book about economics. It is about the rise of a prosperous middle class in the post–World War II era and its subsequent unraveling since the late 1960s. It is not a book about American culture or American social history, nor is it a sociological study of the American middle class. Mainly it defines the middle class in *economic terms* as being a body of wage earners who are able to find meaningful work and receive meaningful compensation to care for their families' physical and medical needs. This group should be able to support its local government and schools and provide for its own retirement through savings. Millions of Americans did just this up until the late 1960s. However, since then a number of forces and individuals have brought about a betrayal, a disintegration, and a demoralization of middle America, complete with deteriorating public schools, crumbling roads, and unsafe streets.

Middle America is not uneducated nor was it born yesterday. Rather, it does not have the time and energy—because it is so hard pressed to survive—to figure out the flaws in the current political system that leaves it unrepresented. It is justifiably angry when major corporations beat up on the local city government to get a tax break. Yet its recourse is to risk being fired for expressing a contrary opinion. It is bombarded with the virtues of free trade, yet it watches the local manufacturing plant close, stripping away many middle-class jobs and benefits. It tolerated the huge business tax cuts such as those in 1981 that were granted for the purpose of new investments and jobs. Yet then the middle class watches these corporations take that money, buy out their competition, lay off workers, or buy back their own stock and privatize their corporation. The managers of these corporations reap huge profits with the middle-class's tax money; and it is left holding the bag, with fewer jobs and higher property taxes.

THE PLAN OF THIS BOOK

What follows might seem to be a complicated argument; however, the average reader who bears with it will understand and grasp its meaning and significance. My plan in explaining the demise of the American middle class is to divide the problem into four parts and accordingly label them as Parts I through IV.

Part I will trace the rise of the American middle class, largely rooted in the New Deal reforms instituted by Franklin Delano Roosevelt. It explains what the New Deal did for the middle class and how the New Deal was unraveled, setting in motion the decline of the middle class.

Part II will explain the magnitude of the middle-class decline as observed by a number of studies. It will also explain the decline due to changing world events—some avoidable, others not. It will also show that the demise of the American middle class is largely associated with the rise of private economic power and the concentration of wealth into fewer and fewer hands at the same time as a decline in the economic and democratic power of labor. Part II also explains the trump card that capital holds in store: the elimination of all corporate taxes and a subsequent shifting of those taxes to the middle and lower classes through a national sales tax, commonly referred to as a "value-added tax" (VAT).

Part III assesses the Reagan role and the decline of the middle class. It discusses Reaganomics and what it was supposed to do, namely promote the United States as a number-one world economic power, creating prosperity and jobs for all. It concludes that its corporate tax cuts, personal income tax increases, anti–wage earner behavior, and scandalous financial mismanagement accelerated the middle-class decline and made America a second-rate economic power behind Germany and Japan.

Finally, Part IV assesses America "at the end of the day"—America at the end of a long era of decline that must, somehow, engineer a new sunrise. It examines the consequences of an American two-class society, such as the loss of the mass market, and the decline of professional jobs along with traditional middle class white- and blue-collar jobs. The decline of the American middle class in manufacturing, retailing, and other services will bring with it a decline in the demand for lawyers,

physicians, nurses, real estate salespersons, and even professional athletes. With an impoverished middle class, we face a more impoverished
government, unable to support educational systems and protect its citizens
from a rising tide of crime and violence associated with poverty, joblessness, and drugs. Under these conditions, the chances for the survival of
political democracy and capitalism as we know it today are dim. Moreover, we may be increasing the odds for the rise of "the messiah" who will
soothe and solve all of our problems. Such messiahs, as we have seen in
the twentieth century, can come in many forms; they show a tendency to
pick many scapegoats, and after their rise to power they have a habit of
suspending or materially curtailing civil liberties.

There is a solution though. There is a road back home to the middle
class. It is a long one, however, since the unraveling of the middle class
has come over a long period of time. The answer lies in the political parties
providing us with a true alternative. The Democrats, to survive, must
become Democrats again and go back to their traditional role of representing those classes of people who are mainly dependent on their labor
or on their small savings for survival. The party of Franklin Roosevelt
should abandon the principles of me-too support for American businesses
that they have recently borrowed and embraced from the Republicans. A
new economic policy should be established in the United States that is
supported by a revitalized labor movement with all labor—not just union
labor—at the heart of its concern. This new economic policy should
include economic thinking that will get back to more philosophical roots
and look at the economy less on a narrow efficiency-based model and
more on a human scale. The United States is greatly in need of a new
national and international economic and industrial policy. Solid arguments have been made in this regard particularly by Robert Reich, but
they have been largely ignored or forgotten.[1]

The initial purpose of this book was to measure the economic impact
of the Reagan economic policies during the 1980s. However, it soon
became evident that the real story of the American economy has been the
decline of the middle class—a phenomenon that became observable in the
late 1960s and early 1970s. Much has been written and documented about
the plight of the American poor and the American underclass yet little has
been done. Perhaps when the plight of the shrinking middle class is made
known, then America will act politically to steer government policy in a
more humane direction.

The author professes to be free from most ideologies save for two: the
principles of political and of economic democracy. This book is written

with the firm conviction that the best way to protect American business and American capitalism is to return to the economics of balance that were practiced by Franklin Delano Roosevelt and that have all but been abandoned. American business and American capital will not be stable nor protected by their government unless politically supported by a strong and vibrant middle class. Nor will business be economically healthy if it is not supported by sufficient purchasing power, and that can only come through a broad-based domestic mass market.

NOTE

1. See, e.g., Robert Reich, *The Next American Frontier* (New York: Times Books, 1983); or Barry Bluestone and Bennett Harrison, *The De-industrialization of America* (New York: Basic Books, 1982).

PART I

THE RISE AND FALL
OF THE NEW DEAL

1

Building the New Deal:
The Foundation for an Expanding
Middle Class

> The important thing for government is not to do
> things which individuals are doing already, and not
> to do them a little better or a little worse; but to do
> those things which at present are not done at all.
>
> John Maynard Keynes

> Just as there must be balance in what a community
> produces, so there must also be a balance in what a
> community consumes.
>
> John Kenneth Galbraith

This book is about the economic condition of the United States. It seeks
to compile information, evaluate it, and, in doing so, place in historical
context the economic impact of the Reagan presidency on the American
people—particularly the middle class. It is written in the hope that
American policymakers—be they government officials, labor leaders,
enlightened members of the business community, or voters—will be
better informed in order to effect changes in the current undesirable
direction of income distribution. It concludes that the American middle
class is shrinking and that this shrinkage is reflected largely in a growing
"under", or lower, class. At the same time it concludes that the economic
quality of life of those still in the middle class is deteriorating. The upper

class is the beneficiary of the above pattern, growing slightly in number but greatly in quality of life, as represented by income and wealth accumulation.

It must further be pointed out that the decline of the middle class did not happen overnight. The story of the decline began with the ascent of capital power in the early 1970s and has continued steadily ever since. Since we are now probably 20 years into a long-run redistribution of income to the wealthy, there will be no quick political fix within the bounds of democracy. Further, since there is no meaningful discussion of the real problem of the American economy, a massive capital–labor power imbalance, the prospects for soon restoring the middle class to its once economic vibrancy are bleak.

This chapter will argue that New Deal measures, which aimed at a better balance of income distribution between labor and capital, were largely conceived by the actions of Franklin Roosevelt and advanced the size and well-being of the American middle class. It will further argue here, as in subsequent chapters, that such New Deal concepts were never fully recognized by politicians or by economists. The result has been an unraveling of the New Deal and thus a reversal in the size and well-being of the American middle class, and great gains in the power of capital.

THE ECONOMIC ACTIONS OF THE NEW DEAL

If you ask the average American what the New Deal was, he or she would probably respond by saying, "The New Deal was a series of measures designed to lift the United States out of the Depression." This answer would have a ring of truth to it. However, the New Deal was more of a series of actions which attempted to address the economic imbalance between capital, as represented by big business, and labor—especially the middle class. Rather than trying to stimulate the economy by massive government spending programs, the New Deal was more one of economic reform, which put in place many programs, to protect the middle class and to allow upward mobility into it, from the ranks of the poor. These measures began in the first 100 days of FDR's first term in 1933 and ended in 1938. By 1938, further extensions of the New Deal to blacks and other minorities were precluded by Roosevelt's need to keep the support of the conservative South for his military buildup in the face of the gathering storm. The president had also been politically damaged by his unsuccessful efforts to pack the Supreme Court.

The overall program is generally divided into two parts. The first New Deal, chiefly beneficial to big business and large farmers, dates from 1933 to mid-1934; after 1934 came the second New Deal chiefly beneficial to labor and smaller farmers.

Greedy business behavior under the first New Deal tipped the scales in favor of making the second New Deal a more prolabor program. The National Recovery Act (NRA), passed on June 16, 1933, sought to ensure a reasonable profit to industry and living wages for labor. Businesses were allowed to form trade associations, and fix or raise prices in such ways as to ensure reasonable profits. In return, business was to observe in good faith the provisions of section 7A of the NRA, which granted to labor newer powers to unionize and elect its own representatives who could enter into collective bargaining. Business practice, however, was generally otherwise. It benefited from the monopolistic practices granted to it by the NRA, but stepped up its anti-union practices of company spies, company unions, discriminatory discharge, and wholesale layoffs. The results were vastly improved profits totally out of line with the continued misery of labor markets. Roosevelt, disgusted with the "economic royalists" of big business, swung the New Deal's weight to directly intervening on the side of labor, ceasing to directly aid capital, and, in many cases, curtailing its power.

After the first Agricultural Adjustment Act, which aided more larger farmers than smaller ones, and the National Recovery Act, which attempted to aid both business and labor simultaneously, the rest of the New Deal legislation (the *second* New Deal) falls primarily into three categories: prolabor, profarmer, or business regulatory. Under the prolabor heading we could list the legislation creating the Tennessee Valley Authority (TVA), the Boulder and Grand Cooley dams, and other electricity-generating plants at Bonneville in the Columbia River and at Fort Peck, Montana. Such plants provided low-cost hydroelectric power that was used not only for the countryside but also for production of electricity for the cities. While businesses benefited from this low-cost power, its main beneficiaries were hundreds of thousands of farmers and ordinary citizens. The Civil Works Administration, which employed some 4 million people on "make work" projects between November 8, 1933, and April 1, 1934, was also a decidedly prolabor measure. Joining the prolabor measures were the Railroad Retirement Act of 1935, the Social Security Act of 1935, and the establishment of the Works Progress Administration (WPA) in the same year. Similarly prolabor was the National Youth Administration, designed in 1935 to educate and employ the disaffected youth of the country. And of course the final passage of the Fair Labor Standards Act to ensure minimum wage standards, and the dramatic passage of the Wagner Act (otherwise known as the National Labor Relations Act), were measures chiefly designed to benefit labor. The Wagner Act guaranteed the right of unions to collective bargaining and established the National Labor Relations Board (NLRB) to investigate unfair employment practices by employers.

Other notable prolabor acts were the creation of the Federal Writers Project and the Federal Theatre Project. In the housing area, the New Deal initiated the Housing Administration (which lent $600 million to communities for slum rehabilitation), the Federal Housing Administration (FHA), which guaranteed mortgages, and also the creation of the Homeowners Loan Corporation, which helped about 1 million distressed homeowners.

For aid to the farmer, there was the Agriculture Adjustment Act of 1933 (and its subsequent amendments) and the Soil Conservation Act of 1936 to aid in the conservation of soil, particularly given the increased erosion in the Dust Bowl. Measures were also taken to help farmers retain their landownership as well as to help the nearly 3 million tenants and sharecroppers who had lost their land. Cooperatives were encouraged, and the Rural Electrification Administration (REA) and the Farm Credit Administration were created.

The business regulatory side witnessed the passage of the Securities Act of May 27, 1933, the Glass Steagal Banking Act on June 16 of that year, the Securities Exchange Act of 1934, and the Communications Act of 1934, which created the Federal Communications Commission (FCC).

In sum, a cursory examination of the major New Deal legislation passed between 1933 and 1938, with the exception of the National Recovery Act and the First Agricultural Adjustment Act, gives the general conclusion that business became more highly regulated while labor as a class was aided either directly through relief payments or assistance with mortgage finance or indirectly through improvements in the unionization process. The farmer received similar aid as did, to a lesser extent, former tenants and sharecroppers who lost their land.

Two other important pieces of New Deal legislation are worth noting in that they both took aim at wealth concentration. The Wealth Tax Act, which was passed on August 30, 1935, created a schedule of corporate income taxes depending on firm size. Smaller corporations paid lower rates, to 12.5 percent, larger corporations paid up to 15 percent, but also additional taxes on "excess profits." Taxes on individual incomes were graduated steeply, particularly on incomes between $1 million and $5 million. The other important piece of legislation was the Public Utility Holding Company Act. This act, passed on August 28, 1935, permitted only two levels of holding companies above operating companies. It specified a "death sentence" of five years, at the end of which term any holding companies that could not show their "useful character" would be forced to dissolve.

NEW DEAL THEORIES
(OR NONTHEORIES) CONSIDERED

Above we have painted in broad-brush strokes the major legislative achievements of the New Deal. There are many theories as to why the New Deal took place. Indeed, there are some theories that the New Deal was not "new" at all. Let us briefly examine some of these notions and their plausibility.

One simplistic theory espoused by many businesspersons and conservatives at the time, and still held by many today, was that the New Deal represented simply a movement toward socialism. While the New Deal did have some socialist elements—such as the Rural Electrification Administration and the establishment of the Tennessee Valley Authority, along with some make-work projects such as the Civilian Conservation Corps and the Works Progress Administration—the vast bulk of legislation prescribed government *regulation* of the *private* market. While the movement in electricity might be called more socialist, what basically survives of that today is the Tennessee Valley Authority. Socialism implies the social ownership and control of capital by the government, and an excellent example of a country moving generally toward a democratic socialism was Britain following World War II and up until the advent of Margaret Thatcher. The New Deal, in contrast, was more regulatory than socialistic, essentially regulating the private economy and redefining the rules of the game. The rules had to do with how labor organized itself, how it might be protected from unemployment and poverty in old age, and how to regulate capital markets and banking. The one significant socialistic program that survives today from the New Deal is the Social Security System. Here was created a government-run, voter-controlled pension system, which one could argue could have been performed by the private sector. But since mixed economies have long included such systems—witness Bismarck's Germany, which introduced social security in the 1880s—it is not very credible to suggest that the New Deal was "socialist" on this basis.

According to economist Rexford Tugwell, perhaps the most genuinely constructive part of the New Deal would consist not in its relieving the misery and anxieties of the Depression, nor even in its introducing long-delayed reforms. According to Tugwell, the key was that the New Deal took the minimum measures to ensure that the depression might not reoccur. Thus, according to Tugwell, it was mainly an anti-Depression action, or set of actions.[1] Tugwell recognized the magnitude of the crisis and also the fact that, given the misery present in the United States among the unemployed, something had to be done—even relief through temporary projects. But Tugwell also emphasizes the more long-run constructive or structural changes in the economy that were designed to prevent future economic disasters of this magnitude. He claims that Roosevelt redefined "traditional" progressivism and called it the "New Deal." Additionally, Tugwell defines the New Deal by stressing the role of Roosevelt's personality in constructing this set of social programs. Indeed, one wonders about the possibility of none or very little of these programs, or set of programs known as the New Deal, coming into existence without the uniqueness of personality of Franklin D. Roosevelt, an accident of political history. Tugwell and others have stressed the willingness of Roosevelt to experiment—to try something and, if it failed, go ahead and try something new. The personality angle reoccurs in many writings. To quote Tugwell, "There were few who ever saw him [Roosevelt] with the mask of confidence removed ... and if he was often uncurtained [sic], as a ... quarterback of a team ... it was not a fundamental uncertainty, only a tentativeness about tactic.... It was his game; and on the whole it was his victory." Tugwell further writes, "The New Deal may have been a progressive interlude in an America predominantly reactionary."[2]

The interesting challenge in arriving at an economic theory of the New Deal is to discern what was really in Roosevelt's pattern of thinking as he acted. Obviously a good part of the program was experimental. Tugwell quotes "Laski's dictum" to the effect that a president cannot always establish institutions which outrun either public opinion or the public's understanding of what is appropriate. The United States was then, as it is today, a very pro-big-business country. So, to a major extent, Roosevelt was constrained in his progressive efforts.

It appears that Roosevelt had a scheme or a plan in mind. To quote Tugwell again, "Roosevelt's team had a purpose. There would be failures but the team would ultimately win.... [I]ndeed they had a singlemindedness."[3] It is this single-mindedness, or scheme which may well have been in Roosevelt's mind, which is the interesting historical question. Indeed, this leads me to what will be my economic theory of the New Deal.

But before I lay my cards on the table, let us examine some other theories of the New Deal. Much that has been written about the New Deal has been done so by historians, economists, or political scientists who had great sympathy with its aims. It is interesting to look at some of those accounts that were more critical. Charles Beard, an often scathing critic of FDR, claimed that "the New Deal was no revolution in class arrangements, no proletarian upheaval, no fabrication designed by socialists. It sprang essentially from the efforts of the property classes in distress to save their claims to farms, homes, banks, railways, financial institutions and investments from … liquidation." They did so by forcing the government of the United States to "underwrite their nominal claims to values with money … borrowed at the risk of coming generations."[4] He states that, if the federal government had not yielded to the outcry of the above groups, the results probably would have been even more disastrous than the dire warnings of the New Deal's conservative critics.[5] In fact, Beard's 1940 article entitled "An Epitome of Characteristics" basically claims that the private economy not only had failed to manage its own affairs but also had failed to accept the economic results of this poor management, which would mean the liquidation to market value of many existing assets. As a result, the federal government stepped in with inflationary techniques to rescue the people, but with the consequence that the people surrendered a certain amount of their independence from the government. There occurred a transference to the executive of a highly discretionary authority in relation to banking, currency, and spending and the "old system of checks and balances, political and economic, was profoundly altered."[6] Indeed Beard sees the New Deal as the establishment of a large political machine composed of government employees steadily growing in number, who created a self-fulfilling prophecy toward more government. This machine would be self-promoting, rally around Roosevelt with its "huge conscript army" and its "immense administrative bureaucracy," so that the phrase *riding into Congress on the president's coattails* is more than a pleasing euphemism. Indeed, Beard saw it as leading eventually to such control of the American populace as to promote the armaments industry, which then might lead further to the likelihood of war.

One especially interesting part of Beard's analysis is his argument that the 1920s created many voters now in the propertied class, who could swing the political spectrum away from the traditional rugged individualism of the average American voter who had previously allowed the conservative wealthy classes to maintain a hands-off government. Suddenly, the small farmer and the small property owner were united with unemployed labor. These perplexed voters, united very quickly, lost their free-market ideology and with it their need to support the aims of the wealthy propertied classes. The very wealthy—the financier, the banking community, the industrialists—were for their part equally perplexed. For the first time they realized that the macroeconomic management of an economy might be beyond the powers of their individual industries. The all-powerful had been brought to their knees!

To give an example, Basil Rauch wrote,

> The bankers were in a chastened mood; they had lost confidence in themselves. Three and a half years of [stock market] attrition ending in the rout of the previous weeks, the disgrace for malpractice of many of their leaders ... and the forceful lesson that their power and privileges derived ultimately from the power of the people's government, brought them to Washington eager to do its bidding.[7]

And again Rauch writes, "The bankers' confusion and willingness to give up responsibility to the government was an extraordinary display of the effects of loss of security in a class ordinarily quite self-reliant."[8]

Another poignant description of the times by historian Arthur M. Schlesinger, Jr., is that the official order in the 1920s presented perhaps the nearest we ever came to the identification of our national interest with the interest and goals of a specific class—in this case, the American business community. The more recent equivalent of that attitude could probably be summed up in a famous remark of a former General Motors president, "Engine Charlie" Wilson: "What's good for General Motors is good for America." But at that point—in 1932—the business community had lost its self-confidence, its bravado, and its all-knowing attitude toward economic affairs. It was willing to abdicate the throne, and to combine with the unemployed, the small property owners, small farmers, and small businesspersons, in allowing the government—that is, all the people—to propose the solution. In sum, a new political coalition was created.

Beard's theory that the New Deal was in essence a response to everybody (including big business) who had lost out in the Depression, clamoring to be saved by the government contains some elements of truth, but overall is still lacking. Roosevelt's first efforts (in the first New Deal) were very business oriented. When this produced an even more skewed distribution of income, he moved to aid labor in general, unemployed labor, the small farmer, the small businessperson, and the small-propertied (homeowners) class through his second New Deal. Beard is correct about the political coalition that brought Roosevelt to power. However, this is the significant theoretical point of the New Deal's actions: the coalition or political phenomenon that produced Roosevelt's election, and that promoted the New Deal, was the traditional coalition of producer groups—that is, capital, or big business, whose leaders played effective roles in shaping New Deal legislation—*and* the labor-dependent classes such as the small farmer and small homeowner, small businessperson, and the insecure laborer. Strange bedfellows indeed. However, the results of the New Deal turned the distribution of economic rewards away from traditional lines of economic theory that were *producer* oriented.[9] The New Deal allowed government to redistribute rewards more toward the *labor-dependent* classes, which in addition to labor includes the small farmer and small businessperson. While big business or capital were well represented (and heard from) in the White House, Roosevelt, with a not inconsiderable amount of support and help from their ranks, particularly the Business Council, created and nurtured his New Deal, whose main beneficiaries were the labor-dependent class.[10]

One of the contentions of this book will be that it is the eventual ignoring of the lessons of history—particularly with regard to identifying a single interest, namely, big business as a god, as capable of prophesying infallible economic policies—that eventually unwound the New Deal. To put it another way, the restoration of the overblown confidence of big business as the economy grew and prospered subsequent to the New Deal is a chief reason for the economic problems we face today. Human memory is short. Lessons are often forgotten—and so are such valuable maxims as, "Be nice to people on the way up; you may need them on the way down."

Another major theory (or nontheory) concerning the New Deal is put forth by Benjamin Stolberg and Warren Jay Vinton. In 1935, Stolberg and Vinton claimed that the New Deal did nothing more than a first-rate earthquake would do, namely, reestablish scarcity and "put all the survivors to work for the greater glory of Big Business."[11]

Their criticism was that, because the New Deal tried to be all things to all people, it was ineffective. Stolberg and Vinton claim that for "big ownership it tried to keep intact its financial domination. For the middle class, its aims to safeguard their small investments only served to reintrench big business, and for labor its efforts to raise wages and employment were negated by its efforts to raise scarcity ... in trying to move in every direction at once the New Deal betrays the fact that it has no policy."[12] It was a "nontheory."

In another revealing observation, they state that the New Deal had no policy "because as a liberal democracy it must ignore the overwhelming fact of our epoch, the irreconcilable conflict between capital and labor."[13] This simple statement raises a number of critical issues.

First, it is my contention that at the root of the New Deal was a reconciliation between the forces of capital and labor, and Roosevelt's theory was to elevate labor. Stolberg and Vinton assert that in a democracy, which must be in fact "liberal," the voices of capital are so powerful that they will dwarf labor. Their continued powerful voice will prevent labor from making little if any headway against capital. However, Stolberg and Vinton were writing in 1935, using 1934 data and foreseeing mainly the results of the first New Deal, in which business profited far more than labor. The second New Deal would go on to favor labor far more substantially. Putting the pieces together, one is led to suspect that the single-mindedness—or the scheme, or the plan—of FDR as the New Deal evolved must have developed into an equalization of the power of capital and labor. To this critical point we will return after one more observation.

In line with this theory, A. A. Berle, Jr., a key Roosevelt advisor, who was writing in the fall of 1933, focused on the "economics of balance." At one point he states, "no longer can we rely on the economics of balance to take care of human needs.... [T]he old economic forces still work and they provide a balance *after a while*."[14] In other words, Berle was referring to the older "Classical" economic theory of an economy where *eventually* even massive unemployment could be cured by falling wages, cheap labor being rehired, and business once again becoming profitable. The theory of a self-balancing economy was still in vogue in the early 1930s, but Berle points out that the economy of his time was different than that of classical economic theory.[15] Berle's description of the 1930s American economy was that large corporations did not simply go out of business easily or reenter business. Massive unemployment and imbalances could persist for a number of years. Government, Berle says, must take hold of the so-called senior controls, such as the banking system, the concentrated domination of certain groups over industry, agricultural legislation and how it affects that industry, and the transportation industry. Further, government must seek to restore "balance" through government management of these senior controls. The key idea in his article, as mentioned earlier, is *balance*. In a telling paragraph the word crops up again: "It was conceived that by mobilizing industry through the National Recovery Administration, and requiring it to meet the responsibilities of an income distributing group, much could done toward achieving the *balance* [emphasis mine] and distribution of income which is required to keep a system of ours afloat."[16]

A final theory of the New Deal to be discussed here is simply a political one. In "Sources of the New Deal," Arthur M. Schlesinger, Jr., claims that there would have been something very similar to it in the 1930s, even without the Depression, given the American "reform pattern."[17] Outsiders get weary of existing leadership. "The Establishment ... was ... exceedingly boring ..., neither bright nor witty nor picturesque nor even handsome and thus produced the human impulse to redress the balance by kicking up heels in the back streets."[18] Schlesinger claims that the political pendulum swings periodically. The United States had witnessed a liberal reform cycle (Theodore Roosevelt and Woodrow Wilson) and then a conservative cycle in the 1920s, and was thus due for another reform cycle. He also says his father predicted that liberal and conservative trends in our national life succeed themselves at intervals of about 15 or 16 years.

I disagree with this proposition. For one thing, I believe that people wanted a change *because* of the Depression. Recent history has shown that a good economy brings a party back, and a bad one throws it out. For another thing, by the "cycle" maxim, George Bush had no business being elected in 1988—particularly by the margin he received—given the string of conservative presidents that started with Richard Nixon in 1968.

The magnitude of the reforms of the New Deal could not have been predicted simply by the political cycle. The case is strong that their magnitude was largely affected by the economic gravity of the times. However, the far-reaching nature of the reforms and their consistency strongly suggest what Roosevelt had in his mind, perhaps not fully developed in 1932, but well on its way by 1934.

A NEW THEORY OF THE NEW DEAL: THE ECONOMICS OF BALANCE

The evidence strongly suggests that the theory of the New Deal as conceived by its author Franklin Delano Roosevelt, the single most important force in the New Deal and its captain and director, was to achieve a better balance between capital and labor by increasing labor's share of income distribution and wealth and by limiting, if not in some cases redistributing, income away from capital or the holders of capital. Roosevelt's genius was to raise the economic power, income, and wealth share of labor, rather than visibly diminishing capital.

As mentioned earlier, a common interpretation of the New Deal is that its primary purpose was to raise the country out of Depression. A common misinterpretation of the means by which the government did this was through increased borrowing and spending. Yet the fiscal policy of the New Deal was only mildly stimulative, or Keynesian. The contention that the Roosevelt administration spent the country back into prosperity, at least prior to 1941, does not hold up. For example, in 1934, the federal deficit was 5.9 percent of gross national product (GNP). In 1937, it had fallen to 2.5 percent and, in 1938, it was a minuscule 0.1 percent of GNP.

However, that the New Deal was a series of anti-Depression measures cannot be denied. Indeed, the New Deal went a good deal farther than expansionary Keynesianism. The New Deal had at its root the purpose, aim, and act of elevating labor and thus balancing in a more equitable fashion the income and wealth distribution between capital and labor. Since the forces of capital had so dominated the American arena as to unbalance the economy, purchasing power had been skewed to the upper classes. Wealth distribution had followed the same pattern. Much wealth was concentrated so that, while there was plenty of money to lend, borrowing was restricted due to the credit-worthiness of the borrower. Fewer credit-worthy borrowers in the Depression meant a weak consumer demand.

Roosevelt first attempted to raise the country out of the Depression by the theory of raising income rewards to *all* factors of production, namely, by raising profits and wages simultaneously. He hoped for a strong revival of purchasing power to raise the economy out of the Depression. But it did not work. Big business fixed prices, took the profits, cut labor, and continued to be anti-union in its activity. The first New Deal resulted not in raising overall purchasing power, but in further strengthening business by increased profits. Roosevelt learned his lesson and changed course. His second New Deal sought to regulate income rewards to capital and to increase income rewards to labor by government-sponsored unionization. The actions of the Roosevelt administration suggest that what was on his mind was to achieve economic recovery in the United States by attaining a better balance in the power between labor and capital. Stimulative measures did not seem to work. Indeed, this is borne out by the fact that when John Maynard Keynes visited Franklin D. Roosevelt in the late

1930s, the meeting did not go well. Roosevelt regarded Keynes more as a mathematician than as an economist. Keynes in turn was disappointed in that he had imagined Roosevelt to be much more economically "literate" than he turned out to be. Keynes's idea of economic literacy was pump priming, while Roosevelt was more interested in equitable income distribution.

In fact, the record of the New Deal suggests that Roosevelt had a more well-defined concept of labor and capital than most economists suspect. Economists define factors of production along classical economic lines as being the following four: land, labor, capital, and entrepreneurship. People control and own these factors of production in various quantities. Capital is the factor of production that accumulates from income in excess of consumption. Indeed, when we look at wealth distribution, we are generally looking at capital accumulation. Further, we regard the person with the most capital as being the wealthiest. Land is another factor of production that, when held in large amounts, signifies wealth. Thus, very large farmers are wealthy if their land is paid for, and if they could sell it off and live off the interest. Thus land and capital in excess of one's normal requirements tend to define wealth, and wealth produces more income independent of labor. Since all factors of production are owned by someone, for income distribution purposes it is better to redefine or reclassify these four factors into two. These two factors can then be evaluated and classified as to their *income distribution* attributes, as opposed to their *income production* attributes—the latter on which classical theory concentrates. Since these factors of income *distribution* necessarily attach to individuals, we can accordingly classify individuals as being of two types given their entitlement to income: Individuals have incomes that are either labor-dependent or capital-enhanced.[19]

A *labor-dependent* individual is one whose livelihood depends primarily on his or her own labor. Thus, in this category we would place the small farmer, the small businessperson, and the laborer. The laborer usually works with the capital of others if he or she works with capital at all. The small farmer and small businessperson might possess capital such as land and buildings, but the capital is of such an insignificant amount that they would not be able to live off its interest were they not to add their own labor. The *capital-enhanced* individuals, on the other hand, are usually not dependent on their own labor for a livelihood, or they control such large amounts of other persons' capital that they are paid an extraordinarily large wage, which represents more of a profit than a wage. Their income is thus capital-enhanced.

When one analyzes the New Deal along these lines, one finds, particularly in the case of the second New Deal, a program to elevate the labor-dependent classes in society, that is, the small farmers, the small businesspersons and labor, unionized or not—all of whom were dependent upon employment and not capital income for their livelihood. It also sought to redress the balance by limiting and realigning the rewards to the capital-enhanced individuals. Some writers have described Roosevelt's actions as experimental, erratic, chaotic and with no central plan in mind. My theory is that FDR had in mind the concept of a more equitable balance between the capital-enhanced individuals in the United States and their labor-dependent cohorts. His actions suggest a balancing act. This congenial-appearing president kept the capital-enhanced individuals at bay while he promoted the interest of the labor-dependent. In the end, he accomplished a peaceful democratic revolution by elevating the economic status of the labor-dependent segment of the society, while not visibly dragging down—or even materially dragging down—the capital-enhanced sector. Relatively, of course, labor became stronger. In other societies, this elevation of the labor-dependent classes has often triggered a process of bloody revolutions. Roosevelt avoided this process by simply elevating, relatively and absolutely, one segment of the society. As A. A. Berle, Jr., wrote, "in a world in which revolutions just now are coming easily, the New Deal chose the more difficult course of moderation and rebuilding. This in a word is the social economics—the political economics, in the old phrase of the New Deal."[20]

Thus, Roosevelt elevated the labor-dependent through his New Deal. The force of his personality and his leadership allowed him to shepherd the reforms around the most powerful and financially influential individuals and corporations of this country. Despite their numerical minority, the capital-enhanced were forces to be reckoned with. It reminds one of another president who, in the 1980s through the force of his congenial and winning personality, elevated the fortune of the capital-enhanced individuals above the labor-dependent and succeeded in economically weakening and further shrinking the size of the American middle class. And in an opposite parallel with the Roosevelt accomplishment, despite the American middle class's relatively weaker per-capita financial position, its huge numbers posed a great political strength that had to be dealt with, and Reagan dealt with it. Both presidents delivered the goods to their constituencies in the face of seemingly insurmountable odds. Capital initially found it difficult to win back the significant victories it had ceded to labor in the New Deal. But it never gave up trying, and in the post-FDR era made the long climb back. It made its greatest strides in the Reagan era, as we shall later see.

SUMMARY AND PROLOGUE

Roosevelt achieved in practice what the economics profession had not done in the 1930s and has not adequately done today. He recognized the distinction between *factors of production*—land, labor, capital, and entrepreneurship—and *factors of distribution*, namely, individuals whose incomes are either capital-enhanced or labor-dependent. He promoted and passed legislation accordingly.

The goal that Roosevelt tried to achieve with the New Deal, and did achieve, was a balance in the economic rewards going to the two factors of distribution: the capital-enhanced classes and the labor-dependent classes. Such a balance would best provide a healthy, strong economy. Early attempts to raise the income levels of *both* factors of distribution failed, since the capital-enhanced individuals were already so far ahead of the labor-dependent that they were able to marshal the resources of government to increase even further their economic rewards relative to labor. That mistake made, Roosevelt felt that the best way to balance an economy was to equalize the relative economic power of the two factors of distribution by raising the incomes of only one: the labor-dependent. The macroeconomic impact of this microeconomic action would take care of itself, in due course.

There are those who argue that the macroeconomic impact of the military deficits during World War II stabilized the economy. To be sure, they created an economic recovery in a short period of time. However, it is my contention that the most stable economic period of the United States was achieved when the factors of distribution were the most balanced, namely, during the 1945–65 period. And it is in this period that the American middle class grew and prospered. Indeed, the attribution to Keynesianism of any economic achievements in Roosevelt's program does not hold water.

However, as the capital-enhanced forces have steadily grown in their power relative to the labor-dependent, the economy has become more and more unstable. This ascent of capital has been achieved most importantly since the early 1960s and has represented an unwinding, withering, and chipping away—and in many cases the nullification—of a large part of the New Deal, and a corresponding shrinkage of the size and well-being of the middle class. The economics of the Reagan and Bush administrations represents a culmination of this unwinding process. It is to the unwinding of the New Deal that we will now turn our attention.

NOTES

1.   Rexford G. Tugwell, "The New Deal in Retrospect," *Western Political Quarterly*, 1, no. 1 (December 1948), pp. 373–85.
2.   Ibid.
3.   Ibid.
4.   Charles Beard and George H. E. Smith, "An Epitome of Characteristics," in *The Old Deal and the New* (New York: Macmillan, 1941) pp. 277–78.
5.   Ibid., p. 277.
6.   Ibid., p. 279.
7.   Basil Rauch, *The History of the New Deal* (New York: Capricorn Books, 1963) p. 61.
8.   Ibid.
9.   The marginal revenue productivity theory of income distribution states basically that capital and labor are rewarded in proportion to their contribution to production.
10.   The Business Council, formed with the aid of the Roosevelt administration, initially consisted of a select group of chief executive officers of major U.S. corporations who met regularly in Washington to advise on economic policy matters. This group has evolved into the Business Roundtable and continues to exercise a powerful influence on the president and Congress. During the 1930s its leaders were considerably more liberal on social issues than the average American businessperson. That generalization, however, appears to be less true today. For an excellent account of this phenomenon, see Kim McQuaid, *Big Business and Presidential Power* (New York: William Morrow, 1982).
11.   Benjamin Stolberg and Warren Jay Vinton, "Roosevelt Panaceas," *The Economic Consequences of the New Deal* (New York: Harcourt, Brace and World, 1935) p. 93.
12.   Ibid.
13.   Ibid., p. 92.
14.   A. A. Berle, Jr., "The Social Economics of the New Deal," *New York Times Magazine*, October 29, 1933; reprinted in William Leuchtenberg, ed. *The New Deal: A Documentary History* (Columbia: University of South Carolina Press, 1968) pp. 34–35; emphasis mine.
15.   John Maynard Keynes pointed this out in the very first chapter of his

famous 1936 work *The General Theory of Employment Interest and Money* (New York: Harcourt, Brace and World, 1936).

16. In Leuchtenberg, ibid. p. 37.

17. Arthur M. Schlesinger, Jr., "Sources of the New Deal," in Morton Keller, ed., *The New Deal, What Was It?* (New York: Holt, Rinehart and Winston, 1963) pp. 94–104.

18. Ibid. p. 96.

19. Retirees could be classified as either transfer-dependent or capital-enhanced. The former group, drawing from pension income and Social Security, would be middle class since they would be most identified with the labor-dependent. Capital-enhanced retirees would be similar to the working capital-enhanced group, i.e., at the upper end of the income distribution scale.

20. In Leuchtenberg, op. cit., p. 35.

2

Undoing the New Deal

Governments can err, presidents do make mistakes,
but the immortal Dante tells us that Divine Justice
weighs the sins of the cold blooded and the sins of
the warm hearted on a different scale. Better the occasional faults of a government living in the spirit of
charity, than the consistent omissions of a government frozen in the ice of its own indifference.

Franklin Delano Roosevelt

The major accomplishment of the New Deal was the elevation of labor-dependent American citizens, to a status more nearly equal to those individuals whose incomes were significantly capital-enhanced. One writer
called it "a New Deal for the common man." And if we accept this
elevation of the labor-dependent as the crux of the New Deal we can more
neatly categorize almost every measure of this set of programs.

The promotion of unionization was a major part of the plan. The
percentage of the workforce unionized went from 6.8 percent in 1930, to
15.5 percent in 1940, and to 21.9 percent by 1945. With this unionization,
with this ascension in the numbers of people able to bargain for a living
wage, came an expanded and more prosperous middle class with the
ability to buy homes and automobiles and to educate children on the salary
of one breadwinner. To this were added income security in the form of
unemployment insurance, and old-age retirement benefits. Security for

the small saver was guaranteed by bank deposit insurance, and the activist role of the federal government ensured that the labor-dependent would be protected from those in possession of large amounts of wealth. Such protection would come through government-sponsored and -regulated collective bargaining, fair labor standards, inspection of banks, regulation of securities trading, control of the money supply, and enforcement of antitrust laws.

The New Deal, in essence, slowed the advancing power of capital, which had been on a steamroller at the expense of the labor-dependent throughout the 1920s. It is important to note, however, that it did not significantly reduce the economic power of capital. It did raise the power of labor so that the power of capital was reduced relative to labor; but in absolute terms, capital remained quite wealthy. To accomplish this protection of the labor-dependent, the federal government evolved into a larger, more influential, and more efficient agent of action that was to have a more direct effect on the lives of average Americans, be they labor-dependent or capital-enhanced.

That the federal government became larger is borne out by the numbers. That the government became more efficient is often a subject for debate. I would contend not only that the government was larger under Roosevelt but also that it was strengthened in quality and efficiency. This position is supported by the observations of a number of scholars and other high-quality talent brought to Washington by FDR. This was no doubt aided by the high purchasing power of a federal paycheck during the period. But the proof of the pudding may be seen in the efficiency and success of the war mobilization effort, the military buildup, the development of the atomic bomb, the defense of the United States, the prosecution of the war, and the conversion to peacetime after World War II. This gargantuan effort could not have been pulled off with an inefficient and underfinanced federal government, whose superstructure demands far more than mere military talent. Indeed, one wonders if the United States could accomplish such a herculean task today after such an immense weakening of the quality and efficiency of the federal government as occurred during the Reagan era.

THE MICROECONOMIC OR NON-KEYNESIAN ACCOMPLISHMENTS OF THE NEW DEAL

The New Deal made remarkable strides by putting into place institutions that would eventually achieve national economic stability. However, it did so largely by operating through *microeconomic* means. The micro-economic means *ultimately had macroeconomic* implications, but micro-economic measures take a long time to take effect. It is thus no accident that in 1940 the unemployment rate in the United States was still 14.6 percent, which, while down from 24.9 percent in 1933, was still very high by historical standards. Nonetheless, macroeconomic stability was achieved by a series of microeconomic measures that included the establishment of the Social Security System, unemployment compensation, and bank deposit insurance—a microeconomic policy with macroeconomic implications. The promotion of unionization would redistribute income from capital to labor, thus increasing mass purchasing power. Programs for systematic financial aid to agriculture and federal relief programs for the poor would accomplish similar results.

By 1940 the economy had recovered somewhat from the massive Depression of the early 1930s, but it had done so largely through micro-economic means. Federal government deficits during the 1930s were minor and not stimulative enough to have a macroeconomic impact. For example the federal government deficit in 1934 was $3.6 billion, in 1937 it was $2.8 billion, and in 1938 it was $1.2 billion. Indeed the economic recovery of the 1930s was non-Keynesian; it was a result of natural neoclassical economic forces working themselves out. Unemployment had risen vastly; labor became relatively cheap and workers were hired back. Incomes also rose through unionization, relief payments, make-work projects and the like. In sum, the economy recovered more along the natural lines of a neoclassical market economy—which is why it did not fully recover by 1940.

Given the magnitude of the Depression, the nearly 25 percent unemployment rates in 1933, a natural recovery along neoclassical economic lines would take more than seven years, if not twelve to fifteen. However, what did occur, which was not immediately evident, was the emplacement of a number of reforms that would ensure that a depression of the magnitude of the early 1930s would never occur again. Laid-off workers would begin receiving unemployment compensation. Older Americans who were forced out of the labor market could draw on their Social Security. The banks would not fail due to a general loss of confidence, and thus the money supply would never again shrink by one-third as it did from 1929 to 1933. Indeed, Roosevelt's priorities were reform first, recovery second.

The Keynesian impact of large deficits on a still-depressed economy would not be felt until the early 1940s when deficits reached a high of

$54.9 billion in fiscal year 1943. Then the unemployment rate dropped swiftly to below 2 percent. The Keynesian revolution then followed somewhat on a de facto basis in World War II, but more explicitly with the passage of the Employment Act of 1946. Roosevelt's real economic revolution was the establishment of balance between not the factors of production, but the factors of distribution, namely, the labor-dependent and the capital-enhanced classes. It was a reform-oriented revolution. The establishment of stability to the labor-dependent in the income they receive and in their ability to retain their housing, and the implications of this new stability for business confidence and national purchasing power (since consumption spending in total represents two-thirds of gross national product), was the real Roosevelt economic revolution. The Keynesian demand management—a by-product of World War II—may never have been tested without such a major war, even following such a period of extreme depression. This is not to say that the Keynesian revolution was not important. But once the balancing act of Roosevelt had taken place, Keynesian measures became more important in enabling a government to stabilize an economy and moderate *recessions*. Roosevelt's reforms would more likely prevent massive imbalances leading to severe downturns or *depressions*.

The recessions of 1973–75 and 1980–82 are cases in point. Both were caused by the macroeconomic impacts of microeconomic oil price shocks. The American imported oil bill in 1972 was $4.7 billion. By 1974 it had risen to $26.6 billion, a $22 billion increase. Thus $22 billion that would have normally been spent in the United States went overseas, bringing with it a massive fall in domestic consumer demand and a multiplier effect felt in all industries, but particularly in autos. A similar occurrence happened with the oil price shocks in 1979. In 1978 the bill for imported oil was $42.6 billion. By 1980 it was $79.4 billion, and again a massive loss of domestic purchasing power occurred, this time $37 billion plus multiplier effects. During both recessions, that loss of purchasing power was compounded by inflation. Interest rates shot to record levels to further compound the macroeconomic misery. The prime rate—the interest rate charged by banks to their best customers—rose from 5.25 percent on average in 1972, to 10.81 percent in 1974. And it rose from an average of 9.06 percent in 1978, to an average 18.87 percent in 1981! Oil prices had delivered the two most severe peacetime shocks to the United States economy since the stock market crash of 1929. Yet the unemployment rate in 1975, at the depths of the 1973–75 recession, averaged only 8.3 percent. In 1982–83 it averaged only 9.5 percent. While such unemployment rates are high, they do not approach the magnitude of the 1930s. The banking system, while strained, did not collapse because there were no runs on banks. Deposits were federally insured. Purchasing power, which fell during those recessions, didn't collapse because unemployed workers received unemployment compensation. Older workers who lost their jobs went on Social Security.

A similar macroeconomic shock of unprecedented magnitude was the stock market crash of October 19, 1987. While predictions of a depression ensued (largely drawing on the 1929 stock market crash experience), the New Deal balancing measures largely saved the day. Insured deposits prevented runs on the banks—which prevented a collapse in the size of the money supply. The Federal Reserve was able to shore up markets largely unhampered by restrictions on their money-creating abilities, thanks to the Glass Steagal Act of 1933. The weathering of the storm by the economy in the 1973–75 recession, in the 1980–82 recession, and in the 1987 market collapse had less to do with Keynesian demand management policies and more to do with a stability of the economy that had its roots in the New Deal, namely, better balance between capital and labor and more complete government management of the monetary system.

Thus, Keynesian economic policies were not an integral part of the New Deal. Their acceptance came later. In fact, they were another important tool of economic management given to the federal government and used as part of the stabilization process from 1946 on. Their use could still be valuable in pulling an economy out of recession, though the reforms of the 1930s have largely precluded a depression.

Because large federal deficits in the 1980s have been a fact of life, there are some who would claim that Ronald Reagan has not repudiated the New Deal, since large deficits and the New Deal are often linked in the minds of many economists and politicians. Nothing could be further from the truth. Keynesian economics was only a minor part—if indeed a part at all—of the New Deal. What did occur in the Reagan years, under the guise of fuller employment and a Keynesian-like deficit stimulus, was a marked undoing of the New Deal by increasing the imbalance between capital and labor.

This process did not begin with Ronald Reagan. The unraveling of the New Deal began with the death of Franklin Delano Roosevelt. Capital, which had been held in check by Roosevelt, began immediately to reassert itself at the completion of World War II. However, so great was the economic prosperity that followed the war and continued through 1965 that the gains made by the capital-enhanced factors went largely unnoticed. The economic pie expanded so much during that time period that the labor-dependent factors also made historically unparalleled economic strides, and thus a growing and more prosperous American middle class. But in the late 1960s, with slowing economic growth and a growing imbalance in the economy as the capital-enhanced factors continued to improve their economic lot, the strains and pressures on the labor-dependent and thus on the American middle class became more evident. The election of Ronald Reagan and his economic policies further widened the imbalance between these two factors ef distribution. A key question of this book is, in fact, this: **Were the Reagan policies merely a continuation of the diminution of the power of labor-dependent individuals in the society and the corresponding enhancement of the economic power of the capital-enhanced groups, or did they represent an acceleration of the process?** We will turn to this question specifically in Chapters 8 and 9. But first we look at the history of the unraveling of the New Deal that began in 1946.

THE GREAT UNRAVELING:
THE BUSINESS COUNCIL AND THE CED

Historian Kim McQuaid has provided a detailed account of high-level business executive influence in Washington.[1] As mentioned earlier, with FDR's encouragement, a group of high-ranking chief executive officers of major corporations in the early 1930s formed the Business Council. The group originally numbered between 40 and 65 chief executive officers of the largest firms in the country. They were a quasi-public advisory agency and included the ranks of such top business leaders as Alfred Sloan of General Motors, Pierre duPont of E. I. duPont, Thomas Watson of IBM, W. Averell Harriman of the Union Pacific Railroad, Robert Wood of Sears Roebuck, and others of equal status. Many of these individuals accepted the idea of expanded federal power. They realized that FDR's mandate came from a changed America where labor and the common person needed federal guarantees and protection. They were in fact far more liberal than the average American businessperson, who was typically represented by such conservative groups as the U.S. Chamber of Commerce and the National Association of Manufacturers (NAM), both of which adamantly opposed most New Deal reforms, including the Social Security Act. The Council was generally helpful in working with Roosevelt to pass much of his New Deal legislation. He further used it as a prominent public sounding board for his pre–World War II mobilization drive.

When in 1943 the National Resources Planning Board (NRPB), a research arm of the White House, issued a report calling for the federal government to become a guarantor of full employment, the Business Council and conservatives all over America were horrified. They managed to get the budget for NRPB voted down by Congress, and the group became defunct. Undaunted, Roosevelt in his State of the Union message in 1944 called for the nation to accept an economic bill of rights that would guarantee essentially the same benefits that the earlier report of the NRPB had advocated. Members of the Business Council realized at that point that they needed to have "a positive business response" to any new reform proposals. The enlightened businessmen of the day realized that more and more reform proposals would be forthcoming from the Roosevelt administration or from more liberal administrations to follow, and that their best bet was to preempt such proposals with programs of their own. This called for an increasingly activist business community, and the result was the Committee for Economic Development (CED).

The CED was an outgrowth of the Business Council and included many of its prominent members as well as leaders of the major labor unions. The group was to be a research and policy body on national economic issues, and prominent in the minds of its members was the conversion of the war economy to a peacetime economy when the war ended. A relatively enlightened group, the CED supported collective bargaining— much to the dismay of organizations like the National Association of Manufacturers and the U.S. Chamber of Commerce. In general it accepted many of the existing New Deal realities. However the CED also wanted to maintain the status quo and prevent any further expansion of federal power.

The CED's first major victory was the watering down of the Employment and Production Act of 1946, euphemistically dubbed the "Full Employment Act." CED members worked long and hard to ensure the federal government would *promote* full employment rather than *insure* it. While the bill created a Council of Economic Advisors (CEA) to inform the president on economic matters, and required that the president give Congress an annual economic report, much of the act was advisory and research oriented and was described by one prominent business leader as a "pretty innocuous" bill.[2] The so-called Full Employment Act of 1946 was probably the last element of economic reform legislation that had intellectual roots to FDR and the New Deal.

"Ole give 'em hell" Harry Truman largely reserved his hell for people other than the business community and leaders of large industrial corporations. He took six months to staff the Council of Economic Advisors fully and appointed conservative economists such as Edwin G. Nourse and Leon Keyserling to chair that body. In an atmosphere of postwar labor unrest, Truman, the leader of labor's liberal Democratic party, turned against labor. He wrote in his private diary, "Like every new rich person who comes into power suddenly labor has gone off the beam. The job now is to bring them back."[3] On the business end of things, the major industrialists had learned their lesson in trying to smash labor by means of direct confrontational techniques, such as hiring strikebreakers and trying to roll back labor legislation. Instead they sought to use the federal government to intervene. Kim McQuaid writes, "Big business activists on the basis of their experiences on war-time mobilization, were finally coming to understand that Washington was a tool that they, too, could use to further their interests."[4] Truman, rather than receiving Business Council members at the White House, paid visits to their gatherings at prominent Washington hotels. The constant pressure of the Business Council resulted in the passage of the tough-on-labor Taft–Hartley Act. Although Truman vetoed the bill, he could not keep Congress in line, and both Houses overrode him.

That business leaders could use Washington to their own ends was evident in the most prominent provision of the Taft–Hartley Act, namely, that, in the event of a strike adversely affecting the national health and safety, the president could order a return to work for a mandatory "cooling-off period" of up to 80 days. This was a severe blow to unions and to organized labor. While big business advocates did not get all they wanted from the Taft–Hartley Act—and many of them wanted to smash completely labor's right to collective bargaining—the New Deal was indeed being unraveled. The retreat had begun. Truman was no reformer. He was no Roosevelt. And the most that he could do would be to contain the probusiness initiative, which was now being carried on by more conservative groups such as the National Association of Manufacturers and the U.S. Chamber of Commerce and the slightly less conservative group known as the Business Council. In general, the record of the Truman White House was one of appeasement toward big business. The year 1952 found America's corporate leaders congratulating themselves on the containment of labor reform legislation since FDR's death and licking their chops in anticipation of an incoming Republican administration headed by Dwight D. Eisenhower.

Table 2-1
Tax Share of Total Federal Receipts during Presidential
Administrations, 1945–1992

	Individual Income Tax (Percent of total)	Change in Share		Corporate Income Tax (Percent of total)	Change in Share	
		Amt.	%		Amt.	%
Roosevelt						
1945	40.7			35.2		
Truman						
1946	41.0			30.2		
		+1.2	+2.9		+1.9	+6.3
1952	42.2			32.1		
Eisenhower						
1953	42.8			30.5		
		+1.2	+2.8		−7.3	−23.9
1960	44.0			23.2		
Kennedy						
1961	43.8			22.2		
		+0.9	+2.1		−1.9	−8.6
1963	44.7			20.3		
Johnson						
1964	43.2			20.9		
		+1.7	+3.9		−2.2	−20.5
1968	44.9			18.7		
Nixon						
1969	46.7			19.6		
		−1.5	−3.2		−4.9	−25.0
1974	45.2			14.7		
Ford						
1975	43.9			14.6		
		+0.3	+0.7		−0.7	−4.8
1976	44.2			13.9		
Carter						
1977	44.3			15.4		
		+2.9	+6.5		−2.9	−18.8
1980	47.2			12.5		

	Individual Income Tax (Percent of total)	Change in Share		Corporate Income Tax (Percent of total)	Change in Share	
		Amt.	%		Amt.	%
Reagan						
1981	47.7			10.2		
		+0.4	+0.8		−4.0	−39.2
1983	48.1			6.2		
1981	47.7			10.2		
		−3.6	−7.5		+0.2	+2.0
1988	44.1			10.4		
Bush						
1989	44.9			10.4		
1991	44.4	(89-92)	(89-92)	9.3	(89-92)	(89-92)
1992 est.	44.5	−0.4	−0.1	8.3	−2.1	−20.2

Source: 1945–1988 data is from *Historical Tables—Budget of the United States Government, Fiscal Year, 1990* (Washington, D.C.: USGPO, 1989). 1989–1992 data is from *Economic Report of the President*, February 1992, p. 387. 1992 data are from White House estimates.

BUSINESS REAPS THE REWARDS OF
ITS WASHINGTON PRESENCE

McQuaid's analysis traces the subsequent influence, relationships, and horsetrading among the Business Council, the Committee for Economic Development, and the Business Roundtable through the Eisenhower administration and up to the early years of the Reagan administrations. What emerges is a portrayal of closeness to some presidents and distance from others. For example, it does not portray, other than Cabinet appointments, a particularly close relationship with Eisenhower. With President Johnson, however, throughout most of the period until Wall Street soured on Vietnam, the relationship was close. With Kennedy it was distant, as it was with President Carter. Yet the overriding theme of McQuaid's analysis is that a constant pressure on presidential administrations and Congress has been exerted by members of this ubiquitous group of chief

Table 2-2
Average Tax Share of Total Federal Receipts, 1934–1992
(in percent)

Administration	Individual Income Tax	Corporate Income Tax
Roosevelt (1934–45)	22.1	23.8
Truman (1946–52)	42.5	27.1
Eisenhower (1953–60)	43.8	26.6
Kennedy (1961–63)	44.7	21.0
Johnson (1964–68)	42.7	21.4
Nixon (1969–74)	45.8	16.1
Ford (1975–76)	44.1	14.2
Carter (1977–80)	46.0	14.2
Reagan (1981–88)	46.2	8.7
Bush (1989–92)	44.8	9.2

Note: Computations of share changes by author.
Source: See Table 2-1.

executive officers of major corporations, calling themselves variously the Business Council, the Business Roundtable, and the Committee for Economic Development. Their philosophy matured to the point of extracting the maximum benefits for the business community from any administration or Congress, be it Democrat or Republican. In short, the Business Council learned to use Washington.

One measure of its success is shown by the changing patterns of tax burdens in the United States. The data show that business pressure was generally more successful in gaining corporate income tax reduction during Republican administrations. Yet the corporate presence managed still to obtain significant tax reductions under the Democrats.

This is borne out by the figures in Table 2-1. Substantial tax reductions were granted to big business as represented by dramatic falls in the corporate income tax during the Eisenhower, Nixon, Reagan, and Bush administrations. In fact, the corporate tax cuts during the first three years of the Reagan administration were so embarrassingly huge that they had to be undone. The pattern of the years 1946–1992 shows a constant pressure to maintain primary reliance on the individual income tax as a source of further revenues while steadily reducing the share of federal taxes paid by the corporations.

Table 2-2 shows the pattern another way by illustrating the average tax share of federal receipts for all years of the postwar administrations. It generally shows materially lower corporate tax receipts during Republican administrations, but the averages hide such things as a dramatic drop in corporate taxes during the last years of the Eisenhower administration that had its primary effects during the Kennedy administration.

One can also count as a major victory of the Business Council its defeat of proposals for a Cabinet-level consumer agency of the federal government. Such an agency might well have exerted more pressure to change this pattern of increasing individual income taxes and decreasing corporate taxes, since its focus would probably have been the economic health of the consumer.

On an average basis the Reagan administration delivered substantially lower tax rates to corporations, particularly with the Economic Recovery Tax Act of 1981. The embarrassment of such low corporate revenues, however, prompted a reversal of some of this legislation in the latter years of Reagan's presidency. Nonetheless, the corporations gained, at least for a temporary period, substantial tax reductions from what was an extremely low tax base to begin with. That Reagan delivered to his business and high-income constituents—that is, what I describe as the capital-enhanced sector—is undeniable. But as we shall see in later chapters, his contribution in the tax field was matched if not surpassed by his generally antilabor policy and by his nonenforcement of the existing antitrust laws (see especially Chapters 4 and 9).

Moreover as Table 2-1 shows, the Bush administration has continued the Reagan and other Republican administrations' policy of corporate tax cuts, with the corporate share falling from 10.4 percent of federal revenues in 1989 to 8.3 percent in 1992 (by the president's own estimate)—an astounding 20 percent drop, and from a very low base.

Thus for nearly 60 years, the Business Council and its offshoots have maintained their presence in Washington and a "yes, but" attitude in the field of reform legislation. In civil rights, as in other fields of social reform, the council maintained a progressive philosophical stance. But while acting progressively on social issues, it continued to stress the need for corporate tax reduction and in the end was very successful.

Its low-profile modus operandi means that the council has gotten little credit for its progressive stances on social issues. However, it also has been little recognized for its successes in achieving corporate tax reduction and maintaining labor's weak bargaining position. One might indeed say of the Business Council (and the corporate presence in Washington) that it had the good sense to follow the old business maxim, "Take the cash and let the credit go!" As later chapters will show, the corporate presence in state capitals and in the councils of city and town governments has also had a substantial payoff in the reduction of corporate, state, and local taxes. These activities are too diverse and myriad to be analyzed in any depth in this book; however a cursory glance is provided in Chapter 6. Suffice it to say, substantially reduced business tax loads at the state and local levels have been the rewards of these efforts. This has correspondingly increased tax rates to individual taxpayers—particularly the middle class.

THE PHILOSOPHICAL UNWINDING OF THE NEW DEAL

While the Business Council labored away with extreme productivity for its efforts in Washington, a philosophical change was occurring in the United States among the electorate. This change in philosophy, which occurred ironically among the American middle class, had economic consequences unforeseen to that class at the time. This philosophical change was sociological in nature representing a less tolerant attitude toward the dispossessed in society—or in other words, a more traditional conservative attitude. This change in middle-class sociological attitudes, which accelerated in the late 1960s, has aligned the power of government away from the liberal toward the conservative spectrum. The conservative financial presence in Washington, as we have seen, never let up during the years of liberal reform kicked off by the New Deal. Thus, with the advent of Richard Nixon and his capitalizing on the frustration and fears of the American middle class (which were largely sociological and not financial) the stage was set for an increased antilabor, antiminority, and pro-law-and-order movement, which traditionally has been the purview of the conservative party in America. The middle class didn't realize it at the time, but it would pay a price for its conservative turn on sociological issues, for aligning itself with the conservatives. Because sociological conservatives are also financial conservatives, the record of such governments is to cut taxes on large corporations, large businesses, large wealth holders, and very high income recipients and to increase taxes and reduce government services for the middle and the lower classes.

The second major event that sent middle-class voters in large numbers to the aid of the financial conservatives was this country's disastrous involvement in Southeast Asia, led by a truly great social and liberal reformer: Lyndon Baines Johnson. Johnson and the Democrats were blamed for Vietnam, and the financial conservatives, who had accomplished an astounding amount with small numbers through the presence of the Business Council in Washington, were now set to accomplish even greater financial and economic advantages for themselves—this time with the unknowing and unrealizing vote of the American middle class.

THE WILLS ANALYSIS

Garry Wills delivers a penetrating analysis of the shift of American middle-class political thinking during the postwar period in his book *Nixon Agonistes*.[5] Wills claims the New Deal ended in 1968 when Nixon was elected. I disagree with this observation. Much of the New Deal was intact at that time although in the process of being dismantled. But my disagreement with Wills is certainly minor, being limited to the above point. The crux of the Wills analysis follows. In describing Richard Nixon's ascent to power Wills states,

> He came to politics at a time when one of the century's great shifts was beginning, a rumble of displacement whose scale and direction were not visible then. It was a shift, though no one knew it, toward Nixon—a vague accumulating lean westward, inward, and backward. What had begun in 1946, when he had been elected to Congress, was fully accomplished in 1968 by his election as president. It was the end of the New Deal.[6]

Indeed there is a recognition in Wills's observation, as in mine, that the unraveling of the New Deal began in 1946. Since that date the capital-enhanced forces that had been slowed down by the New Deal kept up a constant attempt to make their way back, and were successful. Indeed, those forces—the big-money interests, the large corporate interests, the entrenched conservatives—were never really dealt out of the New Deal.

It was merely that others were dealt in. In a sense, the New Deal gave an equal place at the "starting line" to a wide coalition of Americans.

This starting line metaphor is elaborated by Wills. The New Deal, in his mind, was a way of raising up or bringing to the starting line a number of runners who had been left out of the economic race. The Depression, with its 25 percent unemployment, had left many runners out. The New Deal was based on the principle of fairness, since any game or race should have all players begin at the same starting line or on a level playing field. It being quite impossible to bring the rich downward to meet the competition, the idea of a New Deal was to bring those left out—the South, the minorities, the immigrants, and other poor—up to the starting line where they might compete on a fair basis. Those people left out (in my terminology, the labor-dependent people) were dealt back in. During the Kennedy years the thinking was that some especially disadvantaged people, such as inner-city children, might even need a "head start."

Indeed a major contention of Wills is that both the left and the right, the Democrats and the Republicans, generally agreed with the equal-starting-line thesis. Backing up his contention, he quotes a number of conservatives, including Ronald Reagan, Richard Nixon, and Nelson Rockefeller.

However, Wills also points out a central flaw in this metaphor. Once the race has begun, Roosevelt's coalition of runners would necessarily break up. The politics of the starting line loses its appeal for those who get out in front, if there are enough of them. According to Wills, the proletariats' coalition becomes "sufficiently bourgeoisified."

Thus Wills explains an important element in the unraveling of the New Deal. He describes how Nixon used the politics of denigration to capitalize on the frustration and fears of many of the coalition's front runners, who were now successful in the game of life and frightened of the newer minorities. These newer minorities were clawing their way past the starting line, trying to reach the top. Their ranks included blacks, women, and homosexuals. In 1968, Nixon was able to capitalize on the fears of the "silent majority," many of whom were in the group of runners who were already ahead on the track of life, running fast, running hard, making money, doing well, but running scared. Thus by 1968 there were three strong forces working to unravel the New Deal. First, there was the omnipresent lobbying of the Business Council and the CED, the latter supported in large part by the more conservative U.S. Chamber of Commerce and the National Association of Manufacturers. Second, there was the shift of frightened middle-class voters—who were never really economically threatened by the emerging minorities, but who could feel threatened socially, or physically, if the right spokesman drummed the fear into their heads long enough and loud enough. Third, there was the unrest over Vietnam. The middle class began to recognize the war as a political, moral, and economic disaster. It seemed pointless, and increased civil disorder. It increased defense spending, and caused an equal increase in the federal deficit at a time of full employment; and inflation ensued. Everything went the conservatives' way. Rioting blacks, both in disgust at their own ghetto living situations and later disgust over the assassination of Martin Luther King, Jr., provided further unrest. The stage was set for a conservative revival and a continuing inward look that would destroy the equal starting line in American life—an equalization that since the New Deal had swelled the ranks and the prosperity of the middle class.

As the numbers on tax burdens show, Nixon delivered to his conservative constituency in a laudable manner. The further unraveling of the New Deal since the mid-1970s—even after the demise of Richard Nixon—has occurred in a number of ways, some subtle, some explicit. One subtle way has been the decline and fall of the United States as an economic power. While an increase in world competition was inevitable, the rapid rate of economic decline of the United States vis-à-vis such economic powers as Germany and Japan was not as inevitable as the numbers would suggest.

Germany and Japan both prospered economically in domestic and international activity. Their economies were developed by a strong guiding hand from a coalition of government and business leaders who were able to effect what is commonly called a "national industrial policy." Such an industrial policy goes hand in hand with an effective government. As mentioned earlier, a critical element of the New Deal and what it accomplished was a strong and efficient federal government. Thus a key element in the unwinding of the New Deal was an attack on government. Nixon was the kickoff man in this program; and every president since Nixon, except George Bush, has echoed these thoughts. Jimmy Carter was elected to the White House as an outsider who was going in to clean up Washington. And with candidate Ronald Reagan, of course, the problem in America was the government. The Business Council, for its part, acquiesced in this denigration of the government. Its members did not want the government too strong, particularly in the taxation arena (not to mention in its antitrust activities). But Japan has shown that an intelligent and minimal central government can effectively promote and steer an economy, make prosperous a huge middle class, and do all of this with higher corporate taxes than in the United States. Good government was part of the Roosevelt New Deal. It helped promote a large and prosperous middle class. The demise of the government was part of the demise of the New Deal and has been reflected in the demise of the middle class.

In many ways, the American middle class has suffered for lack of an effective government and an effective national economic policy. Consider the oil shocks of 1973 and 1979. No national energy policy was in place, due largely to opposition of the Business Council, the membership of which always contains representatives of major oil companies. In the 1970s, U.S. consumers suffered from oil price increases; and in a perfect correlation, U.S. major oil company profits skyrocketed. No U.S. *government* action to bargain over price on behalf of its citizens was ever put forth to the *government*-controlled oil companies of OPEC. Small wonder!

The final elements in the demise of the New Deal before we reached the Reagan administration might be laid to the wave of deregulation that began under President Carter and then continued under President Reagan. Antitrust activity and bank regulatory policy are two crucial elements examined in an analysis of the economic impact of the Reagan administration in Chapter 9. For now, we shall turn to Part II (Chapters 3–7) for an analysis of what the undoing of the New Deal has meant for the American middle class.

NOTES

1. Much of what follows draws on Kim McQuaid, *Big Business and Presidential Power* (New York: William Morrow, 1982).
2. Ibid., p. 131.
3. Ibid., p. 135.
4. Ibid., p. 137.
5. Garry Wills, *Nixon Agonistes* (Boston: Houghton Mifflin, 1970).
6. Ibid., p. 79.

THE ASCENT OF CAPITAL, THE DESCENT OF THE MIDDLE CLASS

3

The Economic Facts: Middle-class Decline and the New Super Rich

The path to America's future lies down the middle of the road.

Dwight David Eisenhower

A major problem in studying the economic status of the middle class is in finding the right definition or definitions. One even risks criticism for using more than one definition. However, in a study such as this it should be remembered that economics is a *social science*. Hopefully my position will be vindicated by the ensuing discussion.

MIDDLE-CLASS DEFINITIONS AND PROBLEMS THEREOF

What is the middle class? There are various ways of measuring it and also defining it—all fraught with a certain statistical danger, although that danger is not so great as to invalidate the several measures used. In Europe, for example, the middle class is often equated with the working class. My concept of the middle class in America is quite different from this European definition. For years, Americans were able to work in a factory, on road construction, or in a mine, and achieve a dollar income that made them "middle class" even though they earned the money in "working-class" endeavors. In fact, their middle-class incomes earned by working-class endeavors may well have exceeded many white-collar middle-class worker incomes. So America never really got too hung up on a "working-class" definition. Instead, it preferred the definition of middle class. Indeed, this probably served her well by permitting much upward mobility to positions of leadership, such leaders being drawn from a middle-class income range where that income, and hence lifestyle, had little distinction as to the source of its income, whether blue collar or white collar.

Thus, my primary aim in this book is to describe the conditions of the American middle class as it is defined by an income level, without regard to the source of that income. This allows one to escape somewhat from sociological definitions of the middle class. Such sociological definitions are indeed necessary and valuable in certain contexts; but for the purposes of my study, they are irrelevant. I am primarily interested in describing the middle class not in sociological terms, but as it relates to the upper class and the lower classes when all three classes are defined primarily in income but also in wealth terms. Another problem in defining the middle class, particularly by income levels, is that the required income level to live a "middle-class lifestyle" differs markedly between regions of the country. Perhaps the chief reason for this is the differing levels of housing prices. In the Los Angeles area, for example, one is hard pressed to find a four-bedroom home in a desirable neighborhood for under $200,000. By contrast, in southwest Michigan, one can typically find such a home in a decent neighborhood in the $45,000–$60,000 price range. Thus as statisticians come up with a range of family income that is considered to become middle class, it is not surprising that the range is rather wide indeed. For example, statisticians working with the U.S. Census data determined in 1989 that middle-class family income ranged from $18,576 to $74,304. This was the range of family earnings which was equal to one-half the median 1989 family income of $37,152, to twice that level.[1]

Alternatively, Gregory Duncan, a University of Michigan researcher, defines the middle class as the middle 70 percent of American earners. For a family of four, Duncan would place the middle-class income range at between $26,000 and $78,000 per year.[2] As for presidential candidate Governor Bill Clinton of Arkansas, during the 1992 campaign he used a middle-class definition (drawn from census data) that includes families with incomes between $20,000 and $65,000.[3]

With all of these problems of definitions, a number of studies have been done. Such studies have used any and all of these approaches, and the more prominent ones will be quoted in the pages that follow. It is significant to note, however, that no credible studies using any kind of reasonable definition of a middle-class income have concluded that the size and/or the income levels of the American middle class have materially increased over the past 20 years. In fact, they have all showed either a diminution in the size of the middle class and/or a reduction in the growth rate of earnings of that body of wage earners.

Also, I will argue in Chapter 5 that there is another way to define the American middle class. I will start by describing the middle class as being essentially a group of wage earners who are primarily labor-dependent for their livelihoods (to use our income distribution terminology, introduced in Chapter 1). This, of course, is also true of the lower classes, but it particularly fits a middle-class definition well. By contrast, people in the upper class could be defined as those whose incomes are capital-enhanced. The significant difference between these two classifications is that, generally speaking, if people in the upper class (i.e., those whose incomes are capital-enhanced) were to stop working, an income stream would still remain to support them. In other words, they are earning incomes from sources such as capital that are supplemental to the incomes from their labor expenditures. Middle-class wage earners, however, are generally in trouble if they lose their source of income from labor. It goes without saying that the latter is also true for members of the lower income groups. This theme will be developed further in Chapter 5.

Finally, before we turn to some recent studies that detail the decline of the middle class, it must be pointed out that such studies are largely conducted in what economists define as a "partial equilibrium analysis." Since we are measuring middle-class economic rewards, which are often documented before taxes and do not take into account appreciation of assets and wealth (particularly through the use of tax shelters, nontaxable fringes, and hidden assets), the analysis is only partial. Measuring the size of the middle class in this way, we are only comparing it with the size of the upper and lower classes according to a very limited income definition.

However, the welfare of the total labor class is also dependent on how prosperous other factors of production are and on the size of the total income share other factors of production command relative to labor. This is particularly so since other factors of production such as capital compete for rewards with labor and are often substitutable for labor. When we compare the well-being of labor as a whole with the well-being of capital as a whole (as we do in Chapters 5 and 6), then we get the picture that labor and with it the historical middle class have indeed suffered a much greater loss than studies (such as these) cited below would indicate. When we draw capital with its many nonlabor incomes into the picture—many of these incomes do not show up in current income statistics—we are conducting a more complete analysis (what economists term "a more general equilibrium analysis"). Such an analysis reveals that, as the total share of income is increasingly transferred to capital, the middle class finds itself both smaller and with less labor income per capita. One analogy would be to liken it to the unhappy lot of those "middle accommodation" passengers on an ocean liner when the management decides to enlarge the first-class cabins. The middle class, with roughly the same percentage of the population, now finds itself in smaller quarters. To compound the insult, the captain takes away most of their furniture and gives it to the upper-class or first-class passengers.

ESTIMATES OF MIDDLE-CLASS DECLINE

However, we will first begin with a "partial equilibrium" analysis in this and the next chapter, which statistically examines the current and rather limited reportings of incomes to all classes.

Bradbury

Economist Katherine Bradbury[4] classified families by income groups, and further into three income groups, namely, below, middle, and above, as shown in Table 3-1. Middle-class income is defined as the category of income ranging from $20,000 to $50,000 (in 1984 dollars). Bradbury's data indicate that the middle class shrank by 5.1 percent between 1973 and 1984, with the "above" or upper class growing by 0.8 percent and the "below" or lower class expanding by 4.3 percent of the population. When combining the incomes of unrelated individuals and families, the results still held. Bradbury noted "the fact that American society had become less 'middle class' would not be a source of concern if families were generally becoming richer" but, as her data show, median family income in infla-tion-adjusted (1984) dollars fell from $28,048 in 1973 to $26,000 in 1984. Bradbury's data measured "before-tax income."

Levy

Frank Levy, in *Dollars and Dreams, The Changing American Income Distribution*,[5] details the "corrected family income distribution" over

Table 3-1
Distribution of U.S. Families by Income, 1973–1984

Income Class Change (1984 dollars)	Number of Families (in thousands)		Percent of Families			Percent of Families		
	1973	1984	1973	1984		1973	1984	
Below $10,000	6,356	9,332	11.5	14.8				
$10,000–20,000	11,319	13,704	20.6	21.7	Below	32.1	36.4	+4.3
$20,000–30,000	12,458	13,224	22.6	20.9				
$30,000–40,000	10,366	10,246	18.8	16.2				
$40,000–50,000	6,354	6,837	11.5	10.8	Middle	53.0	47.9	−5.1
$50,000–75,000	6,006	6,961	10.9	11.0				
$75,000 & above	2,186	2,928	4.0	4.6	Above	14.9	15.6	+0.8
Total	55,045	63,232	100.0	100.0		100.0	100.0	0.0
Median Income	$28,048	$26,000						

Source: U.S. Bureau of the Census data from Katherine L. Bradbury, "The Shrinking Middle Class," New England Economic Review, Federal Reserve Bank of Boston (September/October 1986), p. 45.

time, that is, corrected for taxes paid and nonmonetary benefits received, such as food stamps. His data show that, while income distribution was more equal in 1984 than in 1949, it was less equal than in 1979. If one were to define the middle class by using Levy's data as the sum of the second, third, and fourth quintiles,[6] its share of income fell from 57.3 percent to 55.9 percent of the total income over the 1979–1984 period. The lower quintile during this period also dropped from 8.7 percent to 7.3 percent. Thus the total income change over the period went to the upper 20 percent which gained 2.8 percent of total income.

Moon and Sawhill

Marilyn Moon and Isabel Sawhill, analyzing the Reagan record,[7] show a shift in family income distribution similar to Levy's figures. Between 1980 and 1984, there was a gain by the top quintile of 1.9 percent and a drop in the sum total of the second, third, and fourth quintiles by 1.1 percent, from a total middle-class (my definition) share of 56.2 percent to 55.1 percent. The bottom quintile also gave up its losses to the top quintile. The data used by Moon and Sawhill were based on disposable (after-tax) income. They also analyze this shift in terms of Reagan policies—a point of analysis that coincides with our own approach (see Chapters 8 and 9).

Danziger, Gottschalk, and Smolensky

A 1989 study by Sheldon Danziger, Peter Gottschalk, and Eugene Smolensky analyzed income distribution with particular emphasis on how the rich have fared.[8] Their findings show that—contrary to what they claim is the "conventional wisdom," which states that income inequality declines during a period of economic recovery—the last economic recovery, the Reagan recovery, showed income inequality worsening.

Danziger, Gottschalk, and Smolensky observe that, even though family income increased and inflation and unemployment declined, inequality increased between 1983 and 1987. Their data show the income shares of the lowest quintile fell to 5.4 percent, only slightly down from 5.5 percent; but the share of the highest quintile rose from 41.1 percent to 41.7 percent over those four years. The middle class (i.e., the second, third, and fourth quintiles) dropped by 0.5 percent. While this is not a large decline, the authors consider its significance to be that inequality grew during a period of economic recovery.

Their results also show that the growth in inequality was due to a marked growth in income in the top two deciles. In 1973, the top two deciles exceeded the bottom two by a ratio of 5.9:1. In 1979 the ratio was 6.1:1. However, in 1987 the ratio had increased to 7.7:1.

U.S. Bureau of the Census Studies, 1991

Two recent measures by the U.S. Bureau of the Census merit mention. First, using a quintile approach the bureau found that, between 1973 and 1990, the top quintile gained 3.2 percent of the total income, the middle three quintiles (the middle class, by my definition) lost 2.2 percent, and the bottom quintile lost 0.9 percent. Of these gains to the top quintile, approximately 60 percent went to the top 5 percent.[9]

Second, as mentioned above, the census also classified incomes as to high, middle, and low. For 1989, a high-income family was one with an income of at least $74,304 (twice the median U.S. family income of $37,152). A low-income family had an income below $18,576 (half of the median income). According to these definitions, from 1969 to 1989 the percentage of middle-income families shrunk from 71.2 to 63.3. The high-income group rose by 3.8 percent and the low-income group rose by 4.2 percent.[10]

THE SHIFT: MIDDLE CLASS TO UPPER CLASS, OR MIDDLE CLASS TO SUPER RICH?

When grouped in quintile data, the redistribution of wealth to the top 20 percent is significant. However, the loss of the middle- and lower-class income becomes shocking when it appears that the lion's share of the gains is not evenly spread among the top 20 percent of the population, but is going mainly to the top 1 percent. Two recent studies confirm these facts.

A Federal Reserve study released in April 1992 showed that the richest 1 percent of the households owned 37 percent of net worth in the United States, up from 31 percent in 1983. Thus, the total net worth of some 834,000 families was $5.62 trillion. By contrast, the bottom 90 percent of the families, numbering 84 million, owned $4.8 trillion.[11]

Reinforcing this are the data released by the Congressional Budget Office on after-tax income between 1980 and 1989. Here the top 1 percent raised their share of income from 8.4 to 12.4 percent and the next 19 percent only increased theirs from 36.5 to 37.3 percent! The middle 60 percent's share went from 50.2 to 46.9 and the bottom quintile's went from 5.4 to 4.3 percent.[12]

Clearly, what has emerged from the data is that the middle-class decline is benefiting not primarily from what used to be called the "upper class" but largely the very upper class—sometimes called the "super-rich"—at the top 1 percent of the income-earning range.

For this reason as well, defining a middle-class income is very difficult, as noted earlier in the chapter. The richest 1 percent take in an average of $550,000 per year, according to IRS statistics.[13] But as noted above, the U.S. Bureau of the Census estimates a high income to be $74,304. While this is certainly a high income in Battle Creek, Michigan, it is middle income in New York City, Chicago, or San Francisco.

AVERAGE WEEKLY EARNINGS

Additional data on average weekly earnings, adjusted for inflation, graphically depict the real-income erosion of the typical wage earner. Chart 3-1 drawn from U.S. Bureau of Labor Statistics (BLS) data shows a strong and steady ascent of real (inflation-adjusted) weekly earnings in the postwar period until 1972 and 1973. From a low of $196.00, real weekly earnings peaked in 1972 at $315.44 and have shown a significant downward trend since then. In 1990 the average was $259.72. In 1991 it fell sharply again to $255.89.

These data, along with those cited earlier in the chapter, reinforce my contention that the postwar ascent of the middle class probably peaked in the early 1970s and that the decline has been generally steady and largely unabated since then.

QUALITATIVE STUDIES ON THE NEW BIPOLARITY

What the previous statistics show, in addition to a declining middle in America, is an increasing income and wealth bipolarization. While economists and statisticians may argue over definitions, contemporary developments in labor markets and corporate behavior clearly herald the new economic bipolarity in American society. Two articles written in 1983 describe it well.

Chart 3-2

Average Weekly Earnings, United States, 1947–1991 (1982 dollars)

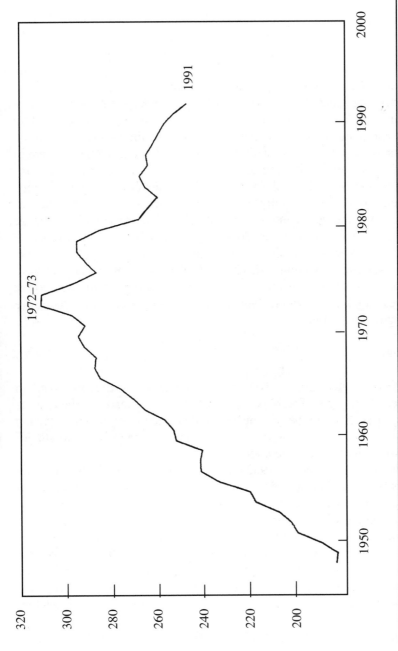

Source: U.S. Bureau of Labor Statistics data, cited in *Economic Report of the President*, Washington, D.C., February 1992, p. 346. Graph of data, 1947–1991, by the author.

Kuttner

Robert Kuttner, in the 1983 article "The Declining Middle Class," logically describes how new technology (particularly computers) in the insurance and banking industries has improved the productivity of workers but does not necessarily translate into better jobs.[14] He points out that the traditionally massive jobs of processing information are more and more being handled by armies of computer clerks at entry-level wages. Training periods are short, and one company makes a practice of locating its offices in areas where the supply of part-time workers is great. Housewives who want to work less than a full day while the kids are in school, or even bright high school students, are sought out by the employer. These workers will forgo the 40-hour-a-week job and thus fringe benefits (most significantly, medical insurance and pension contributions). Yet the new computer technology means new workers can be trained in four weeks; if they don't stay on the job, they can be replaced readily. Indeed, tracing the recent behavior of firms toward their workers—who are now equipped with greater amounts of capital and have higher productivity rates than ever before, but are rewarded with lower wages—makes one wonder where the middle-level jobs of the future are going to come from.

Steinberg

Another interesting analysis comes by way of *Fortune* magazine in Bruce Steinberg's "The Mass Market Is Splitting Apart."[15] The appearance of such an article in a magazine dedicated to accurately advising business can be seen as a strong validation of the economic studies showing an erosion of the middle class.

Steinberg's November 1983 article, following Kuttner's by some four months, reiterates some of the latter's occupational observations particularly with regard to the fact that most recently created new jobs are in the lower-paying occupations. Steinberg cites the fact that families with incomes between $15,000 and $35,000 (constant dollars) have fallen from 51 percent of total families in 1973 to 44 percent in 1982, using before-tax data. Steinberg further attributes much of the recent middle-level job losses to the increase in the service-sector economy and the decline in the manufacturing sector. In general, much of Steinberg's analysis resembles Kuttner's.

However, Steinberg does add something new, namely, the marketing perspective. He quotes an executive at General Electric who sees "more of a bimodal distribution".[16] Executives at Bloomingdale's and Pillsbury agree. And a Ford executive states, "That ... trend ... would be devastating to any durable goods marketing strategy."[17] Thus Pillsbury's restaurants position themselves accordingly: the Steak and Ale group for the upper income class, and Burger King for the lower group. Bloomingdale's moves more toward the high end and leaves the lower end to K-Mart.

While reasonable people might differ about how much the middle class has declined when looking simply at income distribution statistics expressed in a quintile, decile, or similar approach, observations such as those of Kuttner and Steinberg make one wonder if these statistics actually understate the case. It will be my contention that they do.

An Argument to My Thesis—Horrigan and Haugen

One important study by Michael Horrigan and Steven Haugen analyzes the data on middle-class decline and reaches the conclusion that the middle-class decline in the 1969–1986 period was largely due to increased mobility of the middle class to the upper class.[18] Using an approach (the "interval deflator") that adjusts for standard of living, it concludes that the entire decline went to the upper class. Using a second method based on a median family income, about 60 percent of the loss went to the upper class and 40 percent to the lower class. In either case, the study recognizes the increasing disparity between the lower class and the rest of the income distribution.[19]

However, a major shortcoming of this study and several others is that it remains in a partial equilibrium analysis vein. A consistent theme of this book will be that capital has consistently avoided taxes, particularly on income and property, and shifted them to labor—particularly the middle class. However, the Horrigan–Haugen study uses before-tax data, and admits in a footnote, "Note that the ideal data, after-tax income are not available."[20] Another shortcoming is that it uses family income when, increasingly, middle-class lifestyles are now maintained by longer hours worked by more members of the family. Then, too, the increasing home-owner property taxes and decreased government services caused by lack of corporate tax revenues—an increasing source of oppression on the middle class—are not taken into account in this study or in any others that argue with my thesis of middle-class decline.

A FINAL WORD ON DEFINING THE MIDDLE CLASS

It is evident that the American public has some concept of what it means
to be middle class. In a nonstatistical way, most Americans would
probably agree that middle-class status carries with it some sense of
security in income and living standards and also a reasonable hope for
upward mobility. It is when we necessarily try to put statistical boundaries
on the middle class that we have the most problems. Mary Kane, in a
revealing article with the rather descriptive title "The Middle Class:
Politicians Court It but Can't Define It," quotes a number of prominent
politicians and researchers with their definitions.[21] Thus, Tom Harkin, a
presidential candidate at the time, is quoted as setting the range between
$30,000 and $100,000 per year. One Census Bureau official puts it at
between $15,000 and $50,000; and Ted Windt, the University of Pitts-
burgh researcher who specializes in political communication, states, "You
can look at a family of four making $20,000 a year and they consider
themselves middle class. The same family making $120,000 a year
considers themselves middle class." The University of Michigan's Gregory Duncan is quoted in the same vein; "When you tell people that the
typical household income in the United States is $36,000, they can't
believe it. It's interesting to see how high people's definition of the middle
class goes."[22] As mentioned earlier, Duncan defines the middle class as
the middle 70 percent of American earners, which for a family of four
would include income between $26,000 and $78,000. As mentioned
above, 1992 presidential contender Bill Clinton defines the middle class
to be families with an income between $20,000 and $65,000.

Thus there are many definitions of the middle class. While they are
different, their distinctions are not huge. As mentioned earlier, the amount
of income needed to sustain a middle-class lifestyle varies in different
parts of the country. However, because we cannot precisely define the
middle class, the argument that the middle class is shrinking should not
be invalidated.

Earlier in the chapter, a number of well-reasoned definitions and cited
data provide overwhelming evidence that the middle-class situation is
economically deteriorating. These studies are backed up by corporate
behavior as described by Kuttner and Steinberg.

No such body of existing studies backed up by economic data exists
that could effectively deny the shrinkage in the size of the American
middle class, the resulting bipolarization in income levels, the enlarge-
ment of the poverty classes, and the increased income distribution of

wealth at the upper end. Effective challenges to my thesis of a declining middle class should bring forth a reasonable body of statistics to challenge those quoted here and as well contradict the many reasons for middle-class decline set forth in the remainder of this book.

For reasons explained earlier, my preference is to keep in mind that, when we are talking about the middle class, we are essentially talking about a labor-dependent group if currently working or, if retired, a transfer-dependent group, that is, living off Social Security and pension incomes. Keeping in mind the distinction between labor-dependent individuals and those whose incomes are capital-enhanced is helpful when analyzing the data that distinguishes between upper, middle, and lower classes but that naturally varies somewhat according to the specific economic study and its authors.

NOTES

1. Data cited by Barbara Vobejda in "Incredible Shrinking U.S. Middle Class," *International Herald Tribune* (February 21, 1992), p. 3.

2. Mary Kane, "The Middle Class: Politicians Court It but Can't Define It," Newhouse News Service, cited in the Kalamazoo (Mich.) *Gazette*, January 23, 1992, p. A1.

3. Ibid.

4. Katherine L. Bradbury, "The Shrinking Middle Class," *New England Economic Review*, Federal Reserve Bank of Boston (September/October 1986), p. 47.

5. Frank Levy, *Dollars and Dreams, the Changing American Income Distribution* (New York: W. W. Norton, 1988), pp. 186 and 212–13.

6. A quintile is used here as a 20 percent group. Thus the upper quintile of the income distribution would be the 20 percent of the population with the highest incomes.

7. Marilyn Moon and Isabel Sawhill, "Family Incomes, Gainers and Losers," in John L. Palmer and Isabel Sawhill, eds., *The Reagan Record* (Washington, D.C.: Urban Institute), p. 322.

8. Sheldon Danziger, Peter Gottschalk, and Eugene Smolensky, "How the Rich Have Fared, 1973–1987," *American Economic Review* (May 1989), p. 311.

9. Data provided at the request of the author by the U.S. Bureau of the Census.

10. U.S. Bureau of the Census, *Trends in Relative Income: 1964 to 1989*, Current Population Reports, Series P-60, No. 177 (Washington, D.C.: USGPO, 1991), p. 3.

11.   Data cited by David R. Francis, "Economists Suggest More Taxes on Rich," *Christian Science Monitor*, April 23, 1992, p. 15.

12.   Data are from the U.S. Congressional Budget Office quoted by David Wessel in "The Wealthy Watch as Gains of the 1980's Become Political Liabilities," *Wall Street Journal*, April 8, 1992, pp. A1 and A4.

13.   Ibid., p. A4.

14.   Robert Kuttner, "The Declining Middle Class," *Atlantic Monthly* (July 1983), p. 62.

15.   Bruce Steinberg, "The Mass Market Is Splitting Apart," *Fortune* (November 28, 1983), pp. 76–82.

16.   Ibid., p. 82.

17.   Ibid.

18.   Michael W. Horrigan and Steven E. Haugen, "The Declining Middle-class Thesis: A Sensitivity Analysis," *Monthly Labor Review* (May 1988), pp. 3–13.

19.   Ibid., p. 10.

20.   Ibid., p. 11, n.

21.   Kane, op. cit.

22.   Ibid.

4

Washington's Failure at Home and Abroad: The Decline Begins in the Early 1970s

Question:	Who is the largest employer in the United States?
Answer:	Ronald McDonald!

The previous chapter summarized recent studies pointing to a decline in the American middle class. Three major phenomena have caused this decline in the past 20 years: national and international macroeconomic events, adverse labor market developments, and the increasing ability of capital to outcompete labor for factor rewards. This chapter will examine the impact of recent macroeconomic events on labor. Also, labor market developments will be examined. The next two chapters will examine capital's role in the demise of labor and the middle class in a more general equilibrium analysis.

MACROECONOMIC EVENTS

Four major macroeconomic events in the 1970s caused serious world inflation and led to a fundamental change in the structure of the world economy. The benefits would accrue largely to the holders of capital and to those nations more internationally competitive, such as Japan and Germany. Most oil-rich nations would also benefit. The costs of the events would fall on the middle and poorer classes everywhere, and particularly in the United States and Canada. These events were the collapse of the Bretton Woods fixed exchange rate system in May 1973, the OPEC oil embargo of October 1973, the oil shock related to the Iranian revolution in 1979, and the wave of economic deregulation in the United States.

The Collapse of Bretton Woods

The first macroeconomic shock was the abandonment of fixed exchange rates in 1973 and the subsequent U.S. dollar devaluation, which, when combined with America's inability (or unwillingness) to reduce its purchases of foreign oil, caused an enormous increase in world liquidity. This in turn caused an enormous increase in the volume of world trade. In 1970 the total of U.S. exports and imports made up 16.0 percent of GNP. By 1987 this had risen to more than 25 percent. As Table 4-1 shows, the United States increased her imports far more than her exports in the 1980s. Among the major reasons for this were the huge trade deficits with Germany and Japan, which as nations were considerably more attuned to international trade. Also, however, the presence of flexible exchange rates allowed the price of the dollar to reach record heights in the 1980s, pricing many American manufacturers out of the market. The high price of the dollar was in large part caused by the huge federal deficits in the 1980s.

Borrowing to finance such federal budget deficits pushed up American interest rates, the price of the dollar, and with it the price of American products, producing the huge trade deficits. It is unlikely that such an irresponsible federal budget policy as was seen in the Reagan and Bush years would have been tolerated under the Bretton Woods fixed exchange rate system established in 1944. This is because such huge trade deficits would have drained all the gold out of Fort Knox. But since 1973, we have been on a flexible rate system. The strong dollar hurt our exports, encouraged imports, and dealt a severe blow to American manufacturing and to the middle-class jobs that this sector traditionally delivered. This point will be elaborated on in Chapter 9.

The Energy Shocks of 1973 and 1979 and the
Real-wage Decrease

Two additional major shocks to the middle class came with the inflation caused by the oil price increases of 1973 and 1979. The middle class's most valuable generator of real income—namely, labor—lost ground as prices rose and the real wage fell. Prices rose in the 1970s at more than

Table 4-1
U.S. Foreign Trade and Gross National Product, Selected Years (1982 dollars)

	(1) Exports ($bil.)	(2) Imports ($bil.)	(3) Exports Plus Imports ($bil.)	(4) GNP ($bil.)	(5) Exports Plus Imports (% of GNP)	(6) Exports (% of GNP)	(7) Imports (% of GNP)
1970	178.3	208.3	386.6	2,416.2	0.160	0.074	0.086
1980	388.9	332.0	720.9	3,192.4	0.226	0.122	0.104
1987	427.8	556.7	984.5	3,847.0	0.256	0.111	0.145

Source: U.S. Department of Commerce, Bureau of Economic Analysis data cited in *Economic Report of the President*, Washington, D.C., January 1989, pp. 310–11. Computations by the author.

Table 4-2
Change in U.S. Average Weekly Earnings, Productivity,
and Prices, 1950–1991
(average yearly percent change)[1]

	Average Weekly Earnings[2]		Inflation (% change in CPI[3])	Productivity[4] (output per hour)
	Current Dollars	Constant Dollars		
1950–59	4.63	2.54	2.11	2.63
1960–69	3.83	1.45	2.36	2.41
1970–79	6.74	−0.31	7.08	1.33
1980–89	4.27	−0.96	5.55	0.81
1990–91	3.00	−1.60	4.80	0.48

Notes
1. Calculations by the author.
2. Private non-agricultural average weekly earnings U.S. Department of Labor, Bureau of Labor Statistics data cited in *Economic Report of the President*, Washington, D.C., January 1989, p. 359; and *Economic Report of the President*, Washington, D.C., February 1992, pp. 346 and 365.
3. CPI, consumer price index.
4. Nonfarm business sector productivity. U.S. Department of Labor data cited in *Economic Report of the President,* Washington, D.C., January 1989, p. 361 and *Economic Report of the President*, Washington, D.C., February 1992, p. 349 (1991 estimated).

triple the rates of the 1950s and 1960s, as rising oil prices, a weak dollar, and increased foreign trade all interacted to produce the worst inflation since the Civil War.[1]

As Table 4-2 shows, wages, which rose in current dollar terms by 6.74 percent in the 1970s, fell in inflation-adjusted dollars by 0.31 percent. In the 1980s, the fall in real wages was even greater, averaging almost 1.0 percent. This continued in 1990 and 1991, with wage declines averaging 1.6 percent per year. Thus, inflation outpaced wage increases, and labor and the middle class lost ground. But did the middle class lose ground in the 1970s solely because of the oil-based inflation? The evidence is not clear.

Table 4-3 shows that manufacturing jobs in the 1970s grew by 8.6 percent, which was certainly not the 20 percent rate of growth of the 1960s, but was close to the 9.4 percent growth rate of the glory days of the middle class—the 1950s. The difference, however, is evident if we return to Table

Table 4-3

Employment Growth of Selected U.S. Nonagricultural Sectors, 1950–1989 (in percent)

	Total Civilian	Manufacturing	All Government	Federal Government	State and Local Government	Services
1950–59	17.8	9.4	34.1	15.8	42.8	23.1
1960–69	29.8	20.1	45.6	21.5	55.1	36.3
1970–79	26.7	8.6	27.0	1.5	34.1	33.9
1980–89	19.8	–4.1	9.5	4.3	10.5	28.2

Source: U.S. Department of Labor, Bureau of Labor Statistics data cited in *Economic Report of the President*, Washington, D.C., February 1992, p. 345, computations by the author.

4-2. In the 1950s, real-wage increases nearly matched labor productivity. In the 1960s real-wage increases were approximately 60 percent of productivity gains. In the 1970s, 1980s, and 1990s so far, they didn't even come close. Real wages fell, but surprisingly, labor productivity still increased. Something else fundamental was occurring in the 1970s and it continued in the 1980s. In addition to being unable to gain wage increases equal to the rate of *inflation*, labor was unable to gain increases from its employers equal to the gains it delivered to those employers, that is, its rate of increase in output per hour, or *productivity*. The fundamental balance of power was steadily changing, ascending for capital, eroding for labor. Summarizing the data, one must conclude that the middle class and labor lost substantial purchasing power as a result of the falling wage after inflation. It further suffered a slowdown in the growth of middle-class jobs, as imports first slowed the growth of manufacturing jobs in the 1970s, and further reduced the number of such jobs in the 1980s by 4.1 percent. However, beyond these two developments, it appears that labor's fundamental bargaining position eroded still further, as demonstrated by a continual fall of the real wage relative to productivity. This loss of bargaining power should come as no surprise in light of all the pressure brought to bear on labor, as we have seen in the above discussion and in that which follows.

Deregulation

The fourth major macroeconomic event costing middle-class jobs has been the wave of federal deregulation, which, while operating at a micro (or industry) level, has had the collective effect of a macroeconomic event. This process in banking, trucking, airlines, and communications has increased competition in these industries but has also increased failure rates and the probability of merger. Henry Farber, a noted labor economist, observes that the process has caused problems for both the firms and unions involved.[2] Nonunionized workers are doubtless not exempt from these same problems.

LABOR MARKET DEVELOPMENTS AND MIDDLE-CLASS WAGE DEPRESSION

Let us now turn to the labor market itself for several explanations about the recent decline in labor's economic position.

The Baby Boomers and Increased Female
Labor-force Participation

One explanation for the decline in the number of middle-class jobs derives from the enormous increase in the supply of labor, which, in the face of a slower growing demand for labor, caused downward pressure on wages, thus reducing the numbers of what are considered to be "middle-class paying" jobs. Baby boomers entering the labor force in combination with increased numbers of women acted in concert to create this dramatic increase in labor supply.

In 1984, Robert Z. Lawrence, using a shift share analysis, calculated that the proportion of workers receiving middle-class earnings declined between 1969 and 1983 from 50 percent to 46 percent, with 1 percent going to the upper class and 3 percent to the lower.[3] He calculated that on the basis of economic growth the number of middle-class jobs should have grown by 7.3 million over the period, but instead grew by only 4.0 million. The shortfall of 3.3 million jobs is partially explained by sectoral shifts in the workforce, such as movement out of manufacturing into lower-paying jobs (accounting for 270,600 of the middle-class jobs lost) and the changing mix of males and females. More females in the workforce—who traditionally received lower pay—accounted for the loss of 398,700 middle-class jobs. This, however, left an unexplained residual loss of 2,587,600 middle-class jobs. Lawrence suggests that this residual lack of middle-class jobs is due to the increased competition from both male and female job seekers, forcing wage levels down.[4]

Women flooded into the labor force in the 1970s. From 1970 to 1980 female employment grew by 12.4 million—a 41.9 percent increase—while male employment grew by 4.48 percent. And the pace has slowed little. From 1980 to 1990, female employment grew by another 11.4 million jobs or by 27.0 percent—almost as many as the 12.4 million of the 1970s.[5]

Still, the puzzle remains: why did women invade the labor force in such large numbers (and percentages) not only from 1970 to 1988, but also in the 1960s? In that decade there was a 36 percent increase in female employment (almost 8 million new female workers).

While some may claim this was due to influences of the feminist movement, there were clearly other forces at work. With all the increased numbers and percentages of working women, families on average grew poorer in real terms between 1973 and 1984. The evidence strongly suggests that women went out to work to maintain their families' "middle-class" lifestyle, and they were not always successful. In the poorer classes, the evidence suggests they entered the workforce for family survival. As Katherine Bradbury writes, "If the labor force participation of wives had not increased, the fraction of families with middle class incomes and median family income would have declined even more."[6] Thus the picture becomes somewhat bizarre if we stop here. Women rush into the labor force and, in so doing, compete with the baby boomers—also new entrants. This in turn depresses the wages of the entire labor class, and this class ends up no better off than before. Real wages decline; workers are not rewarded with the fruits of their productivity; the size of the middle class declines, and with it, real family income. But this is not the whole story. It is but a partial answer in a partial setting that confines itself to labor. There are other partial answers to labor's dilemma as well, so we will remain in our partial equilibrium mode for a while longer to pursue several other lines of inquiry.

Rising Legal and Illegal Immigration

A second explanation for the inability of labor to maintain its real wages has been increased immigration into the United States—not only legal, but illegal. Adding this factor to the deluge of baby boomers and females pouring into the labor force, we witness a massive rightward shift of the labor-supply curve, depressing wages.

As first to legal immigration, the United States in the 1980s admitted aliens at a rate of about 600,000 per year. The immigration rate from 1971 to 1986 averaged 2.2 per 1,000 U.S. population—the highest rate since the 1920s, which averaged 3.5 per 1,000. In 1989, 1,091,000 new immigrants entered the U.S. legally, over double the 1980 legal number of 531,000. Further, the 1989 rate averaged 4.4 per 1,000 U.S. population, the highest rate since the 1911–1920 period (5.7 per 1,000).[7]

A 1986 study by Leon Bouvier and Robert Gardner estimates that, from 1980 to 1985, immigration (including illegal aliens) contributed 28.4 percent to the total U.S. population growth.[8] Assuming a relatively stable employment-to-population ratio, this would suggest that approximately 28 percent of all job growth during the period would be absorbed by aliens. In fact, the new job absorption by immigrants might be higher due to employer concealment when hiring "illegals."

Higher estimates could therefore be made as to the significance of combined legal and illegal immigrants. Susan Weber writes that estimates vary from 500,000 to 1.5 million entrants per year prior to the implemen-

Table 4-4
"High" Estimate of Immigrant Component in
U.S. Labor-force Growth, 1978–1986

Net illegal immigrants, 1978–86[1]	10,605,269
Legal immigrants, 1978–86[2]	5,730,000
Total	16,335,269
Average civilian employment to population ratio, 1978–86[3]	0.593
Potential new immigrants holding jobs[4]	9,686,815
Total increase in U.S. civilian employment, 1978–86[5]	17,580,000
Percent of "new jobs" held by new immigrants	55.1

Notes
1. The number of illegal aliens actually apprehended was 10,605,269. The INS estimates that two to three enter the United States for every alien apprehended; here we use a conservative estimate that only *one* enters for every one sent home, yielding the 10,605,269 figure. U.S. Immigration and Naturalization Service, *Statistical Yearbook of the INS*, for net detected illegal immigrants (10,605,269).
2. U.S. Department of Labor, Bureau of Labor Statistics, *Statistical Abstract of the United States, 1988* (Washington, D.C., USGPO, 1988), p. 9.
3. Computed by the author from U.S. Department of Labor, Bureau of Labor Statistics data, cited in *Economic Report on the President*, Washington, D.C., January 1989, p. 344.
4. The term new is defined as those immigrants who arrived between 1978 and 1986.
5. *Economic Report*, op. cit., p. 346.

tation of the immigration-reform legislation passed in 1986.[9] She cites the U.S. Immigration and Naturalization Service (INS) estimate "that for every illegal alien apprehended, two to three others cross the border undetected."[10]

As Table 4-4 demonstrates, for the nine-year period 1978 to 1986— using the "high" (but actually quite conservative) figure that only one illegal alien enters the United States for every one detected, plus official U.S. immigration reports on legal aliens—well over half or 55.1 percent of the reported job growth from 1978 through 1986 could have been filled by immigrants. A "low" estimate falls more in line with that of Bouvier and Gardner, based on the "official" figures on illegal immigrants. The official U.S. figure on illegal aliens developed by the U.S. Bureau of the Census for the late 1970s and the early 1980s up until the passage of the Immigration Reform and Control Act (IRCA) of 1986 is a range of 100,000–300,000 per year. Using these data in Table 4-5, the 1978–1986

Table 4-5
"Low" Estimate of Immigrant Component in
U.S. Labor-force Growth, 1978–1986

Net illegal immigrants at 200,000 per year 1978–86[1]	1,800,000
Legal immigrants[2]	5,730,000
Total	7,530,000
Average civilian employment to population ratio[3]	0.593
Potential new immigrants holding jobs[4]	4,465,290
Total increase in U.S. civilian employment[5]	17,580,000
Percent of "new jobs" held by new immigrants, 1978–86	25.4

Notes:
1. U.S. Bureau of the Census estimate quoted to this author.
2. U.S. Department of Labor, Bureau of Labor Statistics, *Statistical Abstract of the United States, 1988* (Washington, D.C.: USGPO, 1988), p. 9.
3. Computed by the author from data in *Economic Report of the President*, Washington, D.C., January 1989, p. 344.
4. See Table 4-4, footnote 4.
5. *Economic Report*, op. cit., p. 346.

estimate is presented based on an average of 200,000 illegals. Here my estimate is that 25.4 percent of new job growth over the nine-year period could have been absorbed by new immigrants. This appears to be the most conservative estimate.

The 1986 IRCA outlawed the hiring of undocumented workers. The statistics indicate, however, that it has probably not done much to stop the illegal flow. For example, the number of apprehensions from 1978 to 1986 was 10,605,269 (see Table 4-4). This is a yearly average of 1,178,000. William Langewiesche, writing in the May 1992 *Atlantic Monthly,* reports an apprehension figure for 1991 of 1,077,000 (along the Mexican border alone!)—barely 100,000 less than the period prior to the IRCA.[11]

The significance of these numbers for labor as a whole is not only that they are large, but that immigrant labor as a general category will accept wages well below U.S. averages— particularly the illegal entrants. The number of middle-class jobs these immigrants took is an open question. However, it must be remembered that many middle-class jobs can be relatively unskilled, particularly in manufacturing, construction, transportation, and other types of labor. That this represents a labor-supply curve shift to the right is a fact that cannot be denied, and any economist would be hard pressed to deny a downward pressure on both lower- and middle-class wages because of this phenomenon. Thus the estimates of new job growth absorbed by immigrants could range from 28 percent to 55 percent in recent years. The high-side estimate is less reliable, given data problems—particularly since many illegal aliens who are apprehended and sent back home simply try again. Nonetheless, the 25–28 percent new job absorption by immigrant labor is both a large relative number and may understate the actual job absorption.

Further, since many illegals written up do eventually make it into the United States, the official estimate at 200,000 per year is very shaky indeed. It would have to mean that the border guards were catching five out of every six people who try to cross the U.S.–Mexican border illegally. In other words, about 1,400,000 people each year attempted to cross the border, about 1,200,000 per year were caught, and about 200,000 a year made it into the country during the 1978–86 period. These are highly unlikely statistics. The odds are that significantly more than 200,000 people are illegally entering the country every year.

Finally, further liberalizations of the immigration law are now allowing approximately 300,000 additional immigrants into the United States annually. If one applied an additional 300,000 legal or illegal immigrants to the 1978–86 data, immigrants would absorb 34.5 percent of all new jobs during that period.

Unlike the French postwar immigration experience, the recent American experience has seen new immigrants able to fill many *sociologically* defined middle-class jobs. This has weakened the *economically* defined middle-class status. In France, by contrast, unions and government policy prevented immigrants (many of them North Africans) from accepting middle-class jobs, and forced them into the lower-paying service areas. Some observers have claimed that this policy of immigrant job exclusion helped build and strengthen the French middle class. No such policy exists in the United States. The net effect of U.S. immigration policy has been to put downward wage pressure on existing middle-class jobs through increased competition for such jobs. This is particularly true in the manufacturing and construction industries.

One might well ask why the American government has allowed such a huge surge of immigration, both legal and illegal, in recent years. The U.S.–Mexican border of almost 2,000 miles *could* be sealed off if the government really wanted to do it. But it does not. As Langewiesche writes, "In the cities the boundary hardens into a steel fence ... and it does not work. In the open desert it dwindles to three strands of barbed wire and it works better, at least for the cattle. For more than half its length, the border is the Rio Grande, a small, swimmable river."[12]

The conclusion one must draw from this situation is inescapable. The Mexican immigration continues at this illegal pace because American industry wants the cheap labor, which puts downward pressure on all wages. And the federal government, particularly under Reagan and Bush, has been most cooperative.

The Decline in Union Membership and Influence

Adding to the increased supply of labor from the baby boomers, the higher female participation rates, and the flood of immigrant labor, we find a fourth factor in labor's decline, namely, the decline in the influence of unionized labor in the United States. Despite the huge growth in employment and with it the many new entrants into the labor field, the American union movement has failed miserably in capturing these workers philosophically, economically, and politically.

Union membership peaked in the United States in the early 1960s. In 1962, 30.4 percent of all nonagricultural employees were union members. Membership held up fairly well through 1975 when 28.9 percent of the workforce was unionized. Suddenly the decline accelerated. By 1980, membership had fallen to 23.2 percent. By 1984, the percentage was 19.4.[13] A quality-of-employment survey conducted by Lewis Harris and Associates for the AFL–CIO and cited by Henry Farber in his analysis of the decline of unionization in the United States gives Current Population Survey (CPS) data that are much more pessimistic, placing union membership at 15.0 percent of the labor force in 1984 and 14.1 percent in 1985.[14] Thus, while there has been a declining pattern of union membership since 1962, the pace of the decline picked up between 1975 and 1980 and further accelerated from 1980 through 1985.

Farber's explanations for the decline are several. First, a shift in employment to the South and West away from the traditionally heavily unionized Northeast and Midwest has dropped members from union ranks. Second, the shift from traditionally unionized blue-collar employment to the service industries, including many white-collar jobs, has had the same effect. However, Farber notes that less than half of the decline in unionization from the mid-1950s through 1978 can be accounted for by such structural shifts. In fact, the percentage of decline in membership was generally greatest in the most unionized sectors. Thus he concludes that "only 1.1 percentage points of the overall 5.4 percent decline in unionization from 1977 to 1984 can be accounted for by changes in the labor force structure." The rest of the decline was in the "union sector probability of membership,"[15] indicating a decrease in the perception of workers as to the effectiveness of the unions.

Farber also notes an increased employer resistance to union organizing as evidenced by an increased number of unfair-labor-practice actions filed by unions under the National Labor Relations Act. In 1960, 1.78 unfair-labor-practice claims were filed per union election. The claim rate rose to 3.99 in 1977 and 7.45 in 1982. Farber states that "the apparent willingness of employers to engage in unfair labor practices makes it more difficult for unions to organize."[16] He notes further that, during the economic recessions of the 1970s and 1980s "more overt anti-union behavior became socially and politically acceptable, turning what had been a stagnation of the union movement into a virtual rout. Explicit anti-union strategies ... have become the standard mode of operation in U.S. industry."[17]

In 1986 Robert J. Flanagan, studying the increase in unfair-labor-practice filings, concluded that a major cause appeared to be the growing differential between union and nonunion wages. He found that a 1 percent increase in the wage differential was associated with an increase of 175 unfair-labor-practice charges against employers per year.[18] This raises the ominous possibility that we will see an increased supply of nonunionized workers who draw an increasingly lower wage relative to those in unions, and of this growing wage differential's inciting the employers to get even tougher in unionized industries. As Flanagan writes, "In general the effect of an increase in the union/nonunion compensation differential is to provide incentives for employers to reduce compliance and for unions and workers to challenge potential noncompliance by filing unfair labor practices."[19] Judging by the decline in union membership, the employers appear to be gaining the upper hand, regardless of the increased number of unfair-labor-practice charges being filed by workers.

The "rout" of unions of which Farber writes was further aided by Ronald Reagan's successful standoff with, and firing of, the striking members of the Professional Air Traffic Controllers (PATCO) union in 1982. Effected amid criticism of union leadership in that strike action, the firing carried with it a none too subtle message on where the Reagan administration stood vis-à-vis unions and management. Margaret Thatcher accomplished a similar psychological blow to British labor as a whole when her government successfully defeated the long, bitter coal miners' strike of 1984–85.[20]

Table 4-6

Government Employees on Nonagricultual Payrolls in the United States, 1950–1989

	All U.S. Employees (000)	All Government		State & Local		Federal	
		in (000)	% of all U.S.	in (000)	% of all U.S.	in (000)	% of all U.S.
1950	45,197	6,026	13.3	4,098	9.1	1,928	4.3
1960	54,189	8,353	15.4	6,083	11.2	2,270	4.2
1970	70,880	12,554	17.7	9,823	13.9	2,731	3.9
1980	90,406	16,241	17.9	13,375	14.8	2,866	3.2
1988	105,536	17,386	16.5	14,415	13.7	2,971	2.8
1989	108,329	17,779	16.4	14,791	13.7	2,988	2.8

Source: U.S. Department of Labor, Bureau of Labor Statistics data cited in *Economic Report of the President*, Washington, D.C., January 1989, pp. 356–57 and *Economic Report of the President*, Washington, D.C., February 1992, pp. 344–45. Computations by the author.

Table 4-7
Goods-producing and Service-producing Employment, 1946–1991

Year	Total Employment (000)	Goods-producing (000)	% of total	Service-producing (000)	% of total
1946	41,652	17,248	41.4	24,404	58.6
1950	45,197	18,506	40.9	26,691	59.1
1955	50,641	20,513	40.5	30,128	59.5
1960	54,189	20,434	37.7	33,755	62.3
1965	60,765	21,926	36.1	38,839	63.9
1970	70,880	23,578	33.3	47,302	66.7
1975	76,945	22,600	29.4	54,345	70.6
1980	90,406	25,658	28.4	64,748	71.6
1985	97,519	24,859	25.5	72,660	74.5
1990	109,971	24,958	22.7	85,014	77.3
1991	108,975	23,820	21.9	85,154	78.1

Source: See Table 4-6.

The Slowdown in the Growth of Government Employment

Another factor in labor's decline—particularly in regard to middle-class jobs—has been the slowdown in the growth rate of government employment. Government work has been a traditional source of middle-class jobs for bureaucrats, teachers, clerks, and even relatively well-paid laborers. As Table 4-3 earlier showed, all government employment grew by leaps and bounds from 1950 to 1979, growing at 34.1 percent in the 1950s, 45.6 percent in the 1960s and 27.0 percent in the 1970s. However, in the 1980s, this growth slowed to 9.5 percent. The major growth during the postwar period took place in state and local government, particularly in education, to accommodate the baby boomers. However, with their maturation, growth rates have slowed. Total government employment as a percent of total employment declined in the 1980s. As Table 4-6 shows, this decline has been particularly dramatic at the federal level, which has shown an employment drop from 4.3 percent of the total in 1950 to 2.8 percent in 1989. These data contradict politicians' warnings of the dire consequences of "big government." They also speak to the unraveling of the New Deal, which had as its cornerstone an effective federal government.

Thus, government employment fell from 17.9 percent of total employment in 1980 to 16.4 percent in 1989. From these data, it is evident that government is no longer the growth sector for middle-class jobs that it used to be.

The Growing Service Sector and Middle-class Job Loss

Related to the stagnation in growth of government employment has been the rapid growth of service-sector employment. As Table 4-7 shows, this trend, which has been evident since the late 1950s, has accelerated since the 1960s. However, the 1970s and 1980s have shown the most marked rates of increase. In the 1960s, the services share rose by 4.4 percent of total employment; it grew by another 4.9 percent share in the 1970s and then leapt by a 5.7 share in the 1980s. Thus, as Table 4-7 shows, service-producing industries employed 77.3 percent of all Americans on nonagricultural payrolls in 1990 and 78.1 percent in 1991! And the growth in services was not in the higher-paying jobs. For example, transportation and public utilities, and government employment—two of the higher-paying service categories—grew by 29.3 percent and 45.6 percent, respectively, from 1970 to 1990. But employment in retail trade and the general services category grew by 79.3 percent and 144 percent over the same period!

What is the significance of the growth of the service sector, when it comes to middle-class jobs? Sadly, while the service sector obviously *can* provide middle-class jobs, the record shows that, proportionately, it does not do as well as manufacturing. In fact, the record shows that there is more of a bipolarization of wages in service industries than in manufacturing. As Bruce Steinberg writes (using Census Bureau data),

> In 1980 ... production workers in manufacturing earned an average of $15,000 per year versus $23,000 for managers and professionals. In the service sector, nonsupervisory employees made an average of just $9,900 per year, while their supervisors averaged nearly $30,000 per year.[21]

The point should be clear. The rapid loss of U.S. manufacturing competitiveness worldwide, particularly since the 1970s, has made us more and more dependent on a service economy. This has resulted in middle-class job decline. In manufacturing, most employees have middle-class jobs. In the service sectors (excluding the professions), it is more likely that the "production workers" do not.

Finally, a recent study using data on a more limited geographic scale—the San Francisco Bay area—echoes this same point. James Simmie and Ray Brady, in an August 1989 study, conclude that the rise of service and high-technology industries are creating more jobs at the lower income levels, more middle-class households have become two-earner families to compensate for the wage decline, and traditional middle-class employment has been eliminated and replaced by jobs in industries with polarized occupational and income structures.[22]

NOTES

1. For one explanation of this interaction of factors and inflation, see A. K. Fosu and F. R. Strobel, "International Impacts of U.S. Inflation in the 1970s," *Eastern Economic Journal* (October–December 1983), pp. 323–31.

2. Henry S. Farber, "The Recent Decline of Unionization in the United States," Reprint No. 1012, National Bureau of Economic Research, Cambridge, Mass., 1988, p. 6.

3. Robert Z. Lawrence, "Sectoral Shifts and the Size of the Middle Class," *Brookings Review* (1984), p. 6.

4. Ibid.

5. U.S. Bureau of Labor Statistics data cited in *Economic Report of the President* (Washington, D.C., February 1992), p. 334.

6. Katherine Bradbury, "The Shrinking Middle Class," *New England Economic Review*, Federal Reserve Bank of Boston (September/October 1986), p. 6.

7. U.S. Immigration and Naturalization Service, cited in U.S. Bureau of the Census, *Statistical Abstract of the United States, 1991* (Washington, D.C.: USGPO, 1991), p. 9, table 5. Calculations by the author.

8. Leon F. Bouvier and Robert W. Gardner, "Immigration to the U.S.: The Unfinished Story," *Population Bulletin*, Population Reference Bureau, 41, no. 4 (November 1988), table 6.

9. Susan Weber, *USA by Numbers, A Statistical Portrait of the United States* (Washington, D.C.: 1988), Zero Population Growth, p. 36.

10. Ibid.

11. William Langewiesche, "The Border," *Atlantic Monthly* (May 1992), p. 62.

12. Ibid., p. 53.

13. Farber, op. cit., p. 1.

14. Ibid.

15. Ibid., p. 3.
16. Ibid., p. 5.
17. Ibid.
18. Robert J. Flanagan, "NLRA Litigation and Union Representation" *Stanford Law Review*, 38, no. 4 (April 1986), p. 980.
19. Ibid., p. 986.
20. For a discussion of labor's decline relative to capital in England, see F. R. Strobel, "Britain Steps Back from Economic Planning," *Forum for Applied Research and Public Policy*, University of Tennessee (Summer 1989).
21. Bruce Steinberg, "The Mass Market Is Splitting Apart," *Fortune* (November 28, 1983), p. 78.
22. James Simmie and Ray Brady, "Middle Class Decline in Post-industrial Society," *Long Range Planning* (Oxford, England, and New York: Pergamon Press, August 1989), pp. 52–62.

5

Methods of Capital Ascent: The Frontal Assault by Corporate America

> You can vote with your feet in this country. If a state is mismanaged, you can move.
>
> Ronald Reagan

In Chapter 3 we saw how a number of measures indicated an increasingly skewed income distribution that has diminished the status, size, and affluence of the middle class. Chapter 4 explained, mainly in a partial equilibrium setting, that a number of macroeconomic factors as well as several factors operating within the labor market have diminished the economic rewards to labor and the labor-dependent, relative to capital.

This chapter will trace and explain the recent increase in strength of capital. We thus move to a general equilibrium analysis since this ascent of capital comes largely from gains at the expense of labor. The two factors of capital and labor are competing resources, and there can be no true picture of the decline of the middle class until we explain what labor has given up to capital in the latter's recent rising power.

The middle class is essentially labor-dependent or transfer-dependent for its well-being. We can lay it out that capital's main route in recent years to self-enhancement, with few exceptions, consists of four major thrusts: (1) to develop and employ new technologies that are capital intensive and labor saving; (2) to use whatever means necessary—be it threat of job loss or union busting—to reduce the real wage; (3) to muster public opinion and ultimately influence the election of politicians who are favorable to capital and less favorable to labor; and (4), to use this influence particularly with government to achieve less regulation of its activities, and lower levels of taxation. In all of these goals, the capital-enhanced regime has been enormously successful. While capital and labor are complementary resources, they are competitive by nature and by the laws of economics. While both can increase their prosperity jointly, as in the 1950s for example, the economic history of the twentieth century has largely showed that capital ascending has meant labor descending, and vice versa. By 1992, however, capital has ascended to a near bruising level of power over labor, over government, and over American life in general. This power is far greater than at any period since the 1920s and perhaps since the 1890s. Further, the trend will quite possibly continue in the foreseeable future to levels that reasonable people could only regard as a threat to the traditional economic democracy of the United States.

REDEFINING CAPITAL, LABOR, AND THE MIDDLE CLASS

In order to explain how capital has gained its present heights, we must first examine and define the nature of capital and its relationship to the forces driving it. That capital which competes with labor we can define as profit-seeking capital. It is footloose and mobile, seeking the highest rewards. This capital and its movement are, of course, human directed. The individuals who direct this footloose capital we can identify as the large holders of capital and/or their professional managers whose livelihoods are not governed by labor alone but rather whose incomes are either capital enhanced or identified strongly with the capital-enhanced group. The identifying feature of the capital-enhanced manager who may not person-ally own the capital, as distinguished from the labor-dependent classes who may also work with the same capital (such as factory workers), is the significantly higher than average income of the manager. This high income is his or her reward for directing capital and for clearly identifying with the holders of capital, as opposed to merely "working with" someone else's capital—often the lot of the labor-dependent. Thus, we will define the capital-enhanced group as the large holders of capital—that is, so large as to render them non-labor-dependent—and their highly paid (well above average) directors or managers. It is this capital under the command of the capital-enhanced individuals that competes with labor.

Most labor does own some capital. Yet, for most of the laboring class the capital that it owns consists of its housing, personal effects, cars, and modest savings. This type of capital, for a large majority of labor and of middle class, is merely self-maintaining. Thus we should redefine *labor*, and thus *most of the middle class*, as that group of individuals whose livelihood or economic well-being is *primarily labor* or *employment dependent*. Without the individual's ability—or the husband and wife's ability—to hold gainful employment, his or her capital holdings would not be sufficient to sustain a given standard of living.

Also, most labor works with some capital. But the distinguishing feature of the labor-dependent is that they work with capital not their own, and that, further, someone else (in the capital-enhanced class) is the significant director of that capital.

The capital-enhanced group also would include those who own and hold command over land and the rents it produces, if in fact that rent is sufficient in size to render an individual non-labor-dependent. On the other hand there are those who have small or moderate amounts of capital, such as the family farm owner or the small shopkeeper or tradesperson, who are still labor-dependent. While they may own and direct the capital, their incomes are labor-dependent, and the capital necessary to the operation is not footloose.

CAPITAL'S SUCCESSFUL BATTLE FOR MINDS AND VOTES

It is thus the capital-enhanced forces, most often represented by the business community, that seek to put forth their views and compete with the labor-dependent forces. Nonetheless the capital-enhanced group will enlist the help of labor-dependent persons—often the middle class—to promote its own self-interest. For example, many employees of large business organizations, particularly from middle management on up, whose small personal assets render them labor-dependent, will frequently align with the capital-enhanced group. They probably believe that their own self-interest aligns with this group. And for one good reason it does: They are in the employ of the large capital holders, and they risk job loss for nonsupport. We might term this combination of capital-enhanced individuals and their otherwise labor-dependent supporters the "capital-enhanced regime." Since the capital-enhanced regime is a minority in the society, it must enlist public opinion and thus garner a sufficient number of votes to ensure its overrepresentation in the Congress and in state and local councils of government. It has of late been enormously successful in elevating the economic well-being of itself over the labor-dependent forces. Paradoxically, it has achieved its elevated position by convincing a sufficient number of the labor-dependent voters to support its political positions, even to the long-run detriment of labor. Quite simply put—rendering Abraham Lincoln's wise pronouncement on the subject obsolete—it has fooled enough of the people enough of the time.

It is here that the role of Ronald Reagan has most prominently figured. His term in office, beginning in 1980, turned what should have been the end of a long period of labor descent and of increasing income inequality, into the middle of such a continuing period. His personal magnetism in putting across the views of his backers fooled most of the people most of the time. His role, or his act, will be examined in more depth in Chapter 8. Suffice it to say that capital continues to exert sufficient control on the governmental machinery to elevate the capital-enhanced and diminish the labor-dependent and thus the percentages of those Americans enjoying the "middle-class" lifestyle. With larger rewards going to capital, there is simply less left over for labor—not enough to support the former percentages of the labor-dependent who were able to achieve that lifestyle. Thus, the middle class must either shrink, or accept a lower standard of living even if it continues to be defined as middle class. The wonder and beauty of the former American middle class was its relative size, its real income levels, and its luxurious lifestyle when compared to its counterparts in other industrial nations. These relative advantages are disappearing.

How is it that a minority, albeit well financed, has effected such a change in the economic landscape of a democratic country, promoting inequality in its own behalf? Quite simply, the capital-enhanced group has been well served by its single-mindedness of purpose. Its leaders are bright, articulate, motivated, well trained and do not lose sight of their own self-interest. Additionally they have the financial power to purchase the expertise that they do not possess, be it legal or managerial. It has thus been able to capitalize on the myriad of new and often complex developments in politics and in the national and international economic arena. The former intellectual leaders of the labor-dependent classes have been weakened, have lost interest, or have been co-opted by the opposition. A combination of complex events, developments, and power shifts have occurred over the past 25 years that have rendered ineffective the leadership of the labor-dependent. But the single-minded self-interest of the capital-enhanced has adapted effectively.

THE COMPLEXITY OF NATIONAL ISSUES

The increasing intricacy and size of the economy and its relation to government has provided capital with a natural avenue to elevate its interests.

The size of the federal budget is one such example. Perhaps no group better understands its size and complexity, and the implications as to how monies are allocated within the federal budget, than the capital-enhanced group. In contrast, a rising and alarmingly large percentage of those in the labor-dependent group either have no interest in comprehending that important instrument of national policymaking or else are unable to understand it since many can't tell the difference between millions and billions of dollars. To a similar degree, voters are showing little interest in state or even municipal budgets except in the case where their taxes might be affected.

Or, to take another example, consider the intellectual prowess required to understand the world of international finance. The technology and expertise needed to deal with floating exchange rates, capital flight, and transfer of funds is simply not possessed by the average or less-than-average citizen. While the business or capital-enhanced class has always held an edge over the labor-dependent in these matters, the complexity of today's open economy—complete with fluctuating exchange rates and rapidly mobile capital—has greatly elevated the relative power of the capital-enhanced group. Other examples abound; but the expertise now possessed by capital over labor, combined with the inability of the latter either to hire such expertise or to assure that its interests are protected by the expertise of a benevolent and caring government, has changed the equation of power in the United States. Along with this, the distribution of income is now more skewed than at any time in the post–World War II era. Let us turn to the methods employed by the capital-enhanced and its representatives in achieving this result.

THE DENIGRATIVE METHOD AND THE ATTACK ON GOVERNMENT

In general, the capital-enhanced regime has used the traditional means of supporting conservative political candidates who will work for minimal government size and less control over the economy. While conservative forces have generally worked to hold down the size of the government, the capital-enhanced regime has, since 1968, added a new element in the strategy. It has become explicitly antigovernment to the point of smearing, slandering, and being generally denigrative. The denigrative approach works better for these forces than simply a minimal-government approach.[1]

The denigrative method seeks to label virtually all actions of the government as being counterproductive. The government becomes the problem. Richard Nixon was the first president openly to run against the government. He was followed in this by Jimmy Carter, who ran an antigovernment campaign of sorts as a "Washington outsider." Ronald Reagan—by far the most denigrative—was the culmination of this approach, stating many times in one way or another that the government of the United States was the problem. Thus the aim becomes to cut the size of the government—delivering in the process two important benefits to the capital-enhanced group, namely, lower taxes and less government regulation—points to which I will return in this chapter and the next.

Success in rallying the voters behind such antigovernment campaigns probably rests on several factors. First, there has always been the natural deep-seated resentment of the American citizen to any kind of control— but particularly government. Second, the job security of the government employee has always been a thorn in the side of the private-sector worker and thus no doubt makes him somewhat receptive to antigovernment campaigns. Then too, the government's role in the extension of civil rights in the 1960s and 1970s left much resentment in enough souls to be capitalized on. Finally, if an antigovernment campaign, particularly in the form of the denigrative or slander method, is successful, the new administration can create what amounts to—with a nudge—a self-fulfilling prophecy.

The Reduction of Government Services

The Reagan administration's huge corporate tax cuts, particularly combined with its antigovernment rhetoric, made the direction toward less government and poorer government inevitable. Such revenue losses to the federal government require—in order to escape even more obscene budget deficits than occurred—cuts in government services and in spending on programs that in the main were designed to benefit the labor-dependent segment of the society. And so, cuts were made in the Head Start programs, in welfare programs, in inner-city programs, in mental health services, in education, in revenue sharing to the states, and in funds for statistical data collection by government agencies.

Why did the mass of voters who lost benefits due to cuts in these programs not react politically? Partly because such actions become a self-fulfilling prophecy. In other words, the cutting of the budgets of government agencies not only reduced the services available to the average citizen, but made these agencies appear (as they probably became) incompetent, strained, and inefficient. They lost quality personnel to the private sector; and therefore, in order to retain staffing, the agencies hired younger, more inexperienced, less qualified individuals since that's all the reduced budgets allowed. Thus the government agencies tended to deliver less quality services, and the electorate at large began to believe that the government was in fact, less efficient—that the government, in fact, "was the problem." The confused electorate—confused in many ways by a very likable president—railed at the government, paid higher taxes, and accepted poorer quality in such public services as road maintenance. Perhaps most damaging of all, it accepted lower quality educational services at the elementary and secondary levels for its children.

Reducing the Watchdog Role of Government

Then too the denigrative method, which diminishes the competence of government in the voters' eyes, makes it much easier to allow private-sector capital interests to escape the regulators. It further lessens the government's traditional role in protecting the middle class. Thus it is no accident that along with middle-class decline we have seen less government protection of the right to collective bargaining, less protection against unfair labor practices, and less government protection of the consumer (and labor) from lax enforcement of antitrust laws. Thus, the government slander approach, combined with every attempt possible to weaken government financially and to enhance the possibilities for government agency failure (or appearance of failure) in performing its duties, was perhaps one of the most effective techniques in elevating the capital-enhanced over the labor-dependent.

THE EXTENDED USE OF PACS AND THE DEMOCRATIC PARTY

A second major development elevating the ranks of the capital-enhanced has been the extended use of funds raised through political action committees (PACs). As Thomas Edsall wrote in the June 1988 *Atlantic Monthly*, the decade of 1974–84 saw PACs go from supplying 17 percent of the total cost of House campaigns to 36 percent.[2] Contributions from individuals fell from 73 percent to 47 percent of such total funds raised over that time period. The significance of this development cannot be understated, particularly in the PAC contributions to the Democratic party. PAC contributions to the Republican party, which generally represents the capital-enhanced group, will be—without exception, if in the economic realm—favoring the capital-enhanced positions. PAC contributions to the Democratic party will be of several varieties. First, there will be the traditional PAC contributions from Democratic groups for liberal causes or labor-oriented issues. Second, however, is a new element: PAC contributions from the capital-enhanced interests. Considerably more of business interest PAC contributions have been accepted over the years, so that the traditional role of the Democratic party in representing the labor-dependent classes has become watered—particularly the Democratic party's traditional opposition to lower corporate taxes. The use of PACs by the capital-enhanced forces and its effect on the Democratic party have helped change the fundamental equation between capital and labor.

THE INTELLECTUAL ASSAULT OF CAPITAL

Capital has combined its political forces with an intellectual assault, and nowhere has this been more successful than in its battle for the minds of the economics profession. Since the counterrevolution in economic thought led by Milton Friedman in the 1960s, there has evolved a significant conservative orientation within the economics profession. Some of this thought is a natural evolution in that the experiments with controlled markets, particularly in socialist and communist countries, generally have not worked. Yet a bigger problem exists within the profession. No segment of the economics profession has challenged, tested, and provided a timely and politically effective counter to the public opinion influence of the many conservative economics spokespersons. Rather, the profession has become progressively interested in partial equilibrium analysis on often obscure microeconomic topics, and in the mathematical modeling of any and every economic theory that breathes. Leading economics journals such as the *American Economic Review*, the *Southern Economic Journal*, or the *Journal of Political Economy*, while containing much excellent economic analysis, have little effective policy influence. Yet it is by publishing in these leading journals and others like them that untenured faculty at most of the major universities earn their tenure points and that associate professors become promoted to full professors. Increasingly, such publications are the means by which faculty earn a merit pay increase. Evaluating policy issues and publishing the results will hardly ever deliver tenure or a pay increase.

Thus, the liberal wing of the U.S. economics profession failed, in the early 1980s, to overcome intellectually the grossly overexaggerated claims of economic benefits to be derived from the proposed tax cuts of 1981. These claims were spearheaded by an evangelical group including George Gilder, Jude Wannisky, Arthur Laffer, and David Stockman. The tragedy for the economics profession is that the supply-siders' claims were grossly exaggerated and/or unproven empirically and yet the liberal economists didn't mount a sufficient campaign to cast reasonable doubts on the supply-siders' propositions either through exercising their prestige and influence or proving them empirically wrong in a timely fashion. The tragedy for the republic is that such wild economic claims became law and, with this, the federal government budget was thrown into massive deficit. As Chapter 6 will show, the Economic Recovery Tax Act of 1981 markedly accelerated the pattern of capital ascent and labor descent.

Could not the opposition economists have countered the largely unsupported claims of the supply-siders in the early 1980s? Of course they could have. But the reward system in major universities dictated other areas of concentration. And so, while an occasional opposing newspaper or magazine article may have been written by a leading liberal economist, the supply-side economic bandwagon moved like a steamroller, when in fact its intellectual fuel was barely sufficient to power a paper airplane.

The economics profession has also by and large accepted uncritically a low unemployment rate as an indicator of economic well-being. The unemployment rate says very little about the distribution of income between capital and labor, or about the quality of jobs.

While the profession (like the large corporations) has largely accepted the stabilization function of government, it has largely ignored tax burdens, average real incomes, and quality of jobs. Further there has been a decline in the relative attention paid to the income and wealth distribution effects of the changing U.S. economy and related U.S. government policy. The rewards of the profession are now moving into the more conservative areas of economics.

For example, one significant factor aiding the capital-enhanced regime in its battle for the minds has been its financial support of think tanks espousing conservative philosophies. As Edsall writes, "The creation and expansion of such ideological think tanks as the Heritage Foundation, the Center for National Policy, the Urban Institute, the American Enterprise Institute (AEI), the Cato Institute, and the Hoover Institution have established whole networks of influential public policy entrepreneurs specializing in media relations and in targeted position papers."[3] The emergence of these conservative think tanks, amply financed, has served to dwarf the intellectual voices supporting labor-dependent positions. Add to this the fact that the Brookings Institution—the flagship of the liberal economic intellectual establishment in bygone days—has become increasingly conservative. Robert Kuttner suggests this stance may have something to do with its sources of funding, which are surprisingly similar to those of the AEI and the Hoover Institution. Among the As in the list of contributors to Brookings, he lists "Alcoa...American Express...Atlantic Richfield, AT&T."[4]

SUPPRESSING GOVERNMENT'S
EDUCATIVE FUNCTION

Another intellectual approach taken by the capital-enhanced regime, though more subtle, is no less effective than its other methods. By downgrading and cutting the size of government, it diminishes the educative function of that body. The American Economic Association has recently established a committee to try to restore some of the economic data gathering that has been dropped by the Bureau of the Census and other agencies. Information is power, and no one knows this any better than the capital-enhanced regime. The less information coming out of the government—and indeed it is only the government that can collect much of this information—the more capital is relatively freer from certain aspects of regulation and/or public criticism. But the downgrading of government has still another very subtle but profound effect, namely, the deterioration in the quality of schools. The capital-enhanced regime will always have available to its group and its cohorts the better educational facilities and sufficient information not only to perform its function, but moreover to compete better with a less well informed and less well educated labor-dependent group. The labor-dependent group, which by definition has little capital, simply cannot afford much data gathering, or in many cases, education. Public education deteriorates and thus the chasm widens. The electorate can be more easily misled. The labor-dependent group becomes increasingly susceptible to manipulation because it lacks an understanding of the huge and complex economic issues of the country, and is thus prey to the masters of intellectual confusion such as those who practice the government slander approach. Further, the labor-dependent group becomes more dependent on single-issue politics to release its political emotions. And the capital-enhanced groups cultivate the single-issue groups politically. They thus kill two birds with one stone. First, they pick up the votes of the anti-abortionists, the prayer-in-the-public-schools advocates, and so on; and second, they provide a release for these persons' political passions, and keep the minds of the labor-dependent off of economic issues such as the changing tax burdens.

CAPITAL'S CAMPAIGN: A NATIONAL SALES TAX TO REPLACE THE CORPORATE INCOME TAX

As the power of the capital-enhanced group grows disproportionately large relative to that of the labor-dependent group, large corporations can use a measured amount of their newly acquired wealth and purchasing power to hire brain power and both defend its intellectual positions and put forth new assaults on government or any organization that stands in their way. In addition to capital's financing of think tanks that support its causes, its lobbying position becomes increasingly powerful. Many of its lobbies, such as the Washington-based American Council for Capital Formation headed by Charls Walker ("Mr. VAT"), are extremely well financed and influential.

The "Committee" is currently trying to convince the American electorate that it would be better off paying a national sales tax (a value-added tax, or VAT) and eliminating the corporate income tax. The danger here is that a legislative settlement on these economic policy issues will be reached through the popularity of the ideas and not necessarily their economic merit. The problem is that the popularity of economic ideas has recently led to seriously ill-informed decisions: Witness the Economic Recovery Tax Act of 1981. So far, the economics profession has been relatively silent and has not directly opposed the popular lobbies advocating elimination of the corporate tax. However, the bulk of economic evidence and studies would favor its retention. Corporate spokespersons for the elimination of the corporate income tax use the very appealing but unproven argument that the tax is actually passed on to the consumer. A number of studies have been undertaken to determine who actually pays the corporate income tax. In other words, are the corporations able to raise prices or cut wages to employees in sufficient amounts to compensate for the taxes they pay? The response most commonly accepted by economists is that there is honest disagreement among reputable persons and studies.

In the face of such disagreement, most economists would be hard pressed to conclude that the corporate tax is paid by anyone but the corporation, at least in the short run. But most economists agree that a value-added (VAT) type of sales tax would be shifted forward to the consumer in the short run. Thus, substituting a VAT for the corporate income tax would most likely further increase the tax burden on an already overtaxed consumer and middle class. It would further lighten the tax load on capital, again adding to its power. And a VAT is regressive, hurting lower-income persons proportionately more than the wealthy. The corporate income tax is just the opposite, that is, progressive.

The capital-enhanced spokespersons will, of course, continue their onslaught against the corporate income tax. A popular appeal to the voter/consumer will continue to be that he or she pays it anyway. Enter the puzzle: If the corporate leaders are convinced that corporations don't pay it, and that they shift it to someone else, why are they so worried about it?

THE THREAT OF CAPITAL MOBILITY FOR WAGE AND TAX CONCESSIONS

Lending further power to the capital-enhanced regime is capital's increasing mobility and the threat thereof. The enhanced mobility of capital has been made possible by several recent developments. One such development is the advent of the global corporation. While the global corporation is nothing new, recent changes in information technology have enhanced its status as a consumer of information and thus its ability to look for new opportunities to capitalize on cheap production costs. The exploding volume of international trade between the United States and the rest of the world in the 1970s and 1980s—both absolutely and as a percentage of its GNP—has also promoted larger international financial markets, giving capital much more opportunity to move between countries. Flexible exchange rates and the development of European and Asian dollar markets have provided vast new avenues for capital flow. In the competition between capital and labor, nowhere is the match so unequal as in mobility, or lack thereof. Never can labor hold the trump card of

mobility that capital always possesses. We never hear labor, as an organization or as a group in society, saying, "We don't like to work in the
state of Michigan or the state of Mississippi, or the state of Florida, so we
are going to leave." But the capital-enhanced regime says this all the time.
It threatens state, county, and city governments with its mobility if "the
conditions are not right." It threatens the federal government with its
mobility if national economic policies are not favorable. And most importantly, it threatens labor, whether unionized or not.

The response to the threat of capital mobility is weak on all fronts.
While the United States has been described by many economists as the
most fluid labor market in the world, the fact is, American labor is at a
disadvantage in this regard. Mobility on the part of labor requires selling
houses, paying moving expenses, uprooting children from schools, and,
increasingly, uncertainty as to whether or not the spouse can find work in
the new location. The two-earner family has made labor more susceptible
to the mobility threats of corporations. It is much easier these days for a
corporation to achieve take-backs, wage concessions, pension concessions, and so on, as more married laborers share in a codependence for
survival, both working needed jobs in the local area.

Another major factor promoting the mobility of capital is an increase
in willingness of that part of local, county, and state economic-develop-
ment agencies to influence their local government bodies toward granting
tax concessions to attract or retain firms. From a national viewpoint, we
see a strange spectacle of competing states, counties, cities, or economic-
development jurisdictions each granting tax concessions and low-cost
services, and in many ways neutralizing each other's attractability as
manufacturing or business sites.

In a 1985 study Michael Wasylenko and Therese McGuire wrote,
"Often policymakers blame slow employment growth on taxes, when, as
in Pennsylvania, the tax variables favored employment growth"; and
further, "variables beyond the direct control of policymakers such as
wages, energy prices, and other variables are the largest contributors to
low employment growth rates. Raiding the state treasury to increase
employment growth may not necessarily produce significant results."[5]

All in all, these concessions, like beer commercials, become largely
self-canceling. Yet there is a cost involved, and that cost is the permanent
or long term erosion of the tax base at the state and local level. Who then
must pick up the difference? Labor—through higher income, sales or
property taxes, or some declining quality of local educational, police, and
sanitation services. As in the oft-heard economic criticism of advertising

when applied to oligopoly or monopolistic competition, much advertising becomes self-canceling, but there is nonetheless a cost. The cost of the product is increased by the cost of the advertising and the consumer ends up paying some of the tab. In a similar way, the bidding for capital by various state and local jurisdictions is largely self-canceling but not without cost. Its cost is one that weakens these jurisdictions and weakens the quality of life of the labor-dependent classes while enhancing the economic power of the capital-enhanced regime.

A number of writers have addressed this problem of immobile labor and mobile capital. Richard Barnet and Ronald Muller, writing in 1974 in their classic work *Global Reach*, provide some of the more memorable and poignant observations on the subject, among them this passage:

> Local communities that waken to the need for their own development programs may not represent a good investment climate and as long as more apathetic and manageable communities exist, corporations would be more likely to move there. For this reason, there should be legal prohibitions on the power of global corporations to exploit their mobility. A corporation should not be allowed to move into a community, pollute it, drain it financially, build dependencies, and then disclaim responsibilities for the problems it creates as it leaves.[6]

Barry Bluestone and Bennett Harrison, writing in 1982, state:

> The capital mobility option provided by the new technology shifted the fulcrum of bargaining power in favor of capital to an unprecedented degree.... The newly enhanced ability to move capital within the same country provides capital corporate management with the necessary economic and political clout to insist upon reductions in local taxation and therefore cuts in community services and the social safety net.[7]

An illustrative case in point is the current effort made by a number of major manufacturers to reduce their local property tax liabilities. Ford Motor Company was successful in doing this in Dearborn, Michigan, in the 1980s. In the mid-1980s, General Motors launched a nationwide campaign to reduce local property taxes in order to increase its competitiveness in world markets, as its press releases explained. Pointed out by consumer advocate Ralph Nader in 1985, fifteen Michigan communities with GM plants were fighting GM attempts to drastically cut property tax assessments.[8] The small town of Comstock (population: 11,000) spent and borrowed heavily for a legal defense fund in attempting to preserve its tax revenues from the Fisher Auto Body plant where many of its citizens were employed. What General Motors spent on this case is unknown, but it was rumored to be paying its attorneys a contingency fee. The company denied this, but one thing *is* certain: GM's legal expenses were tax deductible. After a 37-month legal battle, the Michigan Tax Tribunal on July 1, 1991, ruled in favor of the town.[9] General Motors saved a total of $300,000 for the tax years 1984, 1985, and 1986, as opposed to the $3 million tax reduction it sought.[10] The cost to Michigan taxpayers of the defense against the suit was $3.8 million.[11] Indeed, the matchup of a "GM" against a "Comstock, Michigan" is like a football game between the San Francisco Forty-Niners and Amherst College. Thus, many local governments understandably back down when faced with a threat from a major taxpayer. The cost of fighting is too great. They cut the big employer's taxes and raise homeowner taxes.

The results that corporations and, in reality, the entire capital-enhanced regime have achieved through their enhanced mobility are startling. As will be shown in the next chapter, corporations are paying state and local taxes at the lowest levels in years. Doubtless, capital's ability to move internationally is also a factor in its currently paying nearly the lowest level of federal taxes that it has in years—a point to which we shall also return in Chapter 6.

MERGER, ACQUISITION, AND MIDDLE-CLASS JOB LOSS

Mergers and acquisitions, which increased during the 1970s, accelerated to unprecedented levels during the Reagan administration. Traditionally federal regulation of such acts has come mainly from the Sherman Antitrust Act of 1890 and the Clayton Act of 1914. The Sherman Act, as the grandfather of antitrust legislation, dwells on combinations in restraint of trade, declaring such arrangements illegal and providing substantial penalties for violators. The Clayton Act sharpened and clarified many of Sherman's provisions.

Walter Adams and James Brock, in 1988, detailed the record of corporate acquisitions and mergers over the period of 1980–86.[12] Citing statistics published in the journal *Mergers and Acquisitions*, they reported that the number of corporate acquisitions went from the 1980 total of 1,565 to a 1986 annual total of 4,022. This represented $667 billion as the value of the corporate acquisitions—a historically unprecedented amount. Also over this seven-year time period, there were 106 takeovers involving more than $1 billion each.

The effect on labor of the recent unparalleled relaxation of the antitrust laws—and the ensuing levels of corporate takeovers—cannot be minimized. The simple fact is, a takeover often means a new labor agreement must be made. Insidious actions often follow, such as the raiding of pension funds that are suddenly deemed to be excessively funded. Labor forces are cut to save costs, and the highest paid workers—often those with the most longevity—are dismissed in what the courts are increasingly terming "age discrimination." The Justice Department in the 1980s looked the other way, allowing nonunion companies to acquire unionized companies. Labor's position is seldom enhanced by these combinations except in the case where the combination prevents the firm being acquired from going out of business, which only occurs in the minority of circumstances. The current antitrust laws are applied (when applied) mainly in product markets—such as how the combination will affect the purchase price of the product to the consumer (and even these price-competition effects have been relaxed). A production factor market such as labor is largely ignored, both by government regulators and the economics profession at large. The creation or promotion of monopsonies (single powerful buyers of a product or factor of production) and oligopsonies through the recent relaxation of antitrust laws has served—as economic theory would predict—to weaken the labor-dependent, unionized or not, in their ability to compete with the capital-enhanced regime for economic rewards. In sum, the combination of such firms has probably had the effect of higher prices, higher profits to capital, and a further weakening of the economic well-being of labor.

NOTES

1. I am indebted to Garry Wills for the categorization of this antigovernment method as denigrative. See Garry Wills, *Nixon Agonistes* (Boston: Houghton Mifflin, 1968), especially pp. 72–90.

2. Thomas Byrne Edsall, "The Return of Inequality," *Atlantic Monthly* (June 1988), p. 88.

3. Ibid., p. 89.

4. Robert Kuttner, "The Revenge of the Democratic Nerds," *New Republic* (October 22, 1984), p. 17.

5. Michael Wasylenko and Therese McGuire, "Jobs and Taxes: The Effect

of Business Climate on States' Employment Growth Rates," *National Tax Journal*, 38, no. 4 (1985), p. 509.

6.   Richard J. Barnet and Ronald E. Muller, *Global Reach: The Power of Multinational Corporations* (New York: Simon and Schuster, 1974), p. 382.

7.   Barry Bluestone and Bennett Harrison, *The Deindustrialization of America* (New York: Basic Books, 1982), p. 18.

8.   "GM Tax Request," *New York Times* (April 24, 1985), p. D14.

9.   Al Jones, "Comstock 'Wins' GM Fight," *Kalamazoo Gazette* (Michigan: July 1, 1991), p. B1.

10.   Ibid.

11.   Ibid.

12.   Walter Adams and James W. Brock, "Reaganomics and the Transmogrification of Merger Policy," *Anti-trust Bulletin*, published by the *Journal of American and Foreign Anti-trust and Trade Regulation* (Summer 1988), p. 310.

6

Shifting the Tax Burden: "The Great Escape" of Corporate America

> The entire graduated income tax structure was created by Karl Marx.
>
> Ronald Reagan

In order to assess more completely the decline of the labor-dependent classes (and the accompanying middle-class slide) and the ascent of capital, we must look closer at several key elements that measure each factor's financial health. When analyzing this comparative welfare, one must look for a common measure of economic well-being. Only then can the analysis be in a general equilibrium, or more complete, framework.

One way to do this is to consider taxes on both labor and capital. Governments always need a growing amount of revenue to meet expenditures for growing population needs. Taxes are levied on both labor and capital, most commonly through income and property taxes on each factor. And generally, if tax reductions are given to one group, tax increases must be imposed on the other group to make up for the revenue shortfall.

In Chapter 3 we focused mainly on pretax income available to individuals. Here we will focus on taxes paid by consumers and large businesses (corporations). We will also examine what's left over after all the taxes and expenses have been paid, that is, savings. The analysis of Chapter 3 was rather limited or partial. The following analysis will be more general or complete since what businesses escape in taxes, the consumer—mainly the middle class—must pay. The data presented will verify an important factor in middle-class decline: the "great escape" by corporations from taxes, and the shifting of these burdens to the middle class and to the consumer.

Taxes paid are a critical element in producing financial well-being since, as expenses, they directly affect the residual or profit. This chapter looks more closely at the taxes paid by individuals as the bulk of the labor-dependent group and at taxes paid by corporations as the main representatives of the capital-enhanced group.

Savings—the financial residual—is a critical indicator of economic well-being. While net profit data are not available for either labor or families, personal savings data are, as are business savings data (net profits after taxes plus depreciation). While we don't have net profits for labor, we do have personal savings. By comparing these savings data as well as tax burdens between capital and labor, we can get a more informed view of the comparative financial power of the two groups over time.

THE CORPORATE ESCAPE FROM FEDERAL TAXES

Table 6-1, drawn from the federal budget of the United States, shows the percentage contribution of federal receipts by source. This table illustrates the shifting pressures inflicted on the middle class and on labor as a whole by the capital-enhanced regime in avoiding federal taxes. Individual income taxes have, since 1955, averaged in the 44–48 percent range of all federal tax receipts. On the other hand, the corporate income tax which in 1955 made up 27.3 percent of federal tax receipts, has steadily eroded in its contribution to the government. In 1983—two years after the initial Reagan tax reform (the Economic Recovery Tax Act of 1981) with personal income taxes near their highest share of all federal tax receipts over the period covered—the corporate income tax fell to its lowest percentage contribution: 6.2 percent of all federal receipts. The tax cut, which was proclaimed and sold to the country as essentially a tax break for the workers of America to titillate them with the prospect of receiving supply-side incentives and getting the government off their backs, resulted in the individual income tax's contributing almost the highest percentage of total federal receipts in the history of the republic. The highest percentage was reached in 1982—one year after the Reagan tax breaks—when the individual income tax contributed 48.2 percent of total federal reve-

Table 6-1
Percentage Contribution of Federal Receipts by Source,
1949–1991 and Estimated 1992

	Individual Income Taxes	Corporate Income Taxes	Social Insurance Taxes and Contributions	Excise Taxes	Other	Total
1949	39.5	28.4	9.6	19.0	3.5	100.0
1955	43.9	27.3	12.0	14.0	2.8	100.0
1960	44.0	23.2	15.9	12.6	4.2	100.0
1965	41.8	21.8	19.0	12.5	4.9	100.0
1970	46.9	17.0	23.0	8.1	4.9	100.0
1975	43.9	14.6	30.3	5.9	5.4	100.0
1980	47.2	12.5	30.5	4.7	5.1	100.0
1982	48.2	8.0	32.6	5.9	5.3	100.0
1983	48.1	6.2	34.8	5.9	5.0	100.0
1985	45.6	8.4	36.1	4.9	5.0	100.0
1987	46.0	9.8	35.5	3.8	4.9	100.0
1988	44.1	10.4	36.8	3.9	4.8	100.0
1989	45.0	10.4	34.5	3.4	4.8	100.0
1990	45.3	9.1	36.9	3.4	5.4	100.0
1991	44.4	9.3	37.6	4.0	4.7	100.0
1992	44.5	8.3	38.2	4.3	4.7	100.0

Note: Data for 1992 are White House estimates.
Source: For 1949–88 data, "Historical Tables," in the *Budget of the United States Government, Fiscal Year 1990*, Executive Office of the President, Washington, D.C., 1989, pp. 27–29. For 1989–92, *Budget of the United States Government, Fiscal Year 1993*, Executive Office of the President, Washington, D.C., 1992, part 5, pp. 25–26.

nues. However, in 1983 the corporate income tax fell to its nadir at 6.2 percent.

So embarrassing to the government were the corporate tax cuts of 1981 that some (such as the investment tax credit) were eliminated in 1986. However, as can be seen in Table 6-1, the personal income tax in 1991 and projected for 1992 continues to contribute 44–45 percent of all federal taxes. However the corporate income tax, which had risen to a 10.4 percent share in 1988 and 1989, fell to 9.3 percent in 1991 and is projected by the Bureau of the Budget (assuming the Bush administration's tax legislation is adopted) to fall to an *8.3 percent* share! This is less than one-fifth of the personal income tax share in 1992. And, it is less than one-third of its burden in 1955! This is truly the great escape!

Now consider a second burden on the middle class illustrated by Table 6-1. Social Security taxes, which in 1949 contributed 9.6 percent of total revenues, rose steadily and in 1988 made up to 36.8 percent of all federal revenues. However, by 1991 the level had reached 37.6 percent and it is projected to reach 38.2 percent by 1992. While Social Security taxes are shared about equally by both corporations and individuals,[1] corporations have seen a substantial diminution in their corporate income taxes to allow them leeway to make these increased payroll tax payments. No such relief has been granted to those paying the individual income tax. Clearly, the numbers indicate that the shifting burden of federal income tax shares are an increasing burden to labor and the middle class. Further, as the 1993 federal budget projects, the individual income tax will continue to maintain its lopsided contribution to federal taxes, relative to the corporate income tax, for the foreseeable future.

THE CORPORATE ESCAPE FROM STATE AND LOCAL TAXES

In March 1981 the Advisory Commission on Intergovernmental Relations (ACIR) found essentially that the trend of declining tax payments by corporations and increasing tax payments by individuals, which was occurring at the federal level, was also occurring with state and local taxes.[2] As illustrated in Table 6-2, taxes with an initial impact on business fell from 36.8 percent of total revenues in 1957 to 30.6 percent of total state and local government revenues in 1977. Taxes primarily on individuals, however, increased by that exact percentage to make up the difference of 6.2 percent to 69.4 percent of 1977 total revenues. Thus, over the 20-year period, businesses succeeded in lowering their tax payments to state and local governments by about 6 percent and the difference was picked up by the individual taxpayer.

The decline in taxes with an initial impact on business was particularly prominent in the property tax area, with that percentage falling from 20.3 percent of the total to 12.6 percent over the 20-year period. Property taxes on individuals fell by about 1.3 percentage points over the entire period as compared with the eight-percentage-point drop on businesses. Businesses did see their corporate income tax contributions rise by approximately 2 percent of the total over the 20-year period; however, individuals

Table 6-2

State and Local Taxes with an Initial Impact on Business and on Individuals, by Type of Tax, 1957, 1962, 1967, 1977

	Amount (in millions)				Percent of Total			
	1977	1967	1962	1957	1977	1967	1962	1957
TAX COLLECTIONS:								
Excluding Unemployment Taxes	$175,879	$61,000	$41,554	$28,645	100.0%	100.0%	100.0%	100.0%
Including Unemployment Taxes	184,437	63,911	44,209	30,159	—	—	—	—
TAXES WITH AN INITIAL IMPACT ON BUSINESS:								
Total, Excluding Unemployment Taxes	53,874	19,900	14,478	10,553	30.6	32.6	34.8	36.8
Total, Including Unemployment Taxes	62,432	22,811	17,133	12,067	33.9	35.7	38.8	40.0
Property (Real & Personal)	21,642	10,298	8,156	5,808	12.3	16.9	19.6	20.3
Sales & Gross Receipts	15,062	4,076	2,694	1,902	8.6	6.7	6.5	6.6
Corporation Net Income	9,902	2,479	1,332	1,043	5.6	4.1	3.2	3.6
Unemployment Tax	8,558	2,911	2,655	1,514	—	—	—	—
Severance	2,168	577	451	388	1.2	0.9	1.1	1.4
License and Other	5,100	2,470	1,845	1,412	2.9	4.0	4.4	4.9
TAXES, PRIMARILY ON INDIVIDUALS:								
Total	122,005	41,100	27,076	18,092	69.4	67.4	65.2	63.2
Property (Real & Personal)	40,893	15,749	10,898	7,056	23.3	25.8	26.2	24.6
General Sales and Gross Receipts	28,112	8,158	4,712	3,118	16.0	13.4	11.3	10.9
Selective Excises	17,421	8,296	5,602	4,046	9.9	13.6	13.5	41.1
Personal Income	28,517	5,573	3,013	1,644	16.2	9.1	7.3	5.7
License and Other	7,062	3,324	2,851	2,228	4.0	5.4	6.9	7.8

Source: Advisory Commission on Intergovernmental Relations, *A Commission Report, Interstate Tax Competition* (Washington, D.C.: USPGO, 1981), table A1.

saw their income taxes rise by 10.5 percent of the totals over the period. The report concludes that "state and local taxes with initial impact on business have declined in their fiscal importance relative to taxes falling primarily on individuals."[3]

One reason for the drop in property taxes on businesses has been interstate competition in granting tax concessions at the state and local level to attract business. Yet the ACIR report concludes "that the wide-spread state enactment of incentives to businesses in the 1960s and 1970s has tended to neutralize their pulling power."[4] Thus, this interstate tax competition, and the use of this tool by the corporation to exact concessions from the states and localities in which it may stay, have ended up being a zero-sum game for the nation as a whole, with the drop in business tax collections over the 20-year period being shifted to the individual taxpayer.

What has happened since 1977? Table 6-3 calculates the percentage contribution of state and local receipts using Department of Commerce data somewhat different from those used in Table 6-2. Shown here is a decline in the importance of the property tax by about three percentage points and that of federal revenue sharing by almost 6 percent. These differences are made up in two ways: (1) an increased reliance on the individual income tax, which has grown from 10.2 percent to 12.4 percent

Table 6-3
Percentage Contribution of State and Local Receipts by Source,
Selected Fiscal Years during 1977–1990

	Total	Property	Sales & Gross Receipts	Indiv. Income Tax	Corp. Income Tax	Federal Revenue Sharing	All Other
1977	100.0	21.9	21.2	10.2	3.2	21.9	21.4
1982	100.0	17.9	20.5	11.1	3.4	19.1	28.2
1985	100.0	17.3	21.1	11.8	3.2	17.7	28.8
1987	100.0	17.7	21.0	12.2	3.3	16.8	29.0
1990	100.0	18.3	20.9	12.4	2.8	16.1	29.4

Source: U.S. Department of Commerce data, cited in the *Economic Report of the President*, Washington, D.C., January 1989, table B-83, p. 405, and *Economic Report of the President*, Washington, D.C., February 1992, p. 393. Computations by the author.

of the burden; and (2) by an increase in "all other" fees and miscellaneous revenues by 8 percent, mostly falling on individuals as opposed to business. The corporate income tax as a percentage of total receipts has fallen from 3.4 percent in 1982 to 2.8 percent in 1990, continuing to reflect favorable business tax treatment.

THE UNITED STATES TAX STRUCTURE
COMPARED INTERNATIONALLY

How does the tax structure in the United States compare with that of other major industrial nations? The Organization for Economic Cooperation and Development (OECD) compared such tax burdens in 1987. Of the 11 nations studied, the United States was down at the bottom with France and Sweden as having the lowest 1985 tax revenues (as a percent of gross domestic product, or GDP) contributed by the corporate income tax.[5]

Another interesting comparison is the level of taxation between the United States and her chief economic rival, Japan. Japan, which has outstripped the United States in international trade and overall economic growth in recent years, collects corporate income taxes as a share of its GDP at a rate of 5.9 percent—almost three times that of the United States, whose rate is 2.1 percent.[6] In contrast, Japan's total income tax on individuals makes up 6.9 percent of GDP. The American share is 10.4 percent. To top it off, Japanese payroll and property taxes are lower. (American payroll and property taxes are 5.2 percent and 2.7 percent of GDP, respectively. Japan's are 4.8 percent and 1.6 percent.) The often-heard proposition that American corporations cannot compete internationally because of the burdensome U.S. tax levels on capital should therefore be taken with more than one grain of salt. Indeed, these data suggest that we look elsewhere for the reason behind the lackluster performance of many American corporations, particularly in their international operations.

Japan has recently moved to revise her tax structure, lowering the effective corporate tax rate to between 40 and 50 percent from 52.9 percent. That these tax cuts in Japan at the corporate level, coupled with a newly introduced value-added tax in that country, should be taken as a U.S. model is highly questionable, since Japan currently taxes her corporations higher and her citizens lower than does her American trading partner.

The fact of low U.S. taxes was the subject of a January 1987 article in

Financier written by David R. Francis, with the descriptive title "As Nations Vie to Cut Taxes, U.S. Is Envied Leader."[7] My data show that a major reason for the low overall level of U.S. taxation is the low tax burden carried by corporations and business in general. Perhaps the fascination of foreign economists, bankers, and financiers who envy the U.S. tax structure has its basis in this corporate advantage. The same article states that U.S. tax reform has "greatly impressed politicians and tax experts alike and much soul searching is going on about the practicability of the U.S. approach in various countries."[8] Supply-sider George Gilder is also quoted in the article as predicting that governments everywhere will begin to lower their tax rates.[9] Indeed this is not an unlikely outcome if nations try to outbid each other for capital investment.

The Francis article has a disturbing flavor about it in that the tax structure of the United States is seen as wholly favorable and desirable. Nowhere is there any hint that the U.S. tax system may be deficient in some regard, such as exhibiting an increasingly onerous load on the middle class. Nor does it note that the tax structure is abdicating its role as a social control against the real or potential abuses of unduly large masses of wealth concentration.

There are actually very few positive measures with which to compare the economic well-being of the labor-dependent class with the capital-enhanced regime. Further, there is very little work being done in this field by the mainstream economics profession. However, one measure of economic well-being that makes a meaningful comparison is found in the data on saving. Saving is, after all, a residual activity. It is an accumulation after other expenses have been met. Business savings include funds set aside for depreciation, and that adjustment is specifically made by the U.S. government statisticians by adding depreciation to net profit after taxes. In fact, businesses can deduct depreciation as an expense from revenues. Thus, when this figure is added to net profits, it represents cash flow, commonly called "business savings." Personal saving, however, has no such option granted to it either in real life or by the Internal Revenue Service. Personal depreciation is not deductible, nor is the depreciation of one's home or one's human capital (on which one may have spent considerable sums by investing in college education). Clearly, business savings are treated more favorably by the IRS than personal saving.

Table 6-4 estimates the real personal and business savings per employee for selected years from 1960 through 1990. The total personal savings series and the total business savings series were both adjusted for inflation. They were then divided by total civilian employment to yield a

Table 6-4
Real Personal and Business Savings per Employee in the United States,
Selected Years during 1960–1990

Year	(1) Real Personal Savings per Employee	(2) Real Business Savings per Employee	(3) Ratio: Personal to Business Savings per employee (col. 1/col. 2)
1960	1,130	3,107	36.4
1970	1,887	3,545	53.2
1975	2,174	4,460	48.7
1980	1,886	4,224	44.6
1985	1,646	4,739	34.7
1987	1,116	4,609	24.2
1989	1,156	4,380	26.4
1990	1,341	4,183	32.1

Note: Columns 1 and 2 are in constant dollars (i.e., adjusted for inflation), 1982–84 = 100. Personal and business savings were deflated by the consumer price index (CPI) and then each series was divided by total civilian employment. Computations by the author.
Source: For savings data in columns 1 and 2, U.S. Department of Commerce data, cited in *Economic Report of the President*, Washington, D.C., February 1992, p. 328. For employment data, U.S. Department of Labor data, cited in ibid., p. 334, (civilian employment). For prices, U.S. Department of Commerce data, cited in ibid., p. 361 (consumer price index).

measure of a residual or savings accumulation per employee. The trend is one of increased personal savings per civilian employee worker through 1975 and then a drastic decrease by 1987. On the other hand, real business savings per employee grew strongly over the period from 1960 to 1985–87. A peak appears to have been reached in 1985, but the 1987 real savings by business per worker are 67 percent higher than in 1960. On the other hand, the real personal savings per worker of 1987 were virtually unchanged from 1960 and 41 percent lower than in 1970.

While business savings have historically been greater than personal savings on a per-worker basis, the latter have lost significant ground both absolutely and relatively since 1970, as exhibited by the historically low 1987 personal to business savings ratio of 24.2 shown in column 3 of Table 6-4.

Table 6-5
Business Savings, Personal Savings, and U.S. Gross National Product,
Selected Years during 1946–1990

Year	(1) Ratio: Business Savings to GNP	(2) Ratio: Personal Savings to GNP	(3) Business Savings Ratio to Personal Savings Ratio (col. 1/col. 2)	(4) Ratio: Total Savings to GNP
1946	0.079	0.064	1.23	14.3
1950	0.110	0.044	2.50	15.4
1955	0.121	0.039	3.10	16.0
1960	0.117	0.040	2.93	15.7
1965	0.126	0.034	3.71	16.0
1970	0.105	0.057	1.84	16.2
1975	0.124	0.065	1.91	18.9
1980	0.125	0.050	2.50	17.5
1985	0.134	0.031	4.32	16.5
1987	0.124	0.023	5.39	14.7
1989	0.126	0.032	3.93	15.8
1990	0.117	0.037	3.16	15.4

Note: Based on current dollars (i.e., unadjusted for inflation).
Source: For savings data, see Table 6-4. For GNP data, U.S. Department of Commerce, various reports. Computations by the author.

It is accumulation, or ability to save, that is important in measuring economic well-being. Both revenue *and* expenses are germane. It is meaningless to assess my economic welfare by comparing my income in southwest Michigan with what my income would be in New York City without also making an estimate of my living expenses in southwest Michigan and my living expenses in New York City. Only if these expenses are considered can we derive where I would be better off economically. A savings figure can measure that residual from income and expenses and, in the business case, can indicate an ability to replace worn-out assets and accumulate new ones. Shown clearly above, *business* savings per worker have been growing faster than *personal* savings per worker since 1970, and at an alarming rate. Another way of saying this is that the fruits of labor, per employee, are increasingly awarded to the capital-enhanced class and decreasingly paid to the labor-dependent class—significantly so.

Table 6-4 is especially startling because of the fact of the tremendous increase in employment in the United States due particularly to working wives entering the labor market—which, as Katherine Bradbury observed,[10] has mostly served to maintain the middle-class lifestyle. With all of this, the personal savings of the family, when adjusted on a per-worker basis, have gone down. But the business savings per worker and per family have risen dramatically. Again, what such data point to is a significant increase in financial pressure on the middle class. Such data dovetail neatly with the falling real compensation per worker that has been detailed in Chapters 3 and 4. The conclusion is inescapable. The power of capital has been enhanced to such a degree that it is able to increase substantially its own factor rewards and accumulation, and it is doing so at the expense of the employment-dependent class.

Table 6-5 looks at the problem from a slightly different perspective. It details the ratios of business, personal, and total personal savings to GNP. Business savings in ratio to GNP have shown a slight upward trend since 1970. The personal savings to GNP ratio has shown a marked downward trend since 1975. Comparing the two ratios in column 3, we move from a situation in 1946 where business savings were 23 percent higher than personal savings, to that in 1987 where the business savings ratio was more than five times the personal savings ratio, relative to GNP.

Finally, in column 4, we note that the ratio of total savings to GNP has been stable over the years in the 15–16 percent range. Nevertheless, the table illustrates that from 1975 to 1990 there has been an increasing business savings to GNP ratio and a strongly decreasing personal saving to GNP ratio. These measures of accumulation add another explanation for the tendency of the American middle class to be shrinking.

Further, if one were to adjust these figures for the personal savings of individuals in the upper quintile of the distribution, where most of the saving is done, the accumulation per employee in the middle and lower classes would look woefully worse.

NOTES

1. The initial burden of the Social Security taxes fall about equally on individual taxpayers and employers. For example, in 1982, if one apportions the Social Security taxes paid by both employers and employees from general tax

funds for retirement of federal employees, total employer contributions to Social Security were $136.4 billion and total employee contributions were $133.2 billion.

2.   Advisory Commission on Intergovernmental Relations, *A Commission Report, Interstate Tax Competition* (Washington, D.C.: USGPO, 1981), table A.

3.   Ibid., p. 63.

4.   Ibid., p. 5.

5.   Organization for Economic Cooperation and Development, *Revenue Statistics of OECD Member Countries* (Paris: OECD, 1987).

6.   Ibid.

7.   David R. Francis, "As Nations Vie to Cut Taxes, U.S. Is Envied Leader," *Financier*, Bank Administration Institute, New York (January 1987).

8.   Ibid., p. 13.

9.   Ibid., p. 9.

10.   Katherine L. Bradbury, "The Shrinking Middle Class," *New England Economic Review*, Federal Reserve Bank of Boston (September/October 1986).

7

The Argument Summarized: Eleven Reasons for Middle-class Decline

> Labor is prior to, and independent of capital. Capital is only the fruit of labor, and could never have existed if labor had not first existed. Labor is the superior of capital, and deserves much the higher consideration.
>
> Abraham Lincoln

However vaguely expressed, a very real sense of economic uneasiness has gripped the American public. The poverty rate that measures the number of persons living in poverty as a percentage of the total population has risen since 1979, yet antipoverty programs themselves have become impoverished. There is seemingly no national constituency for the poor that can effectively get its message across in either the U.S. Congress or the various state and local governing bodies.

As shown in Chapter 3, a number of studies have shown that the size and relative incomes of the American middle class have fallen as a percentage of the total population in the past 20 years. Katherine Bradbury details the phenomenon between the 1973–84 period.[1] Frank Levy illustrates similar results between 1979 and 1984,[2] as do the data of Marilyn Moon and Isabel Sawhill between 1980 and 1984.[3] Sheldon Danziger, Peter Gottschalk, and Eugene Smolensky illustrate a middle-class decline or inequality increase between 1983 and 1987.[4] Using other data, they show that the ratio of the top two income deciles to the bottom two has increased dramatically between 1979 and 1987. The U.S. Bureau of the Census has shown that the percentage of Americans classified as middle income fell from 71.2 percent in 1969 to 63.3 percent in 1989.[5] Real average weekly earnings have fallen steadily from a postwar peak of $315.44 to $255.89 in 1991.[6]

Robert Kuttner observes that the recent acceleration in technology has caused a bipolarization in the distribution of jobs, that is, a few high-paying ones, little in the middle, and a number of low-level openings.[7] *Fortune's* Bruce Steinberg writes that retailers are adjusting themselves accordingly to this bipolarization and are aiming less and less at the middle.[8] It is instructive to note there are no convincing economic studies putting forth the idea either that the relative size of the American middle class has increased, or that its economic well-being has increased, over the past 20 years. Likewise there are no economic studies purporting that the number of persons living in poverty has gone down, or that the standard of living of persons living in the poverty classes has gone up.

This book focuses on income distribution in the United States, and it begins with an emphasis on the size and the economic well-being of the middle class. It does so for several reasons. First, the lower classes in the United States have grown both absolutely and in relative percentage terms to the total population over the past 20 years. Yet the federal government since 1980 has ceased to care. Second, there is in the United States a growing economic desperation among middle-class individuals and particularly their offspring who are faced with declining middle-class job opportunities or other income opportunities. If we combine the facts of a relatively increasing lower or poverty class with a shrinking middle class, and reduced overall economic well-being for both classes, these facts might serve to effect some national policy changes. The plight of the "underclass" or lower classes has received less and less political recognition by that class's former champion, the middle class. However, given the increasing decline in economic power of the middle class, one can surely conclude that the situation of the lower classes is nearing desperation. The April 30, 1992, riots in Los Angeles should therefore have come as no surprise to any informed government official. The inner cities of America are bombs with very short fuses, and one can predict with disturbing certainty that more will explode in the future unless government policy is changed.

CAPITAL ASCENDING, LABOR DESCENDING

A demonstrated middle-class decline in the face of rising poverty most dramatically illustrates a decrease in the economic and political power of those who earn their living mainly through their own labor and a significant increase in economic power of a small minority represented by the capital-enhanced forces. To illustrate these trends, however, is more complicated than it at first appears.

For example, looking at the shifts in the size of the middle class as documented by the above-named studies, the percentage changes are fairly dramatic. However, they are not as dramatic as the fear level and the very real economic desperation that is experienced by many persons in the middle class. The reason is simple. The laboring class as a whole has suffered a real-wage decline, so that downward shifts in the size of the middle class, stated as a percentage of the total labor class, understate the loss of economic well-being. Here I will define wages in the very strict sense that they are a return for labor hours spent on the job. The real-wage decline is critical in understanding the circumstances of a growing income inequality, a growing underclass, and a shrinking middle class in the United States. This is because the main source of income of the lower and middle classes (i.e., the labor-dependent classes) is their wage. The incomes of the upper classes, to which power has been steadily accruing, are relatively more capital-enhanced than wage-dependent. In fact, much of what has formerly passed as a wage income for higher income individuals is really a return to capital. High-paid executives, by virtue of their power in the organization, are able to steer the capital rewards (such as huge multimillion-dollar bonuses) their way under the guise of a wage. Thus, if we define the two relevant factors of distribution as either labor-dependent (i.e., the lower and middle classes) and capital-enhanced (i.e., the upper classes) and discover, admit, and accept the fact that the real wage has fallen—particularly if a major reason is the increasing power of capital to capture total factor rewards more readily—then rising inequality in the United States, or in any economy, is no mystery. It is a given. As delineated in Chapter 4, the real-wage decline has three major sources: macroeconomic events, labor market developments, and the increased power of capital and its exercise thereof.

Several macroeconomic events of major import have occurred since 1973. First, the energy shocks of 1973 and 1979 produced major inflationary cycles that redounded mainly to labor's detriment. The record shows an increasing inability of labor to gain wage increases equal to its productivity. This trend was particularly prominent in the 1970s and 1980s. Second, deregulation increased the competitiveness of many firms and, with it, pressured them to reduce all possible costs, including labor. Third, the combination of an overvalued American dollar in the 1980s and a declining American international competitiveness caused U.S. exports to fall as a percent of GNP while imports rose dramatically, thus putting substantial downward pressure on the number of American manufacturing jobs.

A number of labor market developments also contributed measurably to the decline of labor and its ability to command factor rewards. These major labor market developments could be classified as mainly an increase in supply of labor in the face of both sluggish demand and the decline—or some would say, the demise—of the American labor union. The increased supply of labor came from three major sources. First, baby boomers entered the labor force in record numbers and percentages in the 1970s and 1980s, causing huge increases in the labor supply. Second, working women began to flood the labor markets—not only single but also married working women. Female labor-force participation rates grew dramatically in the 1960s but particularly in the 1970s and 1980s. Third, immigration, both illegal and legal, increased at record numbers, absorbing at least 25 percent (perhaps as much as 35 percent) of all job growth in the 1978–86 period.

Finally, the decline of the American labor unions' influence is seen in the fact that they probably represent no more than 15 percent of the American labor force today, compared with 30 percent a quarter century ago.

A MORE GENERAL EQUILIBRIUM ANALYSIS

Economists often use the terms *partial* and *general* equilibrium analysis. The former describes the analysis of a problem in isolation. For example, a particular economist might want to predict the effect that an increase in government spending would have on national income. If he ignores changes in the financial markets, he remains in an isolated or partial equilibrium analysis and gets one estimate. However, if he builds into his model the fact that government borrowing to finance the spending might raise interest rates, he has moved to a general equilibrium analysis, which carries him into financial market reaction. Such higher interest rates might now discourage other forms of spending (such as investment), and his national income estimate will now be lower than it was in the partial equilibrium analysis.

Thus, when analyzing factors that have strengthened capital at the expense of labor as reasons for middle-class and labor decline, we move to a general equilibrium mode. Studying how the corporations have shifted tax burdens to labor and the middle class widens the analysis to a general equilibrium model. When corporations escape income and property taxes, individuals must make up the difference. In a similar way, capital's ability to threaten labor with its mobility, with its ability to merge, and with its newfound ability to hire nonunion workers during a strike calls for an analysis that is more general or complete. While such power may be harder to quantify, it is a major factor in middle-class decline in America.

When sticking mainly to labor market developments, such as an increase in the supply of labor, we are mainly in a partial equilibrium mode. However, even here there may be general equilibrium elements. Certainly an increase in the labor supply due to the maturation of baby boomers would be partial in its origin, since it is mainly a function of an historic birthrate. However, the increase in the supply of labor due to the influx of working women is not clear as purely a labor market development. Could the increase in labor supply caused by more working women—but particularly working wives—be partially due to capital's relatively greater power over labor? (Obviously there are also other reasons for the increased labor-force participation of women: education, and the rise of feminism, to name two.) For example, a falling real wage per worker would induce women to enter the labor market either to hang onto a middle-class living standard or, in the case of the poverty classes, merely to feed the family. The observations of Katherine Bradbury certainly suggest this.[9]

Or could the increased immigration into the United States—now at record levels on a legal basis and who knows what on an illegal basis—be partially explained by capital's desire for an increased labor supply that is both low wage and nonunion? Could capital's desire for this cheap and docile labor supply have been transmitted to its government representatives in such a way as to, for one thing, raise the current legal immigration rate to the highest level since the 1910s and, for another, generally encourage the government to look the other way (until 1986) as illegal immigrants flooded across the Mexican border? Such observations and data make it difficult to analyze the middle-class demise in a strictly partial equilibrium framework as "labor-market developments." Indeed, capital's influence in the picture would suggest a general equilibrium analysis.

Or take the case of declining membership among unions. Studies by Henry Farber,[10] Robert Flanagan,[11] and most recently Richard Freeman[12] conclude that a major reason for the decline in union membership has been the increased power of capital, through its management representatives, to defeat labor unions both at the bargaining table and in labor's ability to organize unions and retain membership.

Thus, we can probably classify the maturation of the baby boomers and the ineffectiveness of union leadership as relatively autonomous factors occurring within the labor markets, and thus apply a partial analysis to isolate their contribution to labor's weakened bargaining power. However, the increased economic, political, and intellectual power of capital must be considered as to its effect on labor and the middle class within a general equilibrium framework since these powers are exercised against labor and since the gains to capital are often at the expense of labor.

Chapter 5 redefines the terms *capital* and *labor* in a more useful way. As a general statement, capital and labor compete with each other for factor rewards. Specifically, however, that type of capital which competes with labor we have defined as profit-seeking capital. It is footloose and mobile and seeks the highest rewards. The individuals who own and/or direct this footloose capital collect rewards that are capital-enhanced. Indeed, the capital-enhanced factor is the relevant one in competing with labor. The capital-enhanced group includes primarily the owners of capital and their highly paid directors of such footloose capital, whose rewards are capital-enhanced and have a relatively low wage content.

Labor must be more narrowly defined as that factor of production which is labor-dependent. This is because many individuals who own some capital and who also work with someone else's capital are nonetheless labor-dependent. The labor-dependent will own some capital such as housing and automobiles, but such is necessary merely to maintain their ability to stay in the labor force. The capital that the labor-dependent work with is generally other persons' capital. Thus, the two relevant groups competing for rewards in the society are the capital-enhanced and the labor-dependent. Many in the capital-enhanced group enjoy the luxury of having an income that is not solely dependent on their labor. High-paid managers of capital—even someone else's capital—are also capital-enhanced and belong to this capital-enhanced group. Thus, the major competition for economic rewards in this society is more specifically defined as that between the capital-enhanced group and the labor-dependent group; and for income distribution purposes, they are the relevant factors. While there are indeed four factors of production—land, labor, capital, and entrepreneurship—income from production accrues to individuals. Economics should analyze income distribution as to how it accrues to the "factors of distribution," of which there are two categories: labor-dependent or capital-enhanced individuals.

Since the capital-enhanced group needs otherwise labor-dependent individuals for political support, we thus broaden its collective interest group into what I call the *capital-enhanced regime*. This regime has been increasingly active and successful in conducting an expensive, well-organized campaign to influence public opinion to support its political positions. Its crowning achievement was the election of Ronald Reagan even after a long period of capital ascension (or, more to the point, a long labor decline). And Reagan's role in the continued ascent of capital has been, and will continue to be, a major factor in the decline of the middle class.

The capital-enhanced group has been served well by its single-mindedness of purpose. Its bright, articulate, motivated, and well-trained leaders have not lost sight of their own self-interest, namely, further capital enhancement. The labor-dependent groups have seen their intellectual leadership falter. The middle class, in addition to looking out for its own economic well-being, has also been left with the political, moral, and intellectual burden of looking out for the lower classes. However, as the middle class has become more pressed financially, it has either lost its will to look out for the latter or else has been persuaded, by the politics of denigration and fear, not to look in that direction.

Capital has, in effect, capitalized on a number of complex events, developments, and power shifts over the past 25 years. One phenomenon is the increased complexity of national issues, particularly in the economic realm. These include the size and the intricacy of the federal budget. Another is the world of international trade and finance, now greatly expanded in its size, mystique, and impact on the American economy. The capital-enhanced regime, having the intellectual prowess and the financial backing to understand, handle, and even profit from such major macroeconomic issues, has also embarked on a very successful campaign to free itself from the control of a government that previously acted as a referee to be sure the allocation of economic power to any one group—whether capital or labor—would not get out of hand. This regime has employed the denigrative method wherein conservative forces have effectively attacked the government, cut its size, weakened its ability to govern—with the end result that it has achieved both lower tax loads on capital and less government oversight into business activities. It has further weakened government by underfinancing it, thus ensuring its relatively poorer performance and contributing to its loss of credibility in the mind of the voters. Capital's trumpeting of the government as the problem has become a self-fulfilling prophecy.

In the use of political action committees, the capital-enhanced regime has provided money to Democratic candidates for its own ends and thus has weakened the role of its opposition. Intellectually, it has financed a number of think tanks that espouse conservative causes and has managed to exert considerable influence for such causes within the ranks of the economics profession. The leaders of the economics profession, who in prior years were more liberally oriented, have been unable or unwilling to counter effectively the conservative, self-seeking, and generally unfounded economic theories of the capital-enhanced regime's chief economics spokespersons.

By weakening government generically, the capital-enhanced regime has weakened the educative function of government. The alarming rise in illiteracy in the United States is but one reflection of this phenomenon. An educationally weakened American electorate has become less able to deal with the complex economic issues of the day and has turned more and more to the relatively simple single-issue type of politics—which frees the capital-enhanced regime to pursue its aims with less government intervention. Further, since most single-issue politics seem to be "conservative" in nature (i.e., concerning moral values), the capital-enhanced regime benefits from its association with money—an association also best handled in a conservative way. Thus, the Republican party, as the collective spokesman for the capital-enhanced regime, courts the single-issue conservative political groups, and gains support from them as necessary.

The threat of capital mobility is a very real one. Mobility is used as a weapon on a national basis to lobby for lower corporate income taxes, claiming the necessity of such to retain jobs in the United States. The same weapon has been used against state and local governments to extract lower taxes and/or special government services. The stick in this strategy is the argument that, if the governmental unit is not "accommodative," the corporation will move on. Yet labor has no such trump card. In reality, labor mobility is a personal and, increasingly, family disruption, particularly with two-earner families. Yet state governments, county governments, and local governments continue to give tax concessions to major corporations despite the fact that responsible economic studies claim these tax concessions do not significantly influence the location of businesses. The threat is there, and the capital-enhanced group uses it. Furthermore, the mobility threat is used to weaken labor both at the bargaining table and in its unionization efforts.

The capital-enhanced regime's success in its intellectual assault and its battle for the minds and votes of the American electorate resulted in the election of conservative governments in the 1980s. These governments have delivered not only lower business taxes, but a relaxed antitrust attitude. Thus in the 1980s, mergers and acquisitions have proceeded at an historically unprecedented rate, many using the 1981 tax cuts as seed money for their mergers. These mergers and acquisitions enhance capital's position and hurt the position of the labor-dependent in three ways. First, the merger permits the cutting of costs and duplicate services—and, in many ways, labor. Second, it serves as a threat in the collective-bargaining process in favor of the capital-enhanced position and against that of the labor-dependent. Third, mergers and acquisitions reduce the level of competition, thus increasing profits for the merged firm by increasing prices, thereby further reducing the purchasing power of the labor-dependent, that is the consumer.

How much has capital increased its power over labor? One problem with the standard measures applied to assess the economic well-being of individuals or families is that generally such data deal with gross revenue either on a per-capita basis or on a per-family basis. Some economists use revenue data after taxes and also adjusted for inflation. Such measures have serious shortcomings in evaluating economic welfare—shortcomings stemming from the fact that the inflation and tax indices are imperfect since they are based on an average. A much more useful measure introduced in Chapter 6—a method that allows some comparability of labor and capital—is the economic unit's ability to save after necessary expenses have been met.

A key element in an economic unit's ability to save is the tax burden it must bear. Here we find that, while individual income taxes averaged approximately 44–48 percent of the contribution to total federal tax receipts from 1955 through 1988, the corporate income tax fell from 27.3 percent of the total to a low of 6.2 percent from 1955 to 1983.[13] Corporate taxes increased since then to a 10.4 percent share in 1988, but were predicted to fall to an 8.3 percent share in 1992. Meanwhile the personal income tax contribution holds steady at about 45 percent. Indeed, the corporation has succeeded in more than halving its federal tax burden over the past 33 years. Viewed in another way, corporate income taxes are one-third of what they were in 1955, while individual income taxes are above their levels of 1955.

At the state and local level also corporations have succeeded in reducing their taxes, thus shifting the burden to individuals. From 1957 to 1977, all corporate taxes fell from 36.8 percent of total state and local revenues to 30.6 percent.[14] Over the same period, however, taxes primarily on individuals *climbed* by exactly the same amount—6.2 percent—with individual taxes rising from 63.2 percent to 69.4 percent of total revenues. In the area of property taxes (which formerly fell primarily on businesses), tax receipts have fallen as a percentage of state and local revenues from 21.9 percent in 1977 to 18.3 percent in 1990.[15] The individual income tax has grown over the period from 10.2 percent to 12.4 percent of total state and local revenues, or by approximately 20 percent. Yet the corporate income tax share has fallen from 3.2 percent to 2.8 percent. Federal revenue sharing has dropped significantly, but all other revenues—mainly user charges, fees, and lottery revenues, all of which fall primarily on individuals—have grown by 8.0 percent of the total over the 1977–90 period.

One might say that reductions in business tax levels would be appropriate if the United States were a high-tax country, particularly in taxes on business. Yet, examining tax revenues as a percentage of gross domestic product between countries in 1985, we find that the corporate income tax in the United States is one of the lowest of 11 major industrial nations.[16] In the United States, corporate tax revenues are a little more than one-third of Japanese levels. And with consumption taxes about the same in the United States and Japan, the United States has higher payroll and property taxes. Indeed, one wonders at the rationale behind such deep cuts in business tax revenues—cuts that have cast the federal budget into an enormous deficit and put such a large burden on the individual taxpayer. One can only conclude that capital in the United States has exercised its growing power effectively in the tax arena, as it continues to do so well in other bruising ways.

The result of such lower taxes for capital and subsequent higher taxes for individuals has been an increase in the financial solvency and liquidity of American business to an unprecedented degree. This has been accomplished by decreasing the financial solvency and liquidity of both the federal government and the middle class (which is an interesting parallel because the insolvency of the government—i.e., the representatives of the people—is mirrored in the growing insolvency of the middle class). *Real personal savings per employee* in the United States between 1970 and 1990 fell by 29 percent to $1,341 per year. *Real business savings per employee* over the same time period rose by 18 percent to $4,183 a year. Another way to look at it is that the ratio of personal to business savings over that time period has fallen from 53.2 percent to 32.1 percent.[17]

Finally, an assessment of the total savings ratio relative to GNP over the past 42 years shows that it has averaged in the 14–18 percent range, with a median figure of about 16 percent.[18] Since 1970 the pattern has been for business savings to grow from 10.5 percent of GNP to about 12.0 percent. Personal savings, however, have fallen over that period from 5.7 percent to around 3 percent of GNP.

In summary, the available data clearly show the recent substantial gains the capital-enhanced regime have made through macroeconomic events, through events occurring within labor markets, and through the exercise of its power over government, over voters, and over labor. These forces have achieved stunning economic advancement in the postwar period, particularly in the past 20 years, and have for all intents and purposes been successful in undoing most elements of the New Deal. Certainly, a few vestiges do still remain, such as Social Security and the right to collective bargaining, although the latter has been weakened considerably.

Economists of late have been wondering why income inequality continues to be on the rise. Part of the problem in isolating the reason for this inequality lies in using partial equilibrium models as the prime mode of analysis.

However, when we take the measures of a partial equilibrium analysis within labor markets and combine them with the forces operating on a general equilibrium basis—measuring capital's power over labor in tax share, merger power, and the threat of mobility—we are able better to understand why income inequality has increased significantly. And we can then answer the question, How much has capital's power increased over labor and the middle class? Our answer will not be provided with a single set of equations, given the complexity of the issues and forces operating. It will be impossible to model. But there is a short response that *would* be acceptable: One hell of a lot!

A BRIEF SUMMARY OF THE REASONS FOR MIDDLE-CLASS DECLINE

We can lay it out thus far that the decline of the middle class has been fostered by at least 11 reasons, many of which are complicated and fundamental. They are as follows:

Lower Wages Due to—

• A huge increase in labor supply as maturing baby boomers flooded into the labor markets in the 1970s and 1980s

- A second labor-supply increase as large numbers of working wives entered the labor markets in the 1970s and 1980s
- A third significant labor-supply increase because of record immigration levels in the 1980s and 1990s—the highest since the 1920s—which gave immigrants at least 25 percent of all new jobs created in the 1978–86 period
- A decline in union membership from 30.4 percent of the nonagricultural workforce in 1962 to 15.0 percent in 1985

Lost Middle-class Jobs Due to—

- A strong dollar and a virtually open import policy that decimated many U.S. manufacturing jobs
- A decline in the growth of government employment
- The corporate merger mania, partly financed by the corporate tax cuts of the 1980s, that has stripped away many middle-class jobs

Increased Financial Burdens on the Middle Class Due to—

- The energy inflation of 1973–74 and 1979–82, which hurt the wage earner more than any other segment in the economy
- The accompanying high interest rate structure, which placed heavy burdens on homeowners in the 1970s and 1980s
- The corporate escape from federal taxes, which have been picked up by middle-class income taxpayers
- The corporate escape from state and local taxes, which have been picked up by middle-class income and property taxpayers

Are these reasons sufficient to depress the middle class economically and financially? I believe so. But hold on. There are at least four more fundamental reasons to be discussed in the chapters that follow (see particularly Chapter 11).

A DISCUSSION ON FACTORS OF PRODUCTION AND FACTORS OF DISTRIBUTION

To better understand income and wealth distribution, one must distinguish between factors of production and factors of distribution since *individuals receive wealth.*

Income is earned by the human factors of production, such as the wage to labor or the profit to the entrepreneur. Rent and interest are earned by the nonhuman factors of production: land and capital. Yet the receipt of all these rewards—wages, rent, interest, and profits—accrues to individuals. The process of creating wealth is production; and in economic theory, the measurement of this wealth creation falls partly to what is known as "marginal revenue productivity" (MRP) theory.

One aspect of MRP theory simply states that the most productive and cheapest factors of production shall be *employed* the most. In other words, if labor is as equally productive as capital, and if it is also cheaper, then relatively more labor will be utilized. The same would hold if labor were more productive but cost the same to employ as capital. Thus, the most productive factors relative to cost are in high demand by managers seeking to employ land, labor, or capital.

Another implication in MRP theory is that the most productive factors will be *rewarded* most. Thus an assumption is commonly made in MRP theory that the proper deployment or mix of these factors (what economists call the "production process") also explains the distribution of the fruits of such production. However, in actuality the distribution of such income accrues to the owners of the factors of production—namely, individuals—and in an imperfect way at that. Simply because a given laborer produces a given valuable product does not mean that he will receive the full fruits of the value he has added to that product, even if the productivity is solely attributable to him, and not to capital, land, or entrepreneurship. He may receive a wage that is lower than his product's value because of imperfect information—that is, he may not be able to sell it or distribute it—or he may be exploited by his employer.

Herein lies the basic flaw of MRP theory when applied to income distribution. Individuals who are labor-dependent are less likely to receive the fruits of their labor productivity than are the possessors of capital, land, and entrepreneurial ability. In fact, for the latter group, the MRP theory of income distribution works well. Further, the latter group, whom I have referred to as capital-enhanced, includes the key players in the recent contest for power between capital and labor.

Thus, the existing theory of production, which explains well the mix of capital, labor, land, and entrepreneurial ability in the production process, should be divorced from a theory of distribution—or in other words, of who gets the rewards. Income is distributed to persons who can be characterized by owning one or more factors of production. The labor-dependent individual is most often at a disadvantage (with a few exceptions such as Michael Jordan or Robert Redford) because, by definition, he or she owns only one factor. But he or she is also a factor of distribution. The other factor of distribution is the capital-enhanced individual, who, in addition to his or her labor, *owns* and thus *receives* the fruits of production of land, capital, or entrepreneurship.

Indeed we must think of these two factors of distribution—labor-dependent individuals and capital-enhanced individuals—when assessing the equity of the current wealth and income distribution scheme. While MRP theory is a valid theory of determining the production mix, it often falls short in determining the *rewards of that production* since these rewards go to *one of the two factors of distribution*. As I have argued, the labor-dependent individual, as a factor of distribution, is usually at a disadvantage relative to his or her only competition, the capital-enhanced individual, who is also a factor of distribution. As we shall see in Chapter 12, the status of these two factors of income distribution has interesting implications for wealth distribution in the United States, as well as for tax policy.

SAVINGS AS A WELFARE MEASURE

A word is in order about my use of personal saving versus corporate saving to measure the comparative health, or power, of labor and capital. Critics might address the fact that many individuals in the labor-dependent category own housing, which, if measured at its true market value, would lend a significant upward bias to their personal wealth. To this my reply is that real estate and other asset holdings of major corporations have also shown a substantial appreciation, adding to their wealth. Additionally, such valuable assets—particularly intangible ones like long-standing trademarks, brand names, or market power—have an incalculable asset value attached to them in today's world economy.

Others might criticize the use and comparison of savings data between businesses and individuals since it is often claimed that U.S. consumers live extravagantly beyond their means and that this is the reason for their low savings rate. One established economic theory that would disagree with this proposition is the life-cycle hypothesis of Franco Modigliani, which states that consumers will save in a traditional way to provide income security for their expected life span. To my knowledge, no economic theory backed up by empirical evidence has established that individual American consumers, or any other consumers, on average, overconsume in such an irrational way as to endanger their ability to compete in the marketplace as healthy and mentally fit laborers (with the exception of drug and alcohol abuse), or systematically overconsume (in the other than alcohol- or drug-related areas) in such a way as to endanger their ability to provide food and shelter for themselves and their family. There are exceptions to this rule, but my contention is that no responsible economic study has shown that this is the average, the model for, or the preponderance of consumer behavior in the United States. Corporations, too, seek to provide in a healthy way for their own future. They seek to maintain their assets and their quality of talent. The tax law favors their saving behavior by allowing depreciation allowances; individuals have no such option and must therefore provide from their even lower savings level the funds for replacing whatever tangible or intangible assets are necessary to their earning power. Thus the corporation is amply favored by tax laws.

A final defense of comparing the savings of individuals and the savings of corporations is found in the startling trend that has taken place over the time period shown in Table 6-4. The data in Chapter 6 show a dramatic increase in the accumulated residual for the corporation on a *per-employee* basis. It can thus be compared to personal savings by the employee. The large increase in real business savings per employee at the expense of personal savings speaks volumes for the real increase in business financial power over the period. The increased business savings in inflation-adjusted dollars per employee, combined with falling real wages, leads to the inescapable conclusion that businesses are absorbing a rapid growth in the labor force and are paying this labor force (on average) less money, particularly relative to its productivity. Also, in employing this labor force, business is profiting more on a per-employee basis—as indicated by the increased business savings per employee.

Finally, the significantly higher business than personal savings in total and per individual employee contradict the traditional proposition found in many texts on economics principles that households form the prime surplus sector in the economy and that businesses constitute the prime deficit sector. In traditional economic theory, the household sector lends, either directly or through financial intermediaries, to the prime deficit units, namely, businesses. Thus, the circular flow model could use updating. A more accurate description of the savings investment process is simply that the business sector saves approximately three-fourths, and the households one-fourth, of total savings in the economy. Who lends to whom is an open question that might be answered by spending a good deal of time in the national income and products accounts or in Federal Reserve flow of funds data. However a lot of households lend to households for home mortgages, either through savings and loan associations or commercial banks or by buying insurance policies. They also do some lending to businesses by buying bonds and stocks. But many businesses lend to households by putting their excess funds to work, particularly in the mortgage market, as well as for consumer credit. Suffice it to say that the U.S. economy has now shifted from a position in 1975 where personal savings made up approximately one-third of total savings, to a situation in 1990 where personal savings made up only one-quarter. The difference has been taken over by business ownership of that savings.

There are those skeptics who will say, What of it? Somebody has to save the money—and isn't it better that business is saving the money since it can plan better and provide for future expansion and jobs? To this there is one simple reply: Wealth means *ownership* of wealth, and that ownership has shifted. The extreme reduction in personal saving by individuals means that their ability to generate revenue via interest income is diminished. Wealth is an accumulation of savings, and the comparison of personal savings with business savings is one instructive way to compare wealth and income distribution in a capitalist economy.

NOTES

1. Katherine L. Bradbury, "The Shrinking Middle Class," *New England Economic Review*, Federal Reserve Bank of Boston (September/October 1986).

2. Frank Levy, *Dollars and Dreams* (New York: W.W. Norton, 1988).

3. Marilyn Moon and Isabel Sawhill, "Family Incomes, Gainers and Losers," in John L. Palmer and Isabel Sawhill, eds., *The Reagan Record* (Washington, D.C.: Urban Institute, 1984).

4. Sheldon Danziger, Peter Gottschalk, and Eugene Smolensky, "How the Rich Have Fared, 1973–1987," *American Economic Review* (1989).

5. U.S. Bureau of the Census, *Trends in Relative Income: 1964 to 1989*, Current Population Reports, Series P-60, No. 177 (Washington, D.C.: USGPO, 1991).

6. U.S. Bureau of Labor Statistics data, cited in *Economic Report of the President*, Washington, D.C., February 1992.

7. Robert Kuttner, "The Declining Middle Class," *Atlantic Monthly* (July 1983).

8. Bruce Steinberg, "The Mass Market Is Splitting Apart," *Fortune* (November 28, 1983).

9. Bradbury, op. cit.

10.   Henry S. Farber, "The Recent Decline of Unionization in the United States," Reprint No. 1012, National Bureau of Economic Research, Cambridge, Mass., 1988.

11.   Robert J. Flanagan, "NLRA Litigation and Union Representation," *Stanford Law Review*, 38, no. 4 (April 1986).

12.   The demise of unions pointed out by Farber (op. cit.) and Flanagan (op. cit.) is supported by Richard Freeman, who observes an unprecedented assault by management on unions during the 1970s and 1980s, particularly in the United States. See Richard Freeman, "On the Divergence of Unionism among Developed Countries," NBER Working Paper No. 2817, National Bureau of Economic Research, Cambridge, Mass., summary in the text cited from *NBER Digest* (May 1989).

13.   *Budget of the United States Government, Fiscal Year 1990*, Executive Office of the President, Washington, D.C., 1989, *Budget of the United States Government, Fiscal Year 1993*, Executive Office of the President, Washington, D.C., 1992.

14.   Advisory Committee on Intergovernmental Relations, *A Commission Report, Interstate Tax Competition* (Washington, D.C.: USGPO, 1981).

15.   Based on U.S. Department of Commerce data, cited in the *Economic Report of the President*, Washington, D.C., January 1989; and *Economic Report of the President*, Washington, D.C., February 1992.

16.   Organization for Economic Cooperation and Development, *Revenue Statistics of OECD Member Countries* (Paris: OECD, 1987).

17.   Based on U.S. Department of Commerce and U.S. Department of Labor data, cited in the *Economic Report of the President*, Washington, D.C., February 1992.

18.   Ibid.; also, U.S. Department of Commerce, various reports.

PART III

THE DECLINE ACCELERATES: AMERICA IN THE REAGAN–BUSH YEARS

8

Reaganomics: A Wolf in Sheep's Clothing

I've finally figured out this politics. It's like show
business. You start with a big opening act, coast, and
close with a great crescendo.

Ronald Reagan

In order to understand middle-class decline in the 1980s, we must examine
the economic picture of the times. Accordingly, to understand these
economic events, many of which flowed from the Reagan economic
policies, we first must understand Ronald Reagan's economic philosophy.
Next, we must examine his management style. Finally, by placing these
two phenomena in the context of the historical time—that is, the late 1970s
and early 1980s, a period of unprecedented peacetime inflation—and the
confused economic thinking of the time, we can contrast the lofty inten-
tions of Reaganomics with its failure to achieve not only its stated
objectives, but also its end result. That end result was the slippage of the
United States from the world's number-one economic power in 1980 to
number three in 1989 when President Reagan exited office.

THE REAGAN ECONOMIC PHILOSOPHY

What was the Reagan economic philosophy? From the writings of

those closest to him, it apparently was no more complex than the traditional, conservative, "old-time religion" of small government budgets,
tight money, and minimal government activity that has characterized
Republican administrations during the twentieth century. As a movie actor
he had been gouged by the ultrahigh tax brackets of the 1940s and 1950s,
so quite naturally tax cutting was a major priority. However, if there was
a single, overriding aspect of his conservative economic theme, it was his
extreme anti-government attitude. No doubt the high marginal tax brackets he suffered as a movie actor influenced this extreme anti-government
stance. William Niskanen, a member of Reagan's Council of Economic
Advisors (CEA), writes that Reagan had conveyed one consistent theme:
"Government is more likely to be the source than the solution to the
perceived problems of the time." [1] And further, "He maintained his general
theme about government as the problem even when serving as governor
of the nation's largest state, a period during which real state spending
increased at a record rate." [2]

In fact, Niskanen concludes—as an answer to the question, How
revolutionary was the initial Reagan program?—that "the initial Reagan
economic program was a conservative program primarily, in the sense
that it represented a rather cautious evolution of a number of policy
changes initiated in the late 1970s." [3]

But the president's economic game plan was very nonspecific, as
confirmed by others close to him in the economic arena. Former Treasury
Secretary Donald Regan found himself, on his own, trying to interpret the
president's economic philosophy. What was expected of Treasury Secretary Regan was never conveyed personally by President Ronald Reagan.
In the personal notes of the treasury secretary we find the following
passage on March 11, 1981: "To this day I have never had so much as one
minute alone with Ronald Reagan! Never has he, or anyone else, sat down
in private to explain to me what is expected of me, what goals he would
like to see me accomplish, what results he wants." [4] Apparently, Reagan's
style was to have his public statements on economic policy form the basis
for his plans, and he left it to his managers to interpret their meanings.
Regan felt the president was a believer in supply-side economics—"a
system of ideas derived from many sources including Adam Smith." [5]
Regan also believed that high income taxes definitely colored or shaded
the president's economic philosophy. Indeed the overall picture of the
Reagan economic philosophy is a generally conservative, antitax, antigovernment framework. Such conservative writers as Milton Friedman of
the Chicago monetarist school, who advocated similar stances—particu-

larly with regard to Federal Reserve monetary policy, or of course good old standbys like Adam Smith—fit well into the general gestaldt.

When describing the heart of the Reagan economic program, former Budget Director David Stockman referred to it as the "Reagan Revolution," which he stated would require a frontal assault on the American welfare state. This Reagan Revolution was to take place in two parts. First, the massive Kemp–Roth tax cuts would reduce personal income taxes by some 30 percent and considerably reduce the corporate income tax. Second, and an equally important part of the program, was that massive cuts in government spending were required. However, to quote Stockman, "the true Reagan Revolution never had a chance."[6] This was because, in Stockman's mind, the forces of history were against it. The long buildup of the size of the government and the built-in system of checks and balances would mitigate against any truly revolutionary reductions in the size of the government. In describing the president and how he would fit into his own revolution, Stockman maintains that "he [Reagan] was a consensus politician not an ideologue. He had no business trying to make a revolution because it wasn't in his bones."[7]

Further, Stockman states,

> The Californians had no strategic plan for launching their government, to say nothing of a Reagan Revolution. . . . The economic indicators were worsening by the day . . . yet the economic team wasn't being assembled with any more urgency than anything else. . . . If others weren't going to get his administration's act together, I would. . . . On December 19th, I wrote a memo to Meese and Jim Baker. It began "Our enemy is time." I sketched out an action plan for launching the entire Reagan Revolution for economic recovery within a few weeks of the inauguration. To my surprise they both agreed with it.[8]

So what emerges from insider accounts of the early days of the Reagan administration in early 1981 is a collection of vacuums. First of all, there was a vague yet sincere presidential economic philosophy of lower taxes, less government regulation, and indeed a smaller government in its everyday presence in American life. There was also a vacuum in the thinking of the American economics profession. No meaningful agreed-upon treatise was propounded by the economics establishment on how to deal with the simultaneous problems of unemployment and inflation. While the evidence was fairly unmistakable that the short-run cause of the 1979–81 inflation was OPEC and rising energy prices, the supply-siders and the monetarists screamed loudly that the real problem was the size of the government and too great a money supply in existence—that huge money supply derived from years of high government spending, high welfare programs, and generally inappropriate government activity financed by a generous monetary policy. Thus, even though it had not caused runaway inflation to date, it was lying fallow, just encouraging and enabling OPEC to do what it did: raise oil prices. The liberal Keynesian wing of the economics profession, which had for years written about such phenomena as cost-push inflation and who were well aware that cost-push inflation could be imposed on an economy by international transmission, were either too busy, didn't bother, or were unable to counter the arguments of the conservative wing of the profession.

There was also a vacuum in experienced personnel, which resulted partly from the Reagan management style and partly from the fact that he was an outsider to Washington. This vacuum was best reflected in his appointment of David Stockman as budget director. Stockman's biggest failure may have been due to his lack of political experience. While he pushed zealously for achieving most of the Kemp–Roth tax cuts, he was overoptimistic and naive in his assessment of the political forces that would eventually prevent most of the spending cuts necessary to prevent the Kemp–Roth tax cuts from becoming an economic disaster. This is what Stockman's book *The Triumph of Politics* is really all about. Stockman underestimated the political forces that opposed government spending cuts, and he also underestimated the ease with which politicians will vote for tax cuts.

As we read Stockman's book, the forecasting process which eventually led to the 1981 administration's budget forecast takes on a disturbing flavor. In order to convince Congress to pass the Kemp–Roth tax cuts, the forecast had to ensure extremely high economic growth as a result of the cuts, i.e., one that would permit sufficient tax revenues, to prevent massive budget deficits. Stockman claimed that Murray Weidenbaum, chair of the president's Council of Economic Advisors, agreed to "keep the real growth rate reasonably high" if David Stockman would keep the projected inflation rate reasonably high to satisfy Weidenbaum in the Office of Management and Budget's economic forecast in early 1981.[9] To quote Stockman's book: "What model did this come out of, Murray?" Stockman asks, and Weidenbaum slaps his belly with both hands and replies, "My visceral computer."[10] Further Stockman states, "The new Weidenbaum forecast added $700 billion in money GNP over five years to our previous consensus forecast. Nearly $200 billion in phantom revenues tumbled into our budget computer in one fell swoop. The massive deficit inherent in the true supply fiscal equation was substantially covered up. Eventually it would become the belly slap that was heard around the world."[11]

And so we have two vacuums: first, the vague economic philosophy of Ronald Reagan; second, his hands-off management style. The first vacuum in economic thinking was filled by generally nonmainstream economists. Garry Wills described the economic problems of early 1981 thusly: "There was little agreement among the experts. So the amateurs took over. Several writers at the *Wall Street Journal*—Robert Bartley, Jude Wanniski, Paul Roberts—had become enthusiasts for the ideas of a weirdly persuasive academic showman named Arthur Laffer."[12]

The so-called Laffer Curve is a fabled bell-shaped curve that economist Arthur Laffer alledgedly drew on a napkin, showing that tax revenues actually decrease as tax rates rise. The Laffer Curve effect, it is said, allowed one to believe that, if there were massive tax cuts such as those proposed by Kemp–Roth, then—through a wondrous supply-side effect—persons and corporations would work harder, invest more, and raise national income to the point at which the tax revenues would be increased sufficiently to cover the revenue losses caused by the original tax cut. Most self-respecting economists doubted this proposition, and Stockman himself found out very early on in the process that this was a fallacious assumption. And so, into the vacuums moved incorrect economic theories. The tax cuts were made along with a few spending cuts which generally affected the weaker political constituencies who lost retraining benefits, public housing rent support, and Social Security benefits. The results, however, were the largest peacetime deficits in history.

OVEREMPHASIZING THE INFLATION PROBLEM

To summarize parts of the above discussion, the administration's game plan was one of tax reductions with simultaneous cuts in the size of the government. This, through the theories of supply-side economics, would produce a flood of goods and production onto the market in order to reduce inflation, increase the productive capacity of the country, and simultaneously fill up the government coffers with tax revenues. This was the Reagan game plan for dealing with inflation.

But was inflation the major economic problem of the time that could be handled by effective government action? That it was a major economic problem of the time there is no doubt. Prices rising at 9, 10, and 11 percent, and gasoline rising from 55 cents a gallon in 1979 to $1.35 in 1982 were certainly real problems for any thinking or even nonthinking consumer. The second part of the question—could the government do anything about it in a quick-fix fashion, or should it?—is a much more difficult one to answer. Inflation, probably more than any other single factor, elected Ronald Reagan in 1980. Yet one of the long-standing truths about good representative government is that elected officials do not always follow every whim of their constituents. After intelligent investigation of a given subject, an elected official may well decide to act against the will of the constituents if he or she knows better. To do so, of course, sacrifices short-run popularity for the elected official; but the primary interest of any dedicated public servant should be the long-run welfare of his or her constituency. Ronald Reagan obviously put his personal popularity first. His economic advisors approved a game plan that, on close examination, had little chance of succeeding against the inflation. In fact, the roots of the inflation of the 1970s, particularly from 1973 on, were based more in oil and energy than in big government. In fact, a bigger government with a national energy policy might have prevented the largely energy-based inflation of the 1970s and 1980s.

It is true that the United States inflation in the late 1960s and early 1970s was due to irresponsible federal government spending. Few economists who examine the record of Lyndon Johnson's administration, with his deficit spending during a period of full employment in the Vietnam era, or the irresponsible overstimulation of the economy by President Richard Nixon in 1971 and 1972 for his own reelection purposes will come away with any other conclusion. But the record of inflation from the mid-1970s on was largely one of oil and energy as the federal government deficit fell steadily as a percentage of GNP and in absolute size until the recession of 1980. As mentioned earlier, the economics profession had a hard time attributing the inflation to rising energy prices. Thus the chorus of conservative business leaders who blamed the inflation on high government spending and a lack of saving by American consumers went largely unchallenged. A prime reason for the drop in saving by American consumers was more probably their need to cope with high energy bills and to spend and borrow money on new low-energy-consuming appliances, automobiles, and even houses.

Indeed the Iraqi invasion of Kuwait in 1990 makes it easier to make the case that all of our energy crises and thus energy-based inflation has been created by a lack of government planning. The United States in the 1970s—having no energy program, and taxing gasoline and heating oil at minimal levels, much to the satisfaction of the major oil companies—found its unorganized consumers dealing with a massive political and economic trading block known as OPEC. With no responsible government to protect them, American consumers had no way of bargaining. And the government, with much encouragement from "big oil," refused to do their bidding.

However, there are many good economic reasons to believe that the high energy prices kicked off by the 1973 and 1979 oil crises would eventually encourage an increased supply of oil through more drilling and oil discovery. Consumers, over time, would also be expected to downsize their automobiles, insulate their homes, and buy more energy-efficient appliances. Further, there is every reason to believe that a one- or two-time burst of inflation will become eventually absorbed into the price system and prices would stabilize. Inflation is the rate of increase in prices, and once an energy inflation is absorbed by the economy the rate of increase in prices should diminish. Thus, with the discovery of new oil and the working-out of consumer adjustments, there should even be a downward pressure on prices. This appears to be exactly what happened to inflation during the Reagan years. It is true that Paul Volker and the Federal Reserve in the early 1980s tightened the money supply and switched to what they claimed was a monetarist policy to reduce money growth rates and thus inflation. But in reality the Volker approach of tight money and high interest rates, while it was anti-inflationary in its early stages in 1981, gradually switched over to a tight-money policy that feared more the inflationary impact of the Reagan deficits.

Thus, it is not clear that the energy-based inflation Ronald Reagan inherited was something he could have done anything about. In fact, he chose to stimulate the economy with massive deficits while at the same time urging the Federal Reserve to pursue a monetarist policy, that is, one that would be deflationary. But the president does not control the Federal Reserve; William Greider's account of the Federal Reserve during this era suggests that Paul Volker was as concerned with the inflationary impact of the Reagan program as he was with other causes of inflation.[13] Greider quotes Volker as saying in 1982, "Before I join the taxpayers revolt I must emphasize the necessary corollary. We can not proceed without concern about the size of the deficit. Prudent tax reduction in the end depends on expenditure restraint."[14] In summary, inflation was a real economic problem when Reagan took office. While some moderate measures such as a freeze or decrease in government spending, or a gradual slowing of money supply growth on the part of the Federal

Reserve, could have been taken, the reality is that inflation was used as an excuse for a planned radical restructuring of the economy. This included massive tax and government-spending cuts. Thus the real goal, the ultimate goal—the reduction of government—would be achieved. But political reality prevented this and government grew. The rise in defense spending aggravated large deficits caused by tax reduction, and stifled investment through high interest rates. High interest rates strengthened the dollar in international markets to such a degree that U.S. manufacturing was nearly decimated in the 1980s. This was perhaps the real cost of the Reagan program, and will be addressed in the next chapter. Suffice it to say that the evidence strongly suggests that the cure for inflation may well have been worse than the disease.

PERCEIVED ECONOMIC PROBLEMS AND THE REAGAN SOLUTIONS

Two documents released by the Reagan White House are in close agreement as to the economic problems in 1981 and 1982, and as to the game plan for their solution. As outlined in the administration's white paper report of February 18, 1981, entitled "A Program for Economic Recovery"[15] and in the 1982 *Economic Report of the President,*[16] the existing government policies would produce a rising government presence in the economy, cause more inflation, stagnate productivity, and raise unemployment. The white paper plan sought to break this cycle of negative expectations by creating some 13 million new jobs by 1986, and achieving an annual growth trend of 4–5 percent.

The Reagan program had four significant parts, as presented in both documents. To quote the white paper, "The plan consists of four parts: 1) a substantial reduction in the growth of federal expenditures; 2) a significant reduction in federal tax rates; 3) prudent relief of federal regulatory burdens; and 4) a monetary policy on the part of the independent Federal Reserve System which is consistent with these programs." The fourth goal was to achieve a monetary policy that would deliver a "predictable and steady growth in the money supply at more modest levels than often experienced in the past."[17]

How should one judge the success of the Reagan economic program? First one should evaluate the four stated goals, that is, assessing to what extent were they accomplished. Second, one should relate the achievement or the nonachievement of these goals to the other major objectives of the economic policy, which, as stated in the *Economic Report of the President*, were an increased economic growth, reduced inflation and unemployment, and a reduced rate of growth in the money supply.[18]

The role of the government in the economy is clearly the villain here. The "stagflation"—a combination of stagnant growth and inflation—was a "development . . . associated with a substantial increase in the federal government's role in the economy."[19] By implication, this included an oversized federal government, an excessive number of federal government regulations, burdensome federal government taxes, and an overly stimulative expansion of the money supply.

The plan of the next chapter will thus be to evaluate the achievement or nonachievement of the four major components of the Reagan plan as set out by White House documents in 1981 and 1982. It will also relate the achievement or nonachievement of these goals and their impact on such implied macroeconomic goals as inflation reduction, unemployment reduction, investment increase, productivity increase, and so on. It will then relate the achievement of these goals to their impact on worker-related or microeconomic goals such as real-wage growth, worker productivity, income distribution, and so forth. Finally, it will attempt to assess the impact of the Reagan economic program on the overall collective health of the U.S. economy, including implications for the economic well-being of the middle class. The strength and performance of the U.S. economy in international markets at the beginning and at the end of the Reagan era will also be evaluated.

NOTES

1. William A. Niskanen, *Reaganomics* (New York: Oxford University Press, 1987), p. 14.

2. Ibid.

3. Ibid., p. 24.

4. Donald T. Regan, *For the Record* (Orlando, Fla.: Harcourt Brace Jovanovich, 1988), p. 142.

5. Ibid., p. 158.

6. David A. Stockman, *The Triumph of Politics* (New York: Harper and Row, 1986), p. 9.

7. Ibid.

8. Ibid., p. 76.

9. Ibid., p. 96.

10. Ibid.

11.   Ibid., p. 97.

12.   Garry Wills, *Reagan's America* (New York: Penguin Books, 1988), p. 431.

13.   William Greider, *Secrets of the Temple* (New York: Touchstone Books, 1987).

14.   Ibid., p. 358.

15.   The White House, "A Program for Economic Recovery," a white paper report, Washington, D.C., February 18, 1981.

16.   *Economic Report of the President*, Washington, D.C., February 1982.

17.   "A Program for Economic Recovery," op. cit., p. 2.

18.   *Economic Report*, op. cit.

19.   Ibid., p. 21.

9

Twilight In America: The Reagan–Bush Economic Legacy

> I see one-third of a nation ill-housed, ill-clad, ill-nourished.
>
> Franklin Delano Roosevelt

The approach of this chapter will be, first of all, to assess the degree of achievement of the four significant parts of the Reagan game plan. Referred to as the "four Rs," they all involved reductions—namely in federal expenditures, in federal tax rates, in federal regulatory burdens, and in growth of the money supply. Next, the degree of success in achieving this plan will be related to the stated goals of the Reagan administration: the reduction of inflation and unemployment, an increase in savings, investment, and worker productivity in order to create 13 million new jobs between 1981 and 1986, and a steady reduction of the federal deficit, "resulting in a balanced budget in 1984 and modest surpluses thereafter."[1]

ACHIEVEMENT OF THE FOUR Rs

The first two parts of the four Rs were only partially achieved. As Table 9-1 shows, the growth rate in government spending in both current and constant or real-dollar terms did slow under the Reagan administration. The slowdown in the growth of government spending in current dollars

Table 9-1
Federal Fiscal Trends, 1961–1992

	Average Annual Percent Change in Federal Spending		Average Annual Percent Change in Federal Receipts		Deficit (current $)	
	Current $	Constant	Current $	Constant	Amount ($mil.)	% of GDP
1961–64	6.5	4.4	5.1	2.8	21,154	0.9
1965–68	10.9	8.1	8.1	4.3	38,913	1.2
1969–72	6.7	2.2	8.4	1.7	46,006	1.3
1973–76	11.8	3.7	9.5	0.9	148,017	2.4
1977–80	12.3	3.5	14.8	5.7	226,863	2.5
1981–84	9.6	3.0	6.8	0.4	600,171	4.5
1985–88	5.8	3.1	8.5	4.6	738,187	4.3
1989–92	8.9	4.2	4.3	1.1	1,042,426	4.7

Note: Constant dollars means that the data have been adjusted for inflation.
Source: "Historical Tables," in the *Budget of the U.S. Government, Fiscal Year 1990*, Executive Office of the President, Washington, D.C., 1989, pp. 19–20; and "Historical Tables," in the *Budget of the United States Government, Fiscal Year 1993*, pt. 5, pp. 14–18. Calculations by the author.

is more dramatic than in inflation-adjusted dollars. In the former the growth of government spending dropped from the 12.3 percent average in the Carter years to 9.6 percent during the Reagan first term and further to 5.8 percent during the Reagan second term. In real terms, however, the drop was to a rate of increase of 3.1 percent during Reagan's second term, from a 3.5 percent average growth rate during the Carter administration. An achievement of the spirit of reduced spending rests in adequate federal revenues to achieve a balanced budget. However, federal revenues in current dollar terms slowed their growth far more dramatically than the drop in federal spending. The highly reduced growth rates of taxes combined with still strong levels of spending led to unprecedented deficit levels. As Table 9-1 shows, the federal deficit rose from 2.5 percent of GNP during the Carter years to an average of 4.4 percent during the Reagan years. This caused nearly a tripling of the national debt (i.e., the accumulated deficits) from $906 billion in 1980 to $2.6 trillion in 1988.

Thus, while some pieces of the first two Rs were achieved, the net effect was in strong contradiction to the other stated goal of a balanced budget by 1984. In that year the federal deficit was $170 billion.

The third R of the game plan was the "prudent relief of federal regulatory burdens." While there was little new deregulation under the Reagan administration, there was a substantial relaxation of existing regulations. This was particularly true in reduced enforcement of antitrust laws and in increased laxity in regulating the nation's thrift institutions. William Niskanen, a member of Reagan's Council of Economic Advisors from 1981 to 1985, writes, "Under Carter there was substantial deregulation of prices and entry into the airline, trucking, railroad, and financial industries and a substantial increase in the regulation of health, safety, the environment and the uses of energy. Under Reagan there was little deregulation and less new regulation."[2] However, the deregulation achieved was more one of relaxed enforcement of existing government regulations. This relaxed enforcement, particularly in the antitrust area and in scrutiny of the savings and loan industry, and its likely impact on the American middle class will be analyzed later in the chapter. Suffice it to say, the third part of the four-R game plan was not overtly achieved through passing new laws, but rather through relaxation of enforcement procedures. To quote Niskanen again, "The total amount of regulation increased during both the Carter and Reagan administrations."[3]

The fourth R of the game plan was to achieve a monetary policy that would deliver a "predictable and steady growth in the money supply at more modest levels than often experienced in the past." As Table 9-2 shows, however, the growth in the money supply as measured by M1 (currency plus demand deposits) grew at only slightly more modest levels during the first term of the Reagan administration than during the Carter administration. The growth rate of M1 slipped from 7.7 percent during the four Carter years to 7.6 percent during Reagan's first term in office, but then jumped to 9.5 percent during his second term.

Indeed, when looking at the basic game plan—that is, the reduction of taxation and expenditures in such a way as to balance the budget in 1984, along with additional deregulation as well as a more "monetarist" or slower money growth economy—one must conclude that none of these policies was essentially achieved. What was achieved, however, was a substantial lowering of taxes on corporations and individuals in the higher income brackets. These tax reductions were supposed to induce supply-side effects such as increased saving, increased investment, gains in productivity, and the related strong performance of similar economic

Table 9-2
U.S. Investment Behavior Measures, 1961–1992

	(1) Net Business Investment Growth (average yearly % change)	(2) Net Non-residential Investment (% of GNP)	(3) Corporate Income Tax as a Percent of Total Federal Revenues	(4) Personal Income Tax as a Percent of Federal Revenues	(5) Growth in M1 (average yearly % change)	(6) Federal Deficit (% of GNP)	(7) Gross Non-residential Investment (% of GNP)
1961–64	12.7	2.7	21.6	44.3	3.3	1.0	9.5
1965–68	12.8	4.3	21.6	42.6	5.3	1.3	10.9
1969–72	-2.1	3.6	16.6	46.4	6.0	1.1	10.8
1973–76	-3.3	3.1	14.7	44.5	5.3	2.4	11.0
1977–80	15.5	3.4	14.3	47.2	7.7	2.4	11.7
1981–84	12.0	2.5	8.2	47.2	7.6	4.4	11.7
1985–88	3.4	2.6	9.2	45.2	9.5	4.2	12.1
1989–90	-3.3	2.4	9.2	44.8	3.3	4.7	11.0
1989–91	—	—	—	—	—	—	11.0
1989–92	—	—	9.2	44.8	—	4.7	

Note: 1992 data are from Office of Management and Banking estimates. GDP data are used for 1989–92, rather than GNP. Columns 1, 2, 6, and 7 are based on constant dollars. M1 refers to currency plus demand deposits.

Sources: Column 1, *Economic Report of the President*, Washington, D.C., 1990, p. 313; and *Economic Report of the President*, Washington, D.C., February 1992, p. 315. Column 2, *Economic Report*, investment, p. 313, GNP, p. 296; and *Economic Report*, op. cit., pp. 300 & 315. Column 3, average of annual percentage, "Historical Tables," in the *Budget of the United States Government, Fiscal Year 1990*, Executive Office of the President, Washington, D.C., 1989, pp. 28–29; and see Table 2-2 of this book. Column 4, ibid. Column 5, *Economic Report*, 1990, op. cit., p. 317; and *Economic Report*, 1992, op. cit., p. 373. Column 6, deficit, "Historical Tables," 1990, op. cit., pp. 19–20; GNP, *Economic Report*, 1990, op. cit., p. 296 and "Historical Tables," in the *Budget of the United States Government, Fiscal Year 1993*, Executive Office of the President, Washington, D.C., 1992, pt. 5, pp. 14–18. Column 7, *Economic Report*, 1990, op. cit., p. 296; and *Economic Report*, 1992, op. cit., p. 300. Computations by the author.

variables that would signify a healthy economy. It is to the Reagan record in these individual areas that we turn next.

LOWER UNEMPLOYMENT THROUGH LOWER REAL WAGES AND BIG FEDERAL DEFICITS

The reduction in unemployment and inflation have often been touted by administration spokespersons and/or supporters as two of the most crowning achievements of the Reagan economic policy. The unemployment rate fell from 7.0 percent for the year in which Ronald Reagan was elected to an average of 5.4 percent for his final year and to a rate of 5.2 percent in December 1988. However, this record of decline belies the average rates of unemployment that prevailed from 1981 to 1988. Though the rate did eventually fall toward the end of the Reagan administration, it did so after rising first from 7 percent in 1980 to an average high of 9.5 percent for both entire years of 1982 and 1983. Indeed, as shown in Table 9-3, the average unemployment rate for the whole of the Carter administration was 6.5 percent. For the first term of the Reagan administration, it averaged 8.6 percent and then fell to just slightly below the Carter average rate to 6.4 percent in the last Reagan term. Nonetheless, the ending overall unemployment rate of 5.2 percent in 1988 was less than any single-year unemployment rate of the Carter administration. Black unemployment rates also averaged generally higher during the Reagan administration than during the Carter years.

To which of Reagan's economic policies can we attribute this fall in the unemployment rate, if any? The supply-side economics that was supposed to promote increased savings and investment—particularly business investment—does not deserve credit for this unemployment drop. Real nonresidential net investment (i.e., business investment), which grew at 15.5 percent during the Carter years, grew at 12 percent during the first term of the Reagan administration and fell to a growth rate of 3.4 percent during Reagan's second term (see Table 9-3). Imports also grew at far more rapid rates of expansion during the first term of the Reagan administration (see Table 9-3). And while the foreign trade deficit improved somewhat in the second term, the trade balance was still a whopping $127 billion in deficit in 1988. With Americans importing so many goods from abroad, and foreigners buying fewer and fewer of our products, this could hardly be expected to turn up as a source of job growth for the United States. My own two major choices for explaining the

Table 9-3
Selected U.S. Economic Performance Measures, Annual Average Percentages, 1961–1991

	(1)	(2)	(3)	(4)	(5)	(6)	(7)	(8)	(9)	(10)
	Unemployment Rate				Business			Export	Import	Living
	All	Black and Other	Inflation Rate	Net Business Investment Change	Sector Productivity Change	Real GNP Growth	Employment Growth	Growth ($ constant)	Growth ($ constant)	in Poverty
1961–64	5.8	10.9	1.2	+12.7	3.9	4.3	0.6	7.0	4.7	—
1965–68	3.9	7.4	3.3	+12.8	3.0	4.7	2.4	4.9	10.9	14.8
1969–72	5.0	8.6	4.6	−2.1	1.9	2.5	2.1	5.9	7.2	12.3
1973–76	6.7	12.2	8.2	−3.3	1.4	2.1	2.0	11.1	4.6	11.6
1977–80	6.5	13.7	10.4	+15.5	0.3	3.1	2.8	9.2	5.4	11.9
1981–84	8.6	17.5	5.1	+12.0	1.5	2.5	1.4	1.8	9.5	14.3
1985–88	6.4	13.6	3.4	+3.4	1.8	3.6	2.2	9.5	7.4	13.5
1989–91	5.7	10.4	4.8	−2.2[1]	0.7	0.9[2]	0.5	8.5	2.0	13.2[3]

Notes: (The above are mostly four-year averages of annual averages, except as noted.):
1. Data for 1989–90. 2. GDP growth. 3. Data for 1989–92.

Sources: Columns 1 and 2, U.S. Bureau of Labor Statistics data, cited in the *Economic Report of the President*, Washington, D.C. 1990, p. 339; *Economic Report of the President*, Washington, D.C., February 1992, p. 34. Column 3, percent change in consumer price index, December to December, *Economic Report*, op. cit., p. 364; *Economic Report* 1992, op. cit., p. 465. Column 4, nonresidential net private domestic investment, *Economic Report*, op. cit., p. 313; *Economic Report*, 1992, op. cit., p. 315. Column 5, output per hour, *Economic Report*, op. cit., p. 347; 1989–91, *Economic Report*, 1992, op. cit., p. 349. Column 6, percent change in GNP, 1982 dollars, *Economic Report*, op. cit., p. 296; and *Economic Report*, 1992, op. cit., p. 301. Column 7, percent change in civilian employment, *Economic Report*, op. cit., p. 332; and *Economic Report*, 1992, op. cit., p. 301. Column 8, percent change in exports, constant dollars, *Economic Report*, op. cit., p. 297; and *Economic Report*, 1992, op. cit., p. 301. Column 9, percent change in imports, constant dollars, *Economic Report*, op. cit., p. 328; and *Economic Report*, 1992, op. cit., p. 330. Calculations by the author.

reduction in the unemployment rate in the United States are a combination of a good old-fashioned Keynesian stimulus brought about by the huge federal deficits, and the reduced real wage of the average American laborer.

The federal deficit, which annually averaged 2.4 percent over the 1973–80 period, jumped to averaging 4.4 percent of GNP during the first Reagan term and then fell slightly to an annual average of 4.2 percent during the second Reagan term (see Table 9-2). This helped raise and sustain respectable real GNP growth rates (see Table 9-3), and these higher GNP growth rates were helped by increased productivity or output per worker hour. However, the increased rates of productivity that were indeed achieved during the Reagan years were nowhere nearly matched by increases in real hourly compensation. Referring to Table 9-4, we find the most striking example of this in the disparities between overall productivity increases in manufacturing of 3.9 percent and 3.7 percent respectively, in the first and second Reagan terms. Real hourly compensation grew only 0.2 percent and 0.5 percent respectively, during those time periods. The same was true in both the nonfarm business sector and in nonfinancial corporations. Quite simply, as observed in earlier chapters, the greater power of capital over labor served to handcuff labor in its ability to extract wage increases anywhere near its levels of increased productivity. This was a period much in contrast to the power of labor in the 1950s and in the 1960s. Indeed, Table 9-4 shows vividly that over the three decades from 1961 through 1987, in all sectors, labor lost most of its ability to match its compensation per hour to its productivity per hour.

Thus, Keynesian fiscal stimulus plus a lower real wage were major factors in the decline in the unemployment rate under Reagan. Further, the employment growth through the 1980s was less than that of the Carter years (see Table 9-3). The fact that family income, in real terms, rose at all during the Reagan years can be more likely explained by the continued sharply increasing labor-force participation rate of females during these years. Quite simply, increases in family income were achieved by the mere fact that more members of the family were working longer hours, for reduced wages.

THE "ACHIEVEMENT" OF LOWER INFLATION

Inflation, which averaged annually 10.4 percent during the Carter years, fell to 5.1 percent during the first Reagan term and averaged 3.4

Table 9-4

U.S. Productivity, Compensation, and Savings, 1961–1988

	Nonfarm Business Sector		Manufacturing		Nonfinancial Corporations		Gross Private Savings Percent of Total	
	Productivity	Real Hourly Compensation	Productivity	Real Hourly Compensation	Productivity	Real Hourly Compensation	Personal	Business
1961–64	3.5	2.7	4.7	2.3	3.7	2.5	27.4	72.6
1965–68	2.4	2.6	1.7	1.7	1.8	2.2	36.4	63.6
1969–72	1.5	1.9	2.8	1.5	1.2	1.6	32.2	67.8
1973–76	1.0	0.8	2.3	1.4	0.8	0.6	34.4	65.6
1977–80	0.1	–0.6	1.4	–0.2	1.8	–0.6	27.0	73.0
1981–84	1.1	0.4	3.9	0.2	1.7	0.1	25.6	74.4
1985–87	1.4	1.0	3.7	0.5	1.6	0.6	17.6	82.4
1985–88	—	—	—	—	—	—	18.2	81.8
1988–Q1	2.8	0.5	3.2	2.0	4.3	0.7	—	—
Q2	1.4	0.7	3.7	–1.7	–1.6	–0.6	—	—
Q3	0.9	0.5	5.2	0.0	–1.1	–0.4	—	—

Notes: Q1, Q2, and Q3 are calendar year quarters. Productivity data (output per worker hour) and real hourly compensation are shown as average annual percent changes. Quarterly data are at annual rates.

Sources: Productivity and compensation figures, and industry analytic ratios, unpublished detail data supplied to the author by the U.S. Bureau of Labor Statistics, Washington, D.C., December 8, 1989. Computation of averages by the author. For savings data, see Table 6-4. Computations by the author.

percent during the second term (see Table 9-3). However, none of the earlier Reagan economic policies in the four Rs appear to have contributed materially to the disinflation. To be sure, a slowdown in monetary growth—that is, tight money—did occur in late 1979, 1980, and 1981, but it is evident that this tight-money phenomenon was more a policy move of the Federal Reserve System, particularly under Paul Volker's direction, than due to any specific policy of Reaganomics. Two far more likely reasons for the fall in inflation of the 1980s are falling oil prices and the subsequent strengthening of the dollar.

In a 1985 article, I argued that what was happening in the 1980s was to a large extent symmetrical to what happened in the 1970s.[4] In 1973 and 1979, oil price shocks greatly accelerated the inflation rate and sent the value of the dollar spiraling south. Americans now had to pay more dollars for the same quantity of foreign goods (particularly oil); and thus, we were importing inflation. In the 1980s, however, a disinflation was led by falling oil prices. The dollar strengthened as a result, and Americans were able to import the same quantities of foreign goods with less dollars—which also had a downward bias on the consumer price index. A third major cause of disinflation in the 1980s was the fall in real compensation per hour, particularly when compared with the increases in worker productivity. This was particularly striking in manufacturing, where productivity rose at an average annual rate of 3.8 percent from 1981 to 1987 while average real hourly compensation rose between 0.2 percent and 0.5 percent (see Table 9-4). The reduction of real wages as a means to fight inflation was never a stated goal of the Reagan economic policy team. However, it is certainly an achievement about which traditional conservatives, most Republicans, and their leader Ronald Reagan could be extremely happy.

DECREASED PERSONAL SAVINGS, INCREASED BUSINESS SAVINGS, AND CORPORATE TAKEOVERS

A supply-side goal in reducing both business and personal taxes was the stimulation of increased personal savings and investment. People would be encouraged to work harder and more, since their after-tax income would be greater. Savings, both business and personal, would increase and would find their way into new productive investment.

The record on savings patterns from the tax cuts of 1981 is one where two distinct trends emerge. First, business savings—that is, net profits plus allowances for depreciation—increased markedly. As Tables 6-4 and 6-5 show, business savings in real terms not only increased markedly but increased on a per-employee basis to record levels during the Reagan years. Second, real personal savings, both in terms of the share of total savings in the economy and on a per-employee basis, fell sharply. In 1980 real personal savings per employee were $1,886; this figure fell to $1,116 in 1987 (see Table 6-4). In 1980 real business savings per employee were $4,224; this climbed to $4,739 per employee in 1985 and averaged $4,609 per employee in 1987. What really happened was that a decided shift took place in *who* was doing the saving in the economy, and that shift was toward less personal saving and more business saving. The business share,

Table 9-5
Business Savings and Investment in the United States, 1980–1988
(in billions of dollars)

	(1) Gross Business Savings	(2) Change in (1)	(3) Non-residential Fixed Investment	(4) Change in (3)	(5) Direct Investment Abroad	(6) Change in (5)
1980	341.5	—	322.8	—	215.4	—
1981	391.1	49.6	369.2	46.4	228.3	12.9
1982	403.2	12.1	366.7	−2.5	207.8	−20.5
1983	461.6	58.4	356.9	−9.8	207.2	−0.6
1984	509.5	47.9	416.0	59.1	211.5	4.3
1985	539.9	30.4	442.9	26.9	230.6	19.1
1986	544.6	4.7	435.2	−7.7	259.6	29.0
1987	562.0	17.4	444.3	9.1	308.0	48.4
1988	593.8	31.8	487.2	42.9	326.9	18.9
Net change	—	+$252.3	—	+$164.4	—	+$111.5
1980–88	—	(+73.9%)	—	(+50.1%)	—	(+50.7%)

Sources: Column 1, undistributed corporate profits, capital consumption allowances (adjusted), and private wage accruals less disbursements, U.S. Department of Commerce article in the *Economic Report of the President*, Washington, D.C., 1990, p. 326. Column 3, U.S. Department of Commerce, in *Economic Report*, 1990, op. cit., p. 294. Column 5, U.S. Department of Commerce data for 1980–86, *Economic Report of the President*, Washington, D.C., January 1989, p. 429; for 1987–88, *Survey of Current Business*, U.S. Department of Commerce report, June 1989, p. 46.

which had been 73 percent of total savings during the Carter years, rose to 81.8 percent during the second term of the Reagan administration (see Table 9-4).

The shift away from personal saving and more decidedly toward business saving was no doubt helped by the tax policies of the Reagan administration. The corporate income tax fell from 14.3 percent of total federal revenues during the Carter years, to 9.2 percent during Reagan's second term (see Table 9-2). However, personal income taxes as a percent of total federal revenues remained virtually unchanged despite personal tax cuts. There is no doubt that the corporate tax cuts—particularly accelerated depreciation, a major part of the early Reagan game plan—increased profits and thus business savings. The question then becomes, What did the business community do with these increased savings? Were they invested in new productive assets?

Table 9-5 shows that gross business savings increased by 73.9 percent between 1980 and 1988—a total increase of $252.3 billion. However, the increase in business savings was invested in about the same proportion domestically and internationally as it had been in prior years. Nonresidential fixed investment in the United States grew by 50.1 percent over that time period, and direct investment abroad grew by 50.7 percent. Further, despite the growth in business saving in the 1980s, domestic investment did not grow until 1984, and foreign investment did not pick up until 1986. This suggests, quite simply, more cash retained within the business organization to be used for purposes other than distribution to stockholders or investment. Where did the increased business savings go?

One purpose for which the newly found cash was used was for corporate takeovers. While the junk bond market certainly contributed here, tax cuts delivered enormous amounts of net cash flow to corporations during the years 1981–84, and these cash inflows were not matched by increased business investment on new plant and equipment. A second purpose to which the increased cash flows were put was for corporations' maneuvers to buy back their own stock, thus privatizing themselves and further insulating managements from stockholder control.

The large increase in gross business savings during the Reagan administration, which was not fully matched by increases in investment, must incline one to assess any achievements of the Reagan supply-side theories as mixed at best. As Table 9-2 shows, gross nonresidential investment—that is, investment that includes both *new* investment and *replacement* for old worn-out capital equipment—increased only slightly as a percent of GNP in the Reagan years over the Carter years. This category of investment, which averaged 11.7 percent of GNP in the Carter years and during the first term of the Reagan administration, edged up to 12.1 percent of GNP during the second Reagan term. However, net nonresidential investment—that is, new investment over and above the mere replacement of worn-out capital equipment—fell as a share of GNP, to the lowest levels of all administrations over the 1961 to 1988 period falling to 2.6 percent of GNP in the second Reagan term.

The slight gains in the replacement of worn-out capital equipment, as represented by a slight increase in the share of gross investment to GNP, may have had some productivity effects. Worker productivity in the overall economy, which had been negative during the Carter years, began to grow again under Reagan. While overall productivity in the economy grew at 1.1 percent during the first Reagan term and 1.4 percent during the second term, manufacturing productivity grew strongly at 3.9 percent and 3.7 percent, respectively, during those time periods (see Table 9-4). Thus there appears to be some puzzle in the record of productivity growth when related to *new* investment, which fell, as opposed to *replacement* investment, which rose slightly during the Reagan years. As Niskanen writes, "The sum of investment in producers' durables and non-residential structures, the two major investment categories most affected by the lower tax rates, increased at a lower rate than during the Carter administration."[5]

One possibility is that the replacement investment was of considerably higher quality than during the 1970s thus delivering greater worker productivity. The computer explosion in many facets of manufacturing during the 1980s would certainly suggest this explanation. Another possibility is that worker productivity increased due to the negative effect of lower real wages, causing workers to work harder and work more. This would agree with the deunionization pattern of the period. Further, the practice of Japanese plants locating in the United States, particularly in the auto and auto-parts industries, also probably contributed to increased productivity. One net result of Japanese-owned auto plants in the United States has been the closing of domestic automobile plants. The Japanese have typically located in labor surplus areas and further in areas where union activity is weak and have largely maintained a nonunionized U.S. workforce. Thus, logic would dictate that the new "transplant" Japanese auto plants, with higher productivity due to new capital equipment and generally a more nonunion labor status, would have raised the productivity averages. Further, these plants would be replacing low-productivity, obsolete U.S. plants, closed because of the existing overcapacity in the industry. American firms, to a certain degree, have relocated their plants with a de-unionization motive as well, particularly to Mexico. Thus the increase in worker productivity during the Reagan years may also be due to the general trend of the increased power of capital over labor—in this case with a bigger foreman's whip, less union protection, and enhanced capital mobility—than due to the rather lackluster investment achievements of supply-side economics.[6]

THE REAGAN PROGRAM AND RISING BUSINESS WELL-BEING

That the Reagan economic program was a boon to the economic health and wealth of business—particularly big business—and to the more selective group of individuals who owned substantial shares of such business can be of little doubt. First, the large transfer of the ownership of savings from individuals to business, which had been steadily shifting toward the latter since the late 1960s, certainly accelerated during the Reagan years. As shown in Table 6-5, the ratio of business savings to personal savings from 1980 to 1987 went from 2.50 to 5.39. Table 6-5 also shows a massive increase in business savings per employee as opposed to personal savings per employee (see also Table 6-4). Indeed the behavior of saving—that is, banking the residual after all expenses are met—is the best measure of wealth accumulation and financial power. Wealth is accumulated by saving; and the saving behavior of the American corporation and business, vis-à-vis the labor-dependent worker, leaves little room for doubt as to the nature of the financial power shift in the 1980s.

Second, another measure of this financial power shift has been the continuing escape by the American corporation from income taxes. As Table 9-2 shows, the total share of income taxes paid by American corporations fell dramatically during the Reagan years, whereas personal income taxes as a percent of total federal revenues remained around the historical 45 percent level of the past two decades.

That the Reagan policies enriched the financial health of the business sector is attested to by William Niskanen, who writes,

> The real equity of U.S. corporations increased substantially during the Reagan years after declining (except in transportation) during the Carter administration.... The average real equity of transportation, utility and financial corporations increased substantially despite the problems of some firms because of deregulation.... This substantial increase in the real

wealth of corporate equity, an increase in real wealth that is not directly reflected in the national income statistics, was one of the more important effects of Reagan's economic policies. Despite the visible problems of some firms and industries the real market value of American firms is now the highest in more than a decade.[7]

However, Niskanen points out that the changes in the real equity of American business was not uniform. His data show vast improvements for industry, transportation, utilities, and finance, ranging from 4 percent to 6.5 percent at an annual rate during the Reagan years. However, the real equity of agriculture diminished at an *annual* average of 10.5 percent. These data further corroborate the trend of the increased financial power of capital-enhanced groups over those who are labor-dependent. Much of the real equity loss during the 1980s in the agriculture industry was the result of bankruptcy of the small farmer—the labor-dependent farmer.

Further enhancing the power of capital during the Reagan administration was its lax antitrust policy. Never before in the history of the republic has there been such an enormous amount of merger activity, both in the number of takeovers as well as in dollar value. Walter Adams and James Brock point out that from 1980 to 1986 the number of acquisitions *per year* went from 1,565 to 4,022![8] The total reported value of such mergers or acquisitions rose from an annual amount of $33 billion in 1980 to $190 billion in 1986. The total for the seven-year period amounted to $667 billion. The number of takeovers worth $1 billion or greater rose from three in 1980 to 34 in 1986—a total of 106 for the whole period.

Thus it is clear that capital, as represented by corporate America, made enormous strides during the Reagan years and greatly improved its financial health. This is evident from falling corporate tax rates, from the increased ownership of the financial assets of America through increased savings, and through an unprecedented ability to combine and merge many of the already large corporations in the United States. We shall later in this chapter return to the question of whether or not this improved health for the capital-enhanced financial regime has been shared by the economic health of the United States as a world power. But before we do that, let us turn to the economic health of the labor-dependent individual.

THE DECLINING ECONOMIC HEALTH OF THE AMERICAN LABOR-DEPENDENT WORKER

Along with a rising level of financial health for the capital-enhanced sector of the American economy during the 1980s there transpired a symmetrical development: the declining financial health of the average American worker. True, the unemployment rate had fallen to 5.2 percent in December 1988 from its 1980 average level of 7 percent and its 1983 average level of 9.5 percent, yet the average for Reagan's second term was barely below the average for the 1977–80 period (see Table 9-3). Inflation had fallen from 10.4 percent during the Carter years to 5.1 percent and 3.4 percent in the two Reagan terms. Certainly, full employment without inflation is, all other things being equal, superior to high unemployment with inflation. Yet all other things were not equal. The evidence strongly suggests that, while many Americans were working, they were working longer hours per family unit at a reduced rate of pay. As cited earlier (particularly in Chapter 4), the labor-force participation rate of women rose substantially in the 1980s. In American manufacturing, average weekly hours rose from 39.7 in 1980 to 41.1 in 1988. Yet average weekly earnings in constant dollars fell over the same time period from $274.65 per week to $266.79 (see Chart 3-1).[9]

Other data support the generally diminished well-being of the American labor-dependent. The percentage of Americans living in poverty rose from 11.9 percent during the Carter years to 14.3 percent and 13.5 percent during the two Reagan terms (see Table 9-3). As earlier noted, the percentage of gross private savings made up by personal savings fell from 27 percent in the Carter years to nearly 18 percent during the second Reagan term (see Table 9-4). While productivity in the American economy increased, most of the fruits of this productivity went to the business owners. Nowhere was this so striking as in the manufacturing sector, where productivity increased on an annual average of approximately 3.8 percent over the Reagan term, but where real hourly compensation decreased from $7.78 in 1980 to $7.69 in 1988 (see Table 9-4). Finally, taxation levels—despite the Reagan income tax cuts in the early 1980s— left the average taxpayer about where he or she was at the start of the decade. Personal income taxes as a percent of total federal revenues averaged 46 percent—exactly where they were during the Carter years and the Nixon years and above those of the approximate 43 percent level of the Kennedy–Johnson years (see Table 9-2). In contrast, the corporate income tax fell dramatically from an average of 21.6 percent during the Johnson and Kennedy years to a total revenue contribution to the federal government of less than 9 percent during the Reagan years.

In summary, the evidence strongly suggests that the increased financial and economic health of the capital-enhanced establishment in the United

States during the Reagan administration came at the expense of the labor-dependent groups: the average American worker, the middle class, the poor, and the homeless.

It is relatively easy to make a case supported by data that the capital-enhanced position in the United States was materially improved during the Reagan years. But it is also difficult to prove that this improved financial and economic well-being was shared by the labor-dependent groups. In fact, the data suggest just the opposite: capital ascended at the expense of labor. The total pie in the United States did not grow materially. Real GNP growth during the Reagan years was about at the average level of the Carter years, and employment growth was below its earlier counterpart. The redistribution of income that took place during the 1980s amounted to an impoverishment of the middle and lower classes, a shrinking in the size of the middle class, and a sending of the "fruits" of that impoverishment upward to the capital-enhanced individuals in the upper classes. Given the data, it is difficult to make a case for any other scenario.

THE ECONOMIC AND FINANCIAL HEALTH OF THE UNITED STATES AS A WORLD POWER

Granted, then, the Reagan years enhanced the financial well-being of capital and of American business. How has this translated into the economic health of the nation? A legitimate reason for redistributing of income from one factor of production to another would be to maintain the benefiting factor's health and thus ensure its productivity. The question thus arises: Did the enrichment of the holders of capital translate into an improved economic performance for the United States economy overall, both domestically and internationally?

THE BORROWED ECONOMIC PERFORMANCE

On the surface, the U.S. economy in the 1980s appeared to have a better-than-average to average performance when measured against other modern economies. Japan led the gains in industrial production, increasing its overall output by 33.7 percent from 1980 to 1988. Canada followed with a 30.1 percent increase, but the United States was third with a 26.3 percent increase. This was far better than the average for the European

Community; that group of 12 nations increased its industrial output by only 12.5 percent over the eight-year period. As far as inflation goes, the American price increase of 43.6 percent over the eight-year period placed it a distant third behind Japan's minuscule 16.2 percent price rise, and Germany's 22.4 percent. For the whole European community from 1980 to 1988, prices rose 65.4 percent. America's unemployment rate in 1988 was the second lowest among the major industrial nations at 5.5 percent, Japan topping her with an extremely low unemployment rate of 2.5 percent. Increases in U.S. manufacturing compensation were the second lowest among the major industrial nations at 47.6 percent over the eight-year period, being bested only by the United Kingdom with a 45 percent hourly compensation rise in constant dollars from 1980 to 1988. It is interesting that, despite Japan's huge gains in international trade, her hourly compensation went up by 150 percent over that time period—almost triple the U.S. rate. Finally, in terms of economic growth, the United States was again third among the major industrial nations during the period 1984 to 1988. Economic growth averaged 4.2 percent in the United States, being bested by Canada's 4.7 percent and Japan's 4.5 percent. The whole European community grew at 2.7 percent.[10]

The U.S. economy did, therefore, have an ostensibly acceptable performance during the 1980s. So why has there been so much criticism? Partly because the decent growth rates in GNP, industrial production, and employment were purchased with a good old-fashioned Keynesian fiscal stimulus that nearly tripled the national debt, sending it from a level of $908 billion in 1980 to $2.6 trillion in 1988. The United States saw its internal national debt rise from 33.2 percent of its GNP in 1980 to 53.2 percent of its GNP in 1988. Interest payments on the federal debt rose from 8.6 percent of total federal outlays in 1980 to 13.5 percent of total federal outlays in 1988. In fact, 1988 interest payments on the federal debt were more than $4 billion greater than the 1988 federal deficit of $145.4 billion.[11]

The United States becoming a huge internal debtor (in other words, with a huge national debt owed to itself) and the fact that this took place over such a short period of time was instrumental in the United States becoming an international debtor nation. Starting the 1980s in a creditor position—that is, with more money owed to it than it owed to other nations—the United States finished up in 1988 in just the opposite position.

THE NATIONAL–INTERNATIONAL DEBT LINK

The huge national debt made us poorer internationally mainly through its effect on interest rates and the exchange value of the dollar. In order to finance the huge internal deficits that resulted from the Reagan tax cuts and expenditure increases, the federal government borrowed massive amounts of money as the national debt increased threefold. When the American government borrowed that much money, it necessarily drove up interest rates to much higher levels than at any time in our nation's history, and also to higher levels than in Japan, Germany, France, and England. Such high U.S. rates caused a great demand for the dollar, and its value strengthened considerably in the 1980s. This demand for the dollar was not to buy U.S. products; it was simply to buy high-yielding U.S. bonds. But a demand is a demand; and when a currency is in demand, it becomes expensive (or strong). Thus, because of the expensive dollar, the prices of U.S. products also rose everywhere. Conversely, however, with the dollar being strong, the prices of goods manufactured everywhere else fell. American manufacturing was hurt severely in two ways. First, Americans bought more and more foreign-manufactured products; and second, foreigners bought less American-manufactured products and more of their own.

Thus, just from trade and investments alone, foreigners earned some $658 billion during the 1980–88 period. This then allowed them to purchase U.S. assets, including bonds and stock—but particularly, entire U.S. companies and U.S. real estate.

Benjamin Friedman, in his book *Day of Reckoning*, gives an account of the decline of the United States as a new national economic power in the 1980s.[12] Friedman refutes those defenders of the Reagan record who claim it is good for foreigners to be investing money to rebuild America. Much of the foreign investment, he points out, has been not for new plant and equipment but rather for the buying of existing assets or land, and thus not for the creation of new productive facilities. Commenting on new Japanese plants such as Nissan in Tennessee and Honda in Ohio, Friedman points out that these are the exception rather than the rule. "In 1987 foreign investors spent $26 billion in fresh investment to buy existing American businesses including sixteen billion dollars worth of manufacturing companies. By contrast, in 1987 foreigners spent only five billion dollars to establish new businesses in America and half of that went into forming new real estate companies."[13]

THE SPENDTHRIFT AMERICAN CONSUMER? THE
SUBSTITUTION AND INFERIOR-GOODS PHENOMENA

Much has been made about "overconsumption" in the United States. Such criticisms have prompted many critics of the American way of life to excoriate Americans' habits of low savings and high consumption, often citing the growing imports consumed by American citizens. Yet this criticism of the American consumer is overdone for several reasons, and perhaps for several motives. The reasons first.

From 1980 to 1988, imports grew by only 1 percent of GNP. In 1980, imports stood at 11.7 percent of gross national product; and by 1988, they had risen to only 12.7 percent of GNP. The problem with our balance of trade deficit was the inability of Americans to export in the 1980s and this problem stemmed directly from the expensive dollar largely created by the U.S. Treasury's pushing up interest rates through its massive borrowing programs. The big story in the balance-of-trade deficit in the United States was not so much increased imports, but the inability to sell U.S. products abroad, given our expensive currency. It must be admitted, of course, that the U.S. imports did not decline during the 1980s in *real* terms; in fact, they increased from 10.4 percent of GNP in 1980 to 15.7 percent of GNP in 1989 showing that Americans, by spending roughly the same relative numbers of dollars as a percent of the economy between 1980 and 1989, received approximately 51 percent more in the way of real goods.[14] This attests to the fact that the dollar was stronger in the 1980s, causing foreign products' relative prices to fall and making them an excellent buy.

Neoclassical economic theory holds that the "substitution effect" causes consumers to substitute products whose prices fall (all other things being equal) for products whose prices have remained stable. All of this is no mystery to us, yet what has been overlooked is the fact that foreign products may have been the "best buys" for Americans, on average, because of a recklessly overvalued dollar.

American marketing professionals have correctly sized up the American market to be one of a declining middle class. The middle class was more and more strapped for disposable income during the 1980s, as evidenced by the increase in the number of working wives needed to support a family and (as mentioned above) the loss in real hourly compensation. Is it any wonder, then, that there was such a massive appetite for low priced goods? Indeed, politicians and economists must be more careful when blaming American high consumption and low saving on some sort of profligate consumerism. Again, neoclassical economics predicts that stagnant or declining real incomes will cause people to purchase "inferior goods," many of which might be imports. Or else they will change their composition of purchases, such as buying more cheap radios and taking fewer vacations. Capital has steadily eroded the economic power of labor, as has been shown to be true time and time again in the earlier chapters of this book. The middle class is under enormous financial and economic pressures. Income taxes remained high in the 1980s while corporate taxes fell. State and local taxes on individuals increased relative to taxes on businesses. There were low wage increases and a large influx of immigrants that further diminished American earning power. The large immigrant population alone, with its low wages, certainly had a huge appetite for imported goods.

Thus the increasing duality of the American economy—the polarization we see in the marketing plans of business executives—virtually screams for cheap imports of all varieties. Huge wage and standard-of-living differentials still exist between the United States and many other parts of the world that are now acquiring a manufacturing base, particularly in the Pacific Rim area. The economies of Korea, Hong Kong, Taiwan, Singapore, and Malaysia will continue to crank out cheaper products facilitated by American as well as Japanese and German foreign investment. It is only natural that the financial pressure on the middle class in general, and on the great bulk of the labor-dependent American consumers in particular, should lead to the consumption of more and more cheaper imported goods.

The reasons for the characterization of the American consumer as greedy and imprudent or as a spendthrift sometimes come from the uninformed who, often in a well-meaning sort of way, wish to cut consumption and increase saving and investment. However, this criticism also comes from a more organized quarter, namely, those people actively lobbying and seeking the imposition of a national sales or value-added tax (VAT). These advocates have their own set of motives behind their criticisms. They wish to impose a national sales tax and fully eliminate the corporate income tax as a way of solidifying, or shoring up, the enormous gains made by corporations during the early 1980s and so they wave the flag of saving and investment.

Yet as shown in Table 6-5, saving is not really the main problem. Total saving in the United States has not materially declined from its levels in the 1950s and 1960s. What *has* happened is that business is doing more of the saving and individuals are doing less of it, but business is *not* investing in America. This is the real crux of the issue. Imposing a consumption tax on individuals would allow still further corporate tax reductions to businesses, which in turn would be able to save more and invest more, wherever they please. The record sadly shows that the investment generated by increased amounts of saving, such as flowed from the Tax Reform Act of 1981, carry with it no guarantee that such savings will be used to revitalize American industry; they would more likely be used for either corporate takeovers or foreign investment.

In fact, the well-known supply-side economist Paul Craig Roberts, writing in *Business Week* in 1990, notes that a number of different accounting standards and methods of measuring saving in the United States—standards that differ from those of other major industrialized nations—make the American saving rate appear lower than it is. Roberts writes, "When U.S. savings and investment are broadened to include education, military capital, consumer durables, and research and development, the U.S. rate of capital formation is equal to the average of the industrialized countries."[15] Roberts then quotes University of Pennsylvania economist Fumio Hayashi and comments, "Once the accounting systems are put on an equal footing, Hayashi finds that the notoriously wide difference in the [Japanese and American] savings rate disappears."[16]

In summary, the Reagan years have seen a decline in the position of the United States as a world economic power, largely due to economic policies of the federal government that have resulted in huge deficits, a strong dollar, and a vast deterioration of America's industry and international trading position.

However, one must not ignore the increase in our foreign trade deficit that is due to a quite normal appetite on the part of a hard-pressed American consumer for cheap foreign products.

REAGAN'S ECONOMIC CHAMPIONS

The economic miracle claims of Reagan's economic champions—mostly former economists with the Reagan administration—are generally unspectacular; and many of these claims, such as disinflation, have been dealt with earlier in this chapter. For example, Murray Weidenbaum, chairman of the president's Council of Economic Advisors from 1981 to 1982, claims that living in a "low inflation environment" was one of the chief achievements of the Reagan administration.[17] For reasons mentioned earlier, the fall in prices had a lot more to do with the drop in oil prices than with the Reagan economic policies. If anything, the Reagan economic policies produced huge deficits, which in a Keynesian sense were extremely stimulative. To take credit for this deflation in the face of such deficits, and further, in the face of such rapid monetary growth (see Table 9-2) flies in the face of generally accepted economic theory. As Weidenbaum admits, a failure of the Reagan legacy was that the federal deficit went from 2 percent of GNP in 1980 to 5 percent of GNP in 1986.[18] Any one who follows Keynesian economic theory, particularly as interpreted by conservative economists, would most likely conclude that such deficits should be inflationary. How then can we explain the fall in inflation, in the presence of such rising deficits?

Again, as Table 9-2 shows, monetary growth between 1977 to 1980 was 7.7 percent as measured by M1. From 1981 to 1984 it averaged 7.6 percent a year, hardly a significant slowdown; and from 1985 to 1988, M1 grew at an average annual pace of 9.5 percent. Such money growth rates, according to monetarist economic theory, would surely predict a continuing inflation. So where is the source of the deflation that apparently followed from the Reagan economic policies? It is hard to escape the obvious. The prime source of inflation in the 1970s and early 1980s were two massive oil shocks that caused what economists have traditionally described as an inflation of the "cost-push" variety. Once these oil shocks had worked their way through the system, and moreover once American consumers and businesses adjusted their energy consumption patterns in response to higher energy prices, the inflation dissipated. In fact, during the Reagan years, falling energy prices helped to hold down the strong inflationary pressures emanating from both the U.S. Treasury with its deficit spending and the Federal Reserve, which continued to churn out money at an excessive rate.

Weidenbaum also points out that economic growth, which was only 0.2 percent in 1980 (a recession year), was a positive 2.5 percent in 1986.[19] However, picking two points in time like this generally does not impress economists, and it should not persuade the lay reader as to the statistical significance of these numbers. As Table 9-3 points out, the *average* rate of economic growth in the Reagan administration was about at the same level as that of the Carter administration. From 1977 to 1980, real economic growth was 3.1 percent. During the Reagan first term it was 2.5 percent, and it improved to 3.6 percent during the second term—an overall average of about the same level as the Carter administration. This was hardly a victory, considering the fact that the national debt had to be tripled in order to achieve these growth rates.

Another claim of Weidenbaum is that savings owned by individuals grew from $219 billion (1982 dollars) to $335 billion over the period of 1980–86.[20] There are several problems with this observation, the foremost being that savings owned by individuals include savings owned by households, personal trust funds, nonprofit institutions, farms, and other noncorporate business. This is a distorted savings figure because it includes personal trust funds (which are notorious for being owned by higher income individuals), other noncorporate business holdings and savings, and that of nonprofit institutions—all of which would tend to skew this savings figure upward. A more accurate description of the change in savings during the Reagan administration is presented in Table 6-5, where the ratio of business savings to personal savings rose between 1980 and 1987 from 2.5 to 5.39. In other words, business savings, which had been 2.5 times greater than personal savings in 1980, grew to be almost 5.4 times greater than personal savings in 1987. This is a much better measure of what has actually happened to savings in the United States during the Reagan years. Businesses have increased their share of total savings at the expense of individuals, while the overall savings rate in the economy has remained about the same.

One other claim Weidenbaum makes for a Reagan success was that median family income rose from $26,481 in 1981 to $27,735 by 1985—a 4.7 percent increase.[21] However, in using 1981 Weidenbaum picked a recession year—which made the increase to 1985 look better. In short, the claimed increases of median family income during the Reagan years are very average when looking at the historical trend in the American economy. Further, median family income in constant dollars in 1988 was $32,191—slightly above the $31,918 level of the last year of the Carter administration (1979), and about where it was in 1973, the start of the second term of the Nixon administration ($32,109). In short, the slightly improved trend of median family income in the Reagan years is unimpressive. As mentioned in Chapter 4 and elsewhere, a major reason for the increase in family income during the Reagan years was already evident in the 1970s: the increased participation of women in the workforce, causing the family unit to contribute more total hours to the economy in order to maintain its middle-class status, or to increase its real income slightly.

One claim that can be taken a little more seriously was made by Martin Anderson. Anderson claimed that a major accomplishment of the Reagan administration was a record boom in terms of number of continuous years of economic expansion, and further an unprecedented number of new jobs created from the period November 1982 to November 1989.[22] During this period 18.7 million new jobs were created, according to Anderson. Indeed the length of the business expansion (i.e., the number of consecutive years and months of continuous economic growth) does seem unusual, and the fall in unemployment as well as the growth in the number of jobs seems impressive. However, in examining past economic expansions we discover that the employment growth rise and the number of consecutive years of this economic expansion is not at all unusual. During the 1982 to 1989 period, as Anderson points out, on an annual average of yearly totals the number of jobs in the American economy grew by 17.8 million. This was a 17.9 percent growth over the seven-year period. However, from 1962 to 1969 the number of jobs grew by 16.8 percent. While Anderson claims that 1982–89 is unusual because Reagan's great expansion was free from any wartime stimulus—as was not the case during the Vietnam era of the 1960s—we must remember that the deficits as a percentage of GNP during the Vietnam War were far less than they were during the Reagan years. In fact, in 1968 at the height of the Vietnam War, the federal deficit was $25.2 billion, or 2.9 percent of GNP. In 1967, the second largest Vietnam-era deficit of $8.7 billion was only 1.1 percent of GNP. In the Reagan years, deficits *averaged* 4.5 percent of GNP!

Further, there is ample evidence that the Vietnam War actually hurt the business expansion. There is every reason to believe that the economy might have proceeded smoothly through the 1960s had the Vietnam War not overheated the economy, thus necessitating that the Federal Reserve clamp on the monetary policy brakes in 1969 and that the federal government also take a tighter fiscal stance.

Other periods of job growth that are comparable to the Reagan era can be found from 1970 to 1977 where the total number of jobs increased 17.0 percent, or from 1972 to 1979 where the total number of jobs grew by 16.7 million or by 20.2 percent—the latter period exhibiting a more than two-percentage-point job growth greater than the 1982 to 1989 Reagan era.[23]

In short, there is nothing about the Reagan economic era and the economy's performance—even since 1982, a recession year—that can be attributed to the Reagan economic policies; the evidence suggests otherwise. To be sure, from 1982 to 1989 there was an economic expansion; it exhibited good growth rates and a good level of job growth. However, this expansion was fueled by the largest sustained growth in federal deficits in American history. And it also featured a period of excessively high monetary growth. It was further characterized by strong deflationary pressures in the commodities markets that had little to do with the Reagan economic policy. Indeed it was a lucky time, with no major shocks to the world economy, no major wars, and a period of relative international calm. One might even characterize the 1981–88 period as a time when the international, political, and economic scene was coated with Teflon.

ACHIEVEMENTS IN TAX REFORM: INCREASED MIDDLE-CLASS TAXES

One of the trumpeted achievements of the Reagan administration was tax reform. However, as pointed out in earlier chapters, the net effect of the Economic Recovery Tax Act of 1981 with its large tax cuts for both individuals and business—but particularly for corporations—was an era of record deficits. As it turned out, the tax cuts for business produced by the 1981 act were so embarrassingly huge that they were reduced somewhat by the Tax Act of 1982 and supposedly further by the "revenue-neutral" Tax Reform Act of 1986. A consistent theme of this book has been the excessive taxation of individuals and the diminished taxation of business (particularly corporations) that have occurred throughout the postwar era but reached their zenith during the Reagan era. And in fact, even the Tax Reform Act of 1986, according to a March 1990 report of the Congressional Budget Office, fell far short of delivering the increased corporate income taxes that were predicted. In 1989 and 1990 the administration's estimate was that corporate taxes would make up 10.5 percent of total revenues while personal income taxes would make up 43.6 percent. In point of fact, corporate taxes made up 10.5 percent but individual income taxes stayed at 45 percent. The net effect, as the Congressional Budget Office showed, was that the Tax Reform Act of 1986, which was supposed to be revenue-neutral, again further increased taxes on individuals above predicted levels and decreased corporate income taxes below predicted levels.

THE LAST WORD ON DEREGULATION

Earlier, economist William A. Niskanen was quoted to the effect that little real deregulation took place in the Reagan era. About the extent of deregulation during the Reagan era, one thing is clear. There was in general a relaxing of the regulatory attitude, causing, among other things, a relaxing of antitrust law enforcement. This resulted in a wave of mergers that was unprecedented in American history; and this, by the admission of one prominent Reagan economist, led to a loss of competitiveness in the airline industry. Murray Weidenbaum, in a 1990 interview with the *Margin* magazine, states, "Because the transportation department was lax in allowing airline mergers, we do not have the kind of competitive airline market that we envisioned would come from the deregulation effort."[24] This is the believable part of the Weidenbaum observations on deregulation in that article. The unbelievable part is his answer to the interviewer's question: "What do you see as the administration's major successes in deregulation?" Toward the end of his answer, Weidenbaum remarks, "The deregulation effort was felt in a variety of areas—most importantly in financial institutions and in transportation."[25] In fact, progress made in deregulation, which actually began under the Carter administration in deregulating commercial banks and some aspects of the thrift industry, was spotty at best. The early deregulation efforts of the Carter administration (via the Monetary Control Act of 1980) played no major role in the economic problems of the banking system that took place in the 1980s. Rather it was the overly permissive Garn–St. Germain Act of 1982, and its implementation by the Reagan administration, that wreaked havoc among the nation's savings-and-loan institutions. This act, signed by Reagan, greatly liberalized the investment possibilities of the thrift institutions. The "too much too soon" permissiveness of the bill and the lax enforcement of bank examinations in the Southwest, particularly in Texas and California, may eventually cause losses to the American taxpayer of at least $300 billion.[26] Thus, Reagan's record on deregulation is an extremely spotty one (and that's being generous) when viewed in the light of promoting competition and when viewed in the light of saving the consumer some money. It did, however, create fortunes in an unprecedented manner for a number of well-placed persons who profited by such deregulation and lack of enforcement of existing regulations.

THE CENTRAL QUESTION ABOUT REAGANOMICS

The central question in examining Reaganomics—the plan and the results—is as follows: Was Reaganomics, with its supply-side tax cuts and its supposedly supply-side incentives for people to save and invest and work, a truly coherent economic theory based on facts, analysis, reasoned economic projections, and carefully thought out economic results? Or was the Reagan economic plan nothing more than a traditional conservative move to redistribute income into the hands of fewer people at the top end of the income scale? This book has attempted to provide some answers. My observations on the coherence of the plan, its design and execution by a limited group of economic theorists, and the deceptive way in which the plan was put across, particularly to the Congress by the budget director of the president of the United States, were presented in Chapter 8. The economic results and benefits that flowed directly from the plan have been described in this chapter. It is my conclusion that the body of thought and the economic results encompassed by the catchy title "Reaganomics" amounted to nothing more than a traditional but successful—indeed far more successful than anyone envisioned—redistribution of income away from the middle and lower classes to the extreme top end of the income scale. The only charitable thing to be said about the plan is that, as some of its proponents actually admitted, it was a trickle-down theory. If one admits it was a trickle-down theory, then there is some faint element of generosity flowing from it. However, such a faint element of generosity is hard to appreciate when wealth concentration and the charity that flows from it have been substituted for economic democracy for all classes of individuals.

THE BUSH FOLLOW-THROUGH

The Reagan years represented the enrichment of the few at the expense of the great middle and lower classes in America, fiscal irresponsibility at the federal level, and further decline of America as an economic power. The Bush years, unbelievably, carried those trends to a higher level.

In the tax arena, burdens still weigh heavily on the personal income tax, which will average 44.8 percent of all federal revenues in the 1989–92 period (see Table 9-2). While this is a slight reduction from the 1985–88 levels, the reduction is insignificant. Corporate taxes as a percent of total federal revenues will hold even at the 9.2 percent share. So, no real tax relief has been given to the American middle or lower classes. Further, average weekly earnings have continued to fall. In the 1990–91 period, as shown earlier in Table 4-2, average weekly earnings fell in inflation-adjusted dollars by an average of 1.6 percent per year. This is despite the fact that productivity growth was positive, although weak, at about 0.48 percent. However, what this does show is a worsening ability of workers to obtain pay increases equal to their productivity gains. Average weekly

earnings after inflation in the United States have fallen steadily since the
1972–73 period from a high in 1972 of $315.44 (see Chart 3-1). Such
earnings fell to $266.79 by 1988, the last year of the Reagan administration.
After that, they steadily fell to $255.89 in 1991.[27] Thus, sadly, the record
of the Bush administration is for worker earnings to fall in real terms, with
an unabated record of continued high taxes. Signs of strain on the U.S.
economy from these conditions became evident in the 1991–92 recession—a long, stagnant one by historical standards, involving a "double-
dip" recession, an extremely cautious consumer, and, in the spring of 1992,
perhaps the worst job market for college graduates since World War II.

The continuation of the Reagan economic policy has left the country
weaker and with less room to maneuver at the federal level. Nowhere is
this more true than in the mushrooming federal deficit, which has been
growing even faster than under the Reagan years. As Table 9-1 shows,
during the 1981–88 period the Reagan administration added $1.34 trillion
to the national debt. The Reagan deficits in those eight years averaged
about 4.4 percent of national income, up from 2.5 percent in the Carter
years. However, in just four years the Bush administration has added $1.04
trillion to the national debt, which is approximately 78 percent of what
Reagan added in eight years; and the deficit as a percentage of national
income has grown from around 4.4 percent to 4.7 percent! With an
economy in a severe and prolonged recession, accompanied by the
festering of poverty, joblessness, and crime in the inner cities that erupted
in late April and early May 1992 in the riots and arson in Los Angeles and
other U.S. cities, the American government finds itself financially
strapped to deal with the root causes of the problems.

The years 1989–91 exhibited other pitiful economic statistics as well.
In 1989 and 1990, net business investment was negative. In other words,
new investment in the United States fell by a 2.2 percent average in those
two years (see Table 9-3). This was down from the 3.4 percent increase
in the last four years of the Reagan era. Productivity in the business sector
edged up an average of 0.7 percent—also well down from the Reagan
years—and overall economic growth was a miserable 0.9 percent average
for three years, the slowest four-year growth era in the postwar period!
Employment exhibited an average growth of 0.5 percent per year—the
slowest four-year performance in the 1961–91 period (illustrated in Table
9-4). And the percent living in poverty dropped a minuscule 0.3 percent
to a still high 13.2 percent, well above the rates of the 1970s and the late
1960s.

Business performance in reinvesting in America during the Bush years attests to the failure of supply-side economic policies, which have given huge tax breaks to corporate America in hopes that it would invest in America and create more jobs. In the 1989–90 period, new business investment averaged only 2.4 percent of national income (see Table 9-2), the lowest average annual rate in 30 years; and gross business investment (i.e., investment to replace worn-out capital goods as well as add new plant and equipment) averaged 11 percent of national income in the 1989–91 period, down from the Reagan years and at its lowest level since the early 1970s.

Clearly, the Bush administration has changed little if any of the Reagan economic game plan that was already starting to show serious economic shortcomings in the second term of the Reagan administration. Now it finds itself in the election year of 1992 with an economy that shows increased joblessness. This is accompanied by a demographic imbalance that sets a large and dispirited populace in the middle and lower classes (with the shrinking middle class manifesting itself in a worried and nonspending consumer) alongside a small affluent group of super-rich at the top of the pyramid and a booming but nervous stock market that largely reflects the concentration of wealth at the upper income levels.

The economic decline of the American middle class, which began in approximately the early 1970s and was accelerated by the Reagan years, has clearly seen that pattern continue under the Bush administration. As to the prospects for economic improvement of the American middle class, we shall evaluate some possible political changes leading to economic change in the final chapter of this book.

NOTES

1. These are the generally agreed-upon goals as stated in two Reagan White House documents: The White House, "A Program for Economic Recovery," a white paper report, Washington, D.C., February 18, 1981; and *Economic Report of the President*, Washington, D.C., February 1982.

2. William A. Niskanen, *Reaganomics* (New York: Oxford University Press, 1988), p. 315.

3. Ibid., p. 315.

4. F. R. Strobel, "The Dollar's Glory Days," *Business Week* (February 1985), p. 16.

5. Niskanen, op. cit. p. 234.

6. Nigel Healy and I have argued this point in "The Productivity Miracle

of the Reagan–Thatcher Years in Perspective," *Banco Nacionale del Lavoro Quarterly Review* (December 1990), pp. 413–30.

7. Niskanen, op. cit., pp. 274–75.

8. Walter Adams and James W. Brock, "Reaganomics and the Transmog-rification of the Merger Policy," *Anti-trust Bulletin* (Summer 1988), p. 310.

9. Two recent works lend credence to the thesis that what income gains have recently accrued to the average American family have been due to more hours worked per family unit. See Juliet Schor, *The Overworked American* (New York: Basic Books, 1991); and Walter Russell Mead, "The New Old Capitalism: Long Hours, Low Wages," *Rolling Stone* (May 30, 1991), pp. 27–29. Also, for information on the rapid growth of low-wage jobs, see Barry Bluestone and Bennett Harrison, "The Great American Job Machine: The Proliferation of Low-wage Employment in the U.S. Economy," Joint Economic Committee report, 99th Congress, 2nd session, December 1986.

10. *Economic Report of the President*, Washington, D.C., February 1992, industrial production data, p. 418 and unemployment rates, p. 419.

11. *Economic Report*, op. cit., national debt data, p. 394, interest on debt data, p. 391. Calculations by the author.

12. Benjamin M. Friedman, *Day of Reckoning* (New York: Vintage Books, November 1988).

13. Ibid., p. 68.

14. *Economic Report of the President*, Washington, D.C., February 1991, pp. 288–89. Calculations by the author.

15. Paul Craig Roberts, "America's Savings Crisis Is a Chimera," *Business Week* (February 12, 1990), p. 20.

16. Ibid.

17. Murry Weidenbaum, *Rendezvous with Reality* (New York: Basic Books 1988), pp. 12–13.

18. Ibid., pp. 10–15.

19. Ibid., p. 15.

20. Ibid.

21. Ibid.

22. Martin Anderson, "The Reagan Boom; Greatest Ever," *New York Times*, January 17, 1990, p. 1.

23. *Economic Report*, 1992, op. cit., p. 334. Calculations by the author.

24. Murray Weidenbaum, interview with the *Margin* (March/April 1990).

25. Ibid., p. 6.

26. There have been several accounts of the Savings and Loan scandal but my favorite is Paul Zane Pilzer (with Robert Deitz), *Other Peoples' Money: The Inside Story of the S&L Mess* (New York: Simon and Schuster 1989).

27. *Economic Report of the President*, Washington, D.C., February 1992, p. 346.

PART IV

AT THE END OF THE DAY

10

Two Nations in America:
The Consequences of
a Two-class Society

Prosperity is just around the corner.

Herbert Hoover

The decline in size and economic status of the American middle class was documented in Chapter 3. Studies by Katherine Bradbury,[1] Frank Levy,[2] Marilyn Moon and Isabel Sawhill,[3] Sheldon Danziger, Peter Gottschalk, and Eugene Smolensky,[4] the Census Bureau,[5] and the Federal Reserve[6] all agree that in general a significant amount of income has moved from the lower 80 percent of the population distribution, to the upper 20 percent. Further, it appears that approximately 80 percent of these gains have gone to the top 10 percent of the population. Data presented by Kevin Phillips in his description of the recent income redistribution under President Reagan leaves little doubt where the middle-class income has gone.[7] Quoting economists Ross LaRoe and Charles Pool, and the Congressional Budget Office, Phillips presents evidence that in the 1977–87 period the top 10 percent of the population received income increases of 24.4 percent and the top 1 percent received 74.4 percent! Further, the most affluent families at the top 5 percent of the population saw incomes rise from $120,253 in 1979 to $148,438 in 1989. In contrast, the poorest 20 percent of all families saw incomes decline from $9,990 to $9,431.[8]

Further, Chapter 4 pointed to a significant weakening of labor's, and thus the middle class's, bargaining position and standard of living—a weakening caused by inflation, deregulation, large increases in labor supply, and a shrinkage in the growth of government employment. In the face of this measured decline of the middle class and a new insecurity in the ability to be gainfully employed over one's working lifetime, Chapters 5 and 6 documented the concurrent ascent of capital, with its concentration of wealth and its attack on government—the traditional protector of middle-class interests.

A central point about the significant decline of the size, the quality of life, and the job security of the middle class is that it is observable in the income distribution data. However, it is more observable when one stacks up the arguments for a weaker middle class caused by a stronger capital-enhanced class. This makes it particularly important to look at the corporate escape from property and income taxes, which have been reflected in declining after-tax income for the middle class. These arguments, in the general equilibrium sense, show the power of the capital-enhanced forces increasing economically and politically at the *expense* of the labor-dependent forces and are even more threatening, more convincing, and more ominous than the data arguments, because the impact of these trends cannot be meaningfully quantified. It goes without saying that this decline of the middle class is reflected in an even further decline and increased desperation of the lower classes. The consequences of these shifts for American society are enormous and frightening in a number of ways. It is to these economic and other implications that we now turn.

THE LOSS OF THE MASS MARKET

A primary economic implication is the loss of the mass market. As mentioned in Chapter 3, retailers are now planning for this eventuality. The inescapable trend is that the mass market will continue to shrink because the relative number and quality of middle-class jobs is shrinking. There may still be full employment in America. Full employment is no longer the issue. In fact the American middle class has tried unsuccessfully to sustain its lifestyle by increasing the number of family workers in the marketplace. As Bradbury pointed out,[9] the decline in the middle class would have been even worse had it not been for the huge increase in working wives. But there are upper limits on the number of working spouses. A man can only have one wife at a time, and a wife one husband, to prop up the family income. The limit of two-earner families having nearly been reached, the continued ascent in the power of capital over labor will be felt even more acutely by the average American family. For American society, the worst aspect of this is the slippage and loss of middle-class status by families with *two* wage earners.

Will there still be a mass market in America? Probably, but not for the high-quality and expensive products it formerly enjoyed. The mass market of tomorrow will be increasingly one of imported goods. Such goods will be concentrated in the low-priced category, produced with low-priced foreign labor. Even the bigger ticket items will be concentrated on the low-priced models because of squeezed middle-class incomes. The auto market will stagnate and that market will turn into a more basic transportation model, increasingly either imported or produced by foreign-owned manufacturers. Perhaps only one of the big three U.S. auto makers will survive. And it will be forced to concentrate its efforts on two kinds of cars, luxury and basic transportation, the latter variety increasingly built with imported parts. This simply underscores a central point: American family income levels will no longer support the consumption levels achieved in the past. This will be further aggravated if the capital-enhanced forces are successful in eliminating the corporate income tax and implementing a value-added tax in the United States.

The decline of American middle-class jobs with the movement of American manufacturing abroad has been eloquently defended by the unbridled capitalists as natural and healthy. The expansion of the service industry, in their minds, is but another stage in the development of a postmodern society. Yet, many services are expensive. And there are signs that the American public can no longer afford a number of such services— not only consumed by the public, but on which the American public depends for many middle-class jobs.

THE DECLINE OF THE PROFESSIONAL CLASS

Health care is a case in point. Rising health-care costs, along with an increasingly economically strapped consumer, are threatening the health-care industry and with it many workers—particularly professionals—who are dependent on it. For starters, the loss of many American manufacturing jobs has brought with it the loss in medical and dental insurance that such jobs often carry. Such health-care policies are far less available to laid-off manufacturing workers—particularly middle-aged males—when they reach the service sector.

Home building is another such industry. While technically a goods-producing industry, it has been, even with the demise of American manufacturing, not only a stable and vibrant industry but one that provides many middle-class jobs. Considering the huge increases in the 25–44-year-old population, the decline in the number of housing starts in the late 1980s may well be indicative of an American middle class that is no longer able to afford new housing. The growing increase in homelessness in the United States certainly underscores this point.

Higher education is another industry that will be materially affected by the middle-class decline. The economic vibrancy of American higher education has been due to the willingness of the American consumer to scrape and provide increasing amounts of savings for the education of his or her children. Concomitantly, legislatures have been historically generous in providing state funds for publicly supported universities. However, there are signs that this too is coming to an end. State legislatures are becoming increasingly parsimonious in funds allocation toward universities. The increased burdens are made up by increased tuition costs and by the reduction in the quality and size of faculty and staff. While we are today primarily a service-producing economy, the demise of the middle class will cause a decline in those industries that provide expensive and high-cost services heretofore supported by—and, as a by-product, acting to sustain—middle-class job growth.

The mass market for the elderly is also endangered, and with it many service providers to that group. Strapped wage earners, particularly on an after-tax basis, are becoming increasingly tax resistant. A particular target for such resistance is the Social Security contribution. Today's payments to the elderly are financed by today's workers. This fact—that is, the fact of an unfunded Social Security System—has dire consequences for the retiring Americans of the years 2000, 2010, and later. As the economic power of the middle class continues to erode, there will be an increasingly shortsighted, but natural, resistance to the current levels of Social Security taxation. Higher Social Security taxes will not be tolerated and there will be pressure for reduced benefits to, and increased taxes on, recipients. This would signal a change in the market for those manufacturers and service producers providing goods and services for the elderly.

Thus it is reasonable to predict that providers of high-priced services, such as home building, medical and dental care, certain legal services, higher education, and even expensive repair services of a highly specialized nature, will find a shrinking market and slower growing (if not declining) sales over the next decade.

The implication of a shrinking mass market are twofold. For American business it has and will continue to spell many financially troubled times. Over and above that, the troubled mass market will mean a further troubled middle class and a further loss of middle-class jobs. Suffice it to say that the American middle class and the American mass market feed on one another. The loss of the middle class will mean the loss of the mass market to American and many foreign businesses.

THE GROWTH OF ECONOMIC INSTABILITY

The New Deal, by creating a huge middle class of financially empowered consumers, also promoted an economic stability that was unparalleled in American history. The mass market created by this middle class saw recessions checked at the tolerable 6 percent or 7 percent unemployment levels throughout the 1940s, 1950s, and 1960s. But as the income distribution became more skewed, the possibility of severe recession increased. The 1973–75 recession and the 1979–82 recessions are cases in point. For the first time in the postwar era—and, not surprisingly, during the period that I have identified with a start of the decline in the middle class, that is, from the early 1970s on—the unemployment rate in recessions rose above 7 percent. With a previous postwar recession high of 6.6 percent for 1958, the unemployment rate averaged 8.3 percent in 1975, fell back during economic recovery, and then rose to the sustained high levels of 7 percent in 1980, 7.5 percent in 1981, and 9.5 percent in both 1982 and 1983. The gradual return to full employment in the Reagan years then proceeded with a 7.4 percent rate in 1984 and a 7.1 percent in 1985. Thus while the Reagan era ended with a relatively full employment rate of 5.3 percent in 1988, the path was a rocky one, studded with high unemployment from 1981 through 1986, averaging well above the worst years of all the preceding postwar recessions. Were it not for the New Deal reforms such as unemployment compensation and Social Security, as well as the welfare programs of the Great Society, one could envision substantially higher unemployment rates during the 1973–75 and the 1979–82 recessions.

Conservatives hailed the 1980s as a period of great economic recovery and growth. Indeed, real GNP growth during the 1980s averaged a respectable 3 percent. Yet also during the 1980s the real wages of American consumers hardly grew, despite the increase in worker productivity. Thus a massive shift took place in ownership of savings in the nation. In manufacturing, where productivity gains averaged 3.8 percent

over the eight-year Reagan period, real hourly compensation in manufacturing grew at about 0.05 percent (see Table 9-4). Not surprisingly, the
personal ownership of private savings went from 27 percent of total
savings during the Carter years to 18.2 percent during the last four years
of the Reagan administration, with business savings increasing from 73
percent to 81.8 percent (again, see Table 9-4). This decided shift in income
and wealth has dire implications for economic stability. The last time a
long period of economic recovery, like the 1980s, was accompanied with
such low growth rates in wages and real earning power was the 1920s.
This, of course, culminated in the most serious economic downturn in U.S.
history.

   For years, there have been in place respected economic theories that
predict economic downturns when income distribution becomes extremely skewed toward the upper end. This generally follows a period of
low wage growth during a business cycle expansion, accompanied by
strong levels of business profit, high business saving, and, generally,
overinvestment. Such overinvestment leads to overproduction of goods
and services that cannot be taken off the market by the underpaid consumer. A severe recession ensues.

   The road to recession because of underpaid labor has a long history in
business cycle theory and follows what are called "underconsumption"
scenarios.[10] The process goes something like this. A prosperity phase of
a business cycle is characterized by a great increase in the amount of
capital goods occasioned by strongly rising profits. Thus, "profit inflation" arises because wages and other incomes fail to advance along with
rising prices or falling costs. Capital goods industries expand relative to
consumption, and they are fed by voluntary private savings as well as by
large amounts of business savings fed by the big profits realized during
the boom. Too much money is invested in capital; too many goods are
produced and they cannot be taken off the market. The lopsided distribution of income once again results in excessive productive power and a
deficiency of consumer demand.

   Today we find further that the wealth concentration of the 1980s has
also introduced more financial instability into financial markets—particularly the stock market. The new ability of the aforementioned transnational financial elite to move funds between countries—funds that are
becoming ever more concentrated—lends to the volatility of these markets. To be sure, there are other sources of instability, such as the large
mutual funds and programmed trading. There are now checks on the
ability of large institutions to unsettle markets, such as the "circuit

breakers" introduced after the 1987 stock market crash. But there are no such regulations governing the huge mega-investor of the new billionaire financial elite or of huge foreign investors. Add to this the massive U.S. national debt—increasingly used by foreigners as a safe haven, often on a temporary basis—and the funds flowing into and out of U.S. financial markets can be volatile and unpredictable. Suffice it to say, the weakening and the shrinkage of the middle class in America have given us new elements of macroeconomic instability and new hardships to endure as well as others to fear. These hardships are felt not only by the middle class, but are also felt, in spades, by the lower class.

THE OPPRESSIVE SOCIETY

The loss of the middle class portends for the United States the rise of an oppressive society the likes of which we have never seen. America will remain a rich country; yet as its wealth and income distribution become further concentrated, the social unrest produced among the poor will meet with more and more cries for law and order, particularly by the "haves." This source of oppression will be manifested in the police force, in the taxation system, and in the influence of a new transnational financial elite.

The first source of oppression will increasingly come through the strengthening of the existing domestic police force. This has already occurred, at the federal, state, and local levels. One ostensible cause for this strengthening is the illicit drug traffic. In 1990 the federal government increased spending to more than $9 billion in antidrug efforts. State and local governments followed suit. Yet it is inescapable that the drug trade has increasingly flourished due to two factors, both of them economic. The first factor is the increased despair among the lower classes of ever obtaining middle-class jobs in America. The hopelessness attached to the typical minimum-wage job, the despair that sets in when such unfulfilling and financially niggardly work is the only employment in sight, carries with it the seeds for the quick fix provided by such relatively cheap drugs as "crack" cocaine. The second factor is that the drug trade goes further than offering middle-class jobs to the poor; it offers upper-class jobs. Its enticement is hard to turn down for the quick, smart, risk-taking, poor, undercapitalized entrepreneur. A $1,000 investment multiplies threefold in a week. The illegality of drugs sustains their high price. The economic appeal of the drug trade is, for many, irresistible.

The symbols of wealth and the good life are everywhere flaunted and are present in the minds of all citizens of this society, whether it be considered to be made up of two or three classes. Researching his highly successful novel *The Bonfire of the Vanities* in the south Bronx, Tom Wolfe speaks of an identity between the symbols of wealth and vanity among the high-paid Wall Street brokers and the poor of the slums. The ghetto youth wear necklaces of linked Mercedes Benz hood ornaments. The drug dealers are no longer content to drive Cadillacs and Lincolns; the ultimate symbol of success for them is the Mercedes. Indeed the money fever has spread from the top to the bottom rung of the social ladder.[11] The lesson is clear: The economic incentive is present for drug dealing; our national economic policy—while it impoverishes the middle class—is truly supply-side economics at its most successful when applied to the drug trade. That same policy also amounts to demand-side economics for the products of the drug trade, given the despair, the homelessness, and the poor employment opportunities for many Americans today.

Rather than promote job opportunities for more citizens, American policy has chosen to fight an interdictive war against the drug trade through increased use of police tactics, with little visible effect. What is taking effect, however, is a buildup of internal police forces, and there are indications that law enforcement in other areas—particularly trivial ones—is working to make the society generally more repressive. Onerous traffic regulations, speed traps, and the spot stopping of motorists for sobriety tests are on the rise. The expanded police forces, ostensibly designed to fight drugs, must surely find traffic enforcement a much less hazardous and easier duty. (It is no surprise to this author that Rodney King's well-documented beating by police in Los Angeles followed his being stopped on a traffic violation.) Further, the need for law enforcement units to win popular support in their competition for tax funds has caused an increase in human rights violations, such as allowing news media coverage of drug busts. Such media coverage rides herd on innocent victims—particularly the spouses and the children of the offending criminals—to say nothing of the fact that some of the suspects may be innocent.

The decline of the middle class brings with it an increase in the oppressive society in a second and more ominous and ubiquitous way, namely, the use of the taxation system. With the demise of the middle class and an even further impoverishment of the lower class, the capital-enhanced forces at the top of the income spectrum are becoming increasingly powerful in their political influence in the day-to-day governance of the country. This includes the influence on taxation law. It is in their best interest to ensure that the tax code remains regressive.

However, the more regressive the tax system becomes, the more pressure there will be for tax evasion. Thus the government necessarily must strengthen its tax-enforcement administrative machinery. With the huge federal tax cuts given to corporations, the individual taxpayer is more and more prone to audit, as the government scrapes harder for money from a declining tax base.

The *Wall Street Journal* recently reported on this trend. IRS Commissioner Fred Goldberg admitted that enforcement efforts since 1980 "have fallen woefully behind in dealing with large corporations, partnerships and upper-income, self-employed individuals."[12] The article leaves no doubt in the reader's mind that it is the middle-class taxpayer who is receiving the most scrutiny: "The agency figures it now gets so much information that its computers could work up standard tax returns for about 40 percent of the country's taxpayers—particularly middle income wage-earners with simple returns."[13] Other startling facts are that 2.5 companies out of 100 are subject to an IRS audit, down from 6.5 a decade ago. The IRS also admits that people with incomes under $100,000 have their taxes tracked more heavily by computers, since their returns are less complex, generally only made up of wages and interest. Further, the IRS has jacked up its penalties on individuals from $1 billion in 1978 to $6 billion in 1987![14] While the article does not report who paid the largest share, a reasonable bet would be that the middle class paid the most, since it is now the prime focus of the IRS. "Lawrence Gibbs, IRS Commissioner from 1986 to 1989, says it's important for the IRS to focus on middle-income taxpayers because they pay most of the country's taxes."[15]

Given the emasculation of the corporate tax base, the machinery of government demands a higher and higher yield from the declining middle-class income earnings. This is not only accomplished by increased audits and by the elimination of deductions for the middle class (thus raising the income tax base). It is also no accident that interest on consumer loans, along with state and local sales taxes, lost their deductibility during the Reagan years. Yet neither interest nor state and local sales taxes lost their deductibility for corporations. The elimination of mortgage interest deductibility was proposed, but the decision was made that this would be too politically unpopular. However, as homeownership in the United States continues to wane, this interest deductibility could lose political support from the millions of Americans whose incomes will not afford them a home of their own.

A third potential source of oppression is the expansion of a transnational, capital-enhanced financial elite. This group of controllers of capital who formerly merely achieved a "kitchen cabinet" status with several American presidents might achieve a "kitchen congress" with its resulting influence over American life. There are some signs now that, their numbers growing, they have achieved enough status to influence congressional legislation substantially, particularly through the use of PACs, and subsequently to control its enforcement. Their power in the United States will generally be directed toward protecting their own interests, which involve, first, capital dominance over labor, second, freedom from government restrictions on their actions, and third, freedom of capital mobility.

Further, the international character of such a transnational elite is foreboding. Its enormous power to shift funds within and between countries raises the specter of an international capital influence on domestic policy. This ubiquitous and invisible force is already presented domestically in the Business Council and the Committee for Economic Development. The presence and growth of this international economic influence peddling now threatens the very principle of economic democracy in the United States. But further, the transnational elite will seek to maintain and increase the regressive nature of the tax system. Control of the senior industries of the country—that is, the oligopolies that account for approximately two-thirds of national manufacturing output—will not be threatened. However, an expanded international financial elite will seek to control the economic policy of the United States—which will make any effort to promote American industries with middle-class jobs much more difficult.

The major interest of the financial elite will be to locate manufacturing primarily where labor is cheapest. Indeed, the impending U.S.–Mexico free trade treaty is a foreboding prospect for American labor and the middle class, but it is strongly advocated by President Bush. How can a small manufacturing town in Ohio support its public school teachers with $30,000 salaries when it is competing with the possibility that the firm might move to northern Mexico? There, the water is undrinkable, sewage runs in the streets, the minimum wage is 50 cents per hour, and children work in the factories.

More middle-class job creation as an aim of national policy goes hand in hand with strengthening the power of labor. As we have seen earlier in Chapter 1, the rise of the American middle class was largely an outgrowth of the New Deal, which enhanced the political and economic power of the labor-dependent individual through unionization and through a strong government that protected the rights of the average citizen. Concurrent with this were antitrust activities, strict regulation of banking and finance, progressive taxation, and a corporate income tax that was on a parity with personal income taxation. The transnational financial elite of capital-endowed, capital-enhanced individuals is determined to avoid a repetition of any such kind of a "New Deal."

THE LOSS OF ECONOMIC DEMOCRACY

The decline of the middle class and the concurrent demise of the lower classes brings closer the likelihood of a disappearance of economic democracy. The lack of economic democracy brings with it a concentration of wealth that subverts the democratic process to influence both the presidency and the Congress. It also allows an oligopolistic or shared-monopoly business structure to exercise a disproportionate control over profits, market share, prices, employment, and indeed the type and quantity of goods produced. Not so very long ago American capitalism, and British capitalism before it, assumed a balance of power between the producer and the consumer. But as we have seen, in the American society the producer power as represented by the capital-enhanced is overwhelming the consumer power as represented by labor and the middle class. We are thus headed toward a more limited democratic capitalism that has wealth concentration, the control of capital, and private property as its primary cornerstones. Free enterprise—the essence of economic democracy—falls by the wayside. Oppressive tax systems fall on middle- and low-income groups, and favor the large corporation and the capital-enhanced whose tax returns are too complicated to audit by computer. The haves continue to accumulate, while new aspiring capitalists are economically, through taxes and market control, shut out of the success game.

A DIMINISHED POLITICAL DEMOCRACY

All of this paints a very dreary picture of representative democracy in the United States. The picture has become one of elected officials whose sense of the issues is increasingly noneconomic, more emotionally charged, and generally meaningless to the life of the average American citizen. Political campaigns today are seldom a forum of economic issues, but instead focus more and more on single-issue politics such as abortion, flag burning, and childbirth out of wedlock (in 1992!). The enormous financial input and waste around the abortion issue is a case in point. Had

10 percent of the political effort expended on the abortion issue been focused on proper regulation of the savings and loan industry we would not have lost a potential $300 billion of the American taxpayers' money. Yet, meaningless political issues are exactly what the capital-enhanced forces want, to maintain the status quo. Meaningful political issues such as income distribution, and even human rights, are swept under the carpet, or trivialized under the guise of sloganeering replete with hackneyed phrases such as "free enterprise" and "patriotism." When Samuel Johnson remarked that "patriotism is the last refuge of the scoundrel," he was referring to ungainly and exploitive use of the patriotism emotion. In the same vein it might be said that free enterprise is the last refuge of the expanded financial elite bent on increasing its grip on American society. What it is arguing for is *private* enterprise, and its brand of enterprise is anything but *free*.

It is often asserted that for democracy to work well the majority of the citizenry should be economically empowered. Barrington Moore registers strong agreement with the thesis that a "vigorous and independent class of town dwellers has been an indispensable element in the growth of ... democracy. No bourgeois, no democracy."[16] Indeed, democracy has historically been established and sustained first by the growth of the new financially independent merchants (i.e., the bourgeois), and later by its incorporation into and alliance with the middle class. The point is that if there is a large number—a majority—of citizens in an economically viable position, democracy remains the most practical and successful way to maintain the status quo and protect all rights. However, when the middle class is lost, or brought to its knees economically, so that it exists only in a sociological sense, dictatorship becomes the more viable option to protect the wealth of those at the top of the income distribution scale.

THE RISE OF THE MESSIAH

If unaddressed by the political parties, the continued deterioration of the middle class could lead to the rise of new and unexpected personalities on the political scene, promising a quick fix to the problems of the day. Such "messiahs" can come in many forms with many different types of messages. Their ease of entry into the political sphere will be oiled by the confused state of the American electorate when it finds answers in neither the Republican nor the Democratic message. As will be discussed in more detail in Chapters 11 and 12, the message of the Democrats is that they can be all things to all people. They can support liberal causes, social causes, civil rights, and still be good for business. But in determining to keep taxes low on business—having bought into the supply-side economic rhetoric, and thus sure that they are creating new jobs—they have not taken care of the consumer. The various levels of government then find themselves starved for revenue, particularly with the loss of corporate income and property tax revenues, and do not address adequately the social needs of the country. So, the cities fester with crime, the inner cities decay and become increasingly dangerous, taxes remain burdensome on the middle class, and a general air of economic insecurity prevails. Still, many Democrats and more Republicans say less and less on meaningful economic issues, preferring their single-issue politics that touch on abortion, flag burning, and single parenthood and thus do less to tackle the real economic issues of the day. Enter the messiah. A new face! This new personality will capitalize on the discontent of the people through tried and true methods that are more suitable to fascist demagogues than to experienced politicians who have worked their way through the democratic process, serving constituents, soliciting their votes, and not being overly willful in their actions.

The danger is that the new messiah will arrive and sweep people off their feet momentarily, capture their votes in the euphoria of fresh ideas, and then trample on the Constitution.

Obviously, a new party realignment would be preferable. This could involve either the Democrats' getting back to representing traditional democratic interests of the middle and lower classes such as collective bargaining, aid to education, a national health service, and so on, or else a new party's forming that would take with it the liberal elements from both the Republicans and the Democrats. In the latter case, we would then have a third party that would be truly a liberal and labor-oriented party. This being so, the existing Democrats and Republicans might themselves form one party out of the more conservative elements of the former two groups.

However, there is no guarantee that this realigning will happen. If the Democrats do not see the light and start to make their distinctions from the Republicans real and known, the odds are greatly enhanced for the sudden entrance of the messiah. Since the founding of the American republic, this has never happened. But the record of events that have occurred in other countries when such messiahs appeared, put themselves above the political process, and then sought to carry out their own private agendas, is indeed a foreboding and ominous lesson of history.

NOTES

1.   Katherine L. Bradbury, "The Shrinking Middle Class," *New England Economic Review*, Federal Reserve Bank of Boston (September/October 1986).

2.   Frank Levy, *Dollars and Dreams* (New York: W. W. Norton, 1988).

3.   Marilyn Moon and Isabel Sawhill, "Family Incomes, Gainers and Losers," in John L. Palmer and Isabel Sawhill, eds., *The Reagan Record* (Washington, D.C.: Urban Institute, 1984).

4.   Sheldon Danziger, Peter Gottschalk, and Eugene Smolensky, "How the Rich Have Fared, 1973–1987," *American Economic Review*, May 1989.

5.   Data provided by the U.S. Bureau of the Census at the request of the author. Also, U.S. Bureau of the Census, *Trends in Relative Income: 1964 to 1984*, Current Population Reports, Series P-60, No. 177 (Washington, D.C.: USGPO, 1991).

6.   Federal Reserve Bank data cited by David R. Francis, "Economists Suggest More Taxes on Rich," *Christian Science Monitor*, April 23, 1992.

7.   Kevin Phillips, *The Politics of Rich and Poor* (New York: Random House, 1990), pp. 12–14.

8.   U.S. Bureau of the Census data, reported in the *New York Times*, September 27, 1990, p. 10.

9.   Bradbury, op. cit.

10.   For a summary of underconsumption theories, see Gottfried Haberler's classic work *Prosperity and Depression* (New York: Atheneum, 1963), pp. 118–41.

11.   Bill Moyers, *A World of Ideas*, Interview with Tom Wolfe (Alexandria, Va.: PBS Video, 1989), vol. 29.

12.   Paul Duke, Jr., "IRS Excels at Tracking the Average Wage Earner, but Not the Wealthy," *Wall Street Journal*, April 15, 1991, pp. A1 and A4.

13.   Ibid., p. A1.

14.   Ibid.

15.   Ibid., p. A4.

16.   Barrington Moore, Jr., *Social Origins of Dictatorship and Democracy* (Boston: Beacon Press, 1966), p. 418.

11

What Happened?
The Failure of Key Institutions

The American people are quite competent to judge a
political party that works both sides of the street.

Franklin Delano Roosevelt

As we saw in Chapter 1, the balance between capital and labor, the balance
between producer and consumer, the balance between the rich and the
vibrant middle class, was achieved most effectively by the actions of the
New Deal. How did we let things slide? How did we let the New Deal get
so unraveled? As I read the past 20 to 25 years, four institutions that helped
protect the middle class were weakened substantially and thus lost their
protective role. They are the American union, the Democratic party, the
economics profession, and the decline of critical voting and political
accountability. The magnitude and depth of the weakening of these
institutions—all failing us in concert—make a reversal of current trends,
and a revitalization of the middle class, highly unlikely. In fact, the most
likely prospect for the near future is that things will get far worse for
middle- and lower-class America before, if ever, things get better.

THE DECLINE OF THE AMERICAN LABOR UNION

The American labor movement is one failing institution that has
contributed to the decline of the middle class. Its actions have primarily
served only its current membership and have often been short-sighted.

First of all, the unions have displayed a remarkable inability to retain membership. As noted in Chapter 4, union membership plummeted from 30.4 percent of all nonagricultural employees in 1962 to 14.1 percent in 1985. As noted by Henry Farber,[1] most probably about 80 percent of the recent decline took place in sectors that would be expected to have a high probability of union membership. Farber's explanation for this is that the unions have not demonstrated the benefits of membership to prospective members.

While this is a possibility, it's hard to imagine being unable to explain the benefits of joining the UAW, or United Mine Workers, or the International Brotherhood of Electrical Workers. A more likely reason for the unions' demise may well lie in the restrictive membership practices that keep union numbers down and allow the current membership to extract above-equilibrium wages, but at the same time increase the pool of hungry workers outside the union. These predominantly black, Hispanic, and often immigrant workers, feel no guilt about acting as strike-breakers, particularly if they feel they weren't welcome in the first place.

Had the American unions given more political support to the rights of the disadvantaged, the poor, the black, and the recently immigrated, two events could have occurred that would have been more advantageous toward labor. First, the new arrivals—particularly immigrants—might have taken on a more favorable voting pattern both toward labor union causes and toward the Democrats. Second, the union membership itself would have been more socially oriented, thus increasing the chances of electing a president with a more prolabor attitude.

In recent elections, two Republicans—Richard Nixon and Ronald Reagan—openly and successfully courted unions such as the Teamsters and PATCO. Nixon won in a close election in 1968; both he and Reagan (in 1980) benefited from labor union members' breaking ranks with the Democrats. The shortsighted aspect of this for the union members was the tremendous power that they gave to a capital-oriented president who would, by turns, smile at them and nonetheless allow record-high legal and illegal immigration rates to depress wages, appoint a conservative secretary of labor, cut government services, appoint an antilabor National Labor Relations Board, favor regressive taxation, and, in general, act in a probusiness, antistrike fashion. Had the unions championed social causes more—particularly civil rights and immigrants' rights—as their European brethren have done, they would be a far more powerful force in American politics today.

Such a strong political force representing labor, minorities, and the poor, acting in concert with other traditional Democrats, could have helped check the rise in the power of capital. Wealth concentration, and the power it wields, occur at the expense of labor. This the union leadership has failed to see. Union membership has been content to restrict its numbers, forget about nonunion labor, collect its pay and benefits, and go home. Grossly myopic in vision, the unions have failed to put on their glasses, thus losing the political support of nonunion labor.

THE CONFUSED MESSAGE OF THE DEMOCRATIC PARTY

A related development that has weakened the Democratic party's support among labor has been its pragmatic "probusiness" stance. This started with the economic activism of John F. Kennedy, who proclaimed that the Democrats, too, could be good for business and at the same time enhance the status of the laboring classes. The "new economics" agenda of the early 1960s—perhaps best asserted by the activist Council of Economic Advisors under Walter Heller—proposed and managed to see legislated such distinctly probusiness measures as the investment tax credit and accelerated depreciation. The Kennedy administration thus went beyond the mere stabilization function of government, that is, its role in ensuring adequate aggregate demand in order to maintain full employment. However well intentioned these "supply-side" measures were at the time, the investment tax credit would be used in subsequent years to enhance capital mobility—particularly by subsidizing companies' moving to "right-to-work" states—and the accelerated depreciation concept expanded, mostly under the Reagan administration, until it practically scuttled the corporate income tax. Thus the pragmatic probusiness approach of the Democratic party has had the unintended result of substantially weakening its message, and with it labor and the middle class. What prominent Democrat has called for a corporate tax increase as a means to reduce the federal deficit or simply as a fairness issue? Yet we have seen that the enormous corporate tax cuts of the past 20 years have merely strapped government for revenue and produced little in the way of added investment in America and middle-class jobs.

The Republican party has been much more single-minded in its aims—specifically, its policy of supporting the positions of the capital-enhanced forces. The Democrats have tried to support labor and business at the same time—many times, an impossible task—and further argue for government help to the disadvantaged, the poor, and/or the uneducated. The effort to do all this confuses the party's philosophy. While the people continue to elect Democrats in the majority to Congress, the national economic philosophy of the Democrats is confusing, contradictory, and hard to sell. This was a major factor in the elections of 1980, 1984, and 1988. The Republican party, representing the capital-enhanced regime, has a clear and unequivocal message: less government, no new taxes, less welfare, keep what you earn. The Democrats on the other hand must juggle welfare, civil rights, the homeless, and the plight of the middle class, but at the same time be probusiness, which generally means antigovernment—precisely the stance you don't need, to accomplish the other goals. The Democrats as the representative of the labor-dependent classes thus have a mixed if not garbled message. It makes them appear contradictory, indecisive, and above all weak. This is not the stuff that wins presidential elections.

THE DECLINING INFLUENCE OF THE ECONOMICS PROFESSION

The 1960s, often described as the "Golden Age of Economics," may well have earned that moniker, particularly during the first half of the decade. Activist economists such as Walter Heller of the University of Minnesota, Gardner Ackley of Michigan, and Arthur Okun were heard and respected as they advised presidents Kennedy and Johnson.

Their analysis and the issues they raised had the air of education, objectivity, and critical thought. The state of the economics debate remained good through the 1970s, but nonetheless showed tell-tale signs of the rout that was to come in the 1980s. These signs were manifested in several key errors of economic policy in the late 1960s and 1970s on which the profession failed to raise meaningful opposition and thus alert public opinion.

The first great silence occurred during the Vietnam era. Federal deficits started to balloon in 1965 and rose steadily through 1968. In a distinctly Keynesian atmosphere—well aware that such deficits at full employment meant demand-pull inflation—the profession said little to break ranks with Lyndon Johnson. The deficit spending continued, the economy overheated, and the Federal Reserve was muscled by President Johnson into an easy-money policy. Inflation was the inevitable result.

Two other major abdications of the opportunity to influence economic policy came with the oil shocks of 1973 and 1979 and the ensuing inflations. The profession advanced little creative thought on how to deal with the OPEC cartel other than accepting its dictates as a free-market phenomenon. The bilateral monopoly model—where one monopoly opposes another and achieves something akin to a competitive price—has been in the neoclassical economics textbooks for years (at the introductory level). Yet the possibility of an American buying monopoly to oppose the OPEC selling monopoly was never seriously promoted by the profession. Instead, the American consumer and American industry faced the monopoly in a disorganized way, and paid dearly with inflation stemming from both the high oil prices and a weakened dollar.

To further compound the economic confusion, many liberal economists retreated to accepting the monetarist proposition that the main cause of the inflation was simply years of excessive money creation by the Federal Reserve. While this was a contributing factor, the real cause of the inflation—and a hard factor for the profession to accept—was the lack of a national energy policy. Such a policy necessarily calls for nonmarket economics, that is, government economic planning—a concept the profession hesitated to advocate.

But the profession's biggest fall from grace occurred during the Reagan years. The failure of any segment of the profession to raise a meaningful dialogue on the exaggerated supply-side claims of Reagan economic spokesmen, and to influence any meaningful change in direction away from a giveaway program to the rich at the expense of the poor and the middle class, was a major disappointment. At the time, few voices of economists were heard advocating a fairer distribution of income.

And as we face a similar economic crisis to those of 1973 and 1979, the profession is again largely silent on the economic need for an energy policy. The August 1990 Iraqi invasion of Kuwait threatened us not only with inflation, but with the loss of American lives; and the lack of a national energy policy was at the root of our involvement. In the face of a diminishing middle class, the economics profession remains largely silent over the recent maldistribution of income; it has been left for a conservative—Kevin Phillips—to protest.[2] There is little opposition when Charls Walker of the American Council for Capital Formation advocates a value-added tax to replace the corporate income tax, despite the fact that, first, the corporate tax is now historically low and, second, there is scant economic evidence that the tax is paid by anyone but the holders of capital. In other words, it is *not* shifted forward to the consumers. Yet the heads of major oil companies press for a broad-based national sales tax to prevent a higher tax on oil. They claim that the corporate tax is passed on to the consumer, despite the lack of economic evidence for their claim. The economics profession remains silent.

Why the acquiescence? Why the silence? There are several plausible reasons. First, the mathematical approach to economic analysis has largely crowded out policy analysis, which often requires much simpler tools. Mathematical "models" become the norms for performance at the graduate student, tenure, and promotion levels of the leading economic think tanks and universities. This is not to downgrade the use of tools such as mathematical economics, econometrics, and statistics in analyzing and measuring economic phenomena. However, such tools are difficult to adapt to meaningful policy issues. And there are many policy issues where institutional, political, and philosophical economic factors are far more relevant.

Second, with mathematical analysis gaining the upper hand, the profession has turned increasingly "micro" in its orientation. Macroeconomic issues of national importance seem to have lost the interest of many economists.

Third, this nonpolitical economy approach has been spread through the profession by the inbreeding of the publishers of the leading economic journals, the graduate schools that run them, and the professors at these schools who invite each other and their students to present papers at annual meetings. While much hard work and good economics is exercised, the irrelevant and/or the abstract is often the result. Further, the exclusivity of the practitioners leaves little room for fresh outside thought, views, and influence.

John Kenneth Galbraith, Lester Thurow, Robert Heilbroner, Robert Lekachman, and a few others remain the exceptions. The Association for Evolutionary Economics—its membership and its focus—provides another exception. It is also significant that recently more innovative thinking in economics is reaching public opinion not from the prestigious halls of academia, but from nontraditional economic thinkers such as Robert Reich, Robert Kuttner, and more recently Kevin Phillips.

The economics profession is badly in need of a reorientation that will stress economic analysis of real national economic problems and objective recommendations and their solutions, regardless of whose toes are stepped on. If American society loses its middle class, much of the American professoriate will go with it, including a good slice of the economics profession. And it will be a shame if this huge loss of talent takes place without a nonconforming whimper.

THE DECLINE OF POLITICAL ACCOUNTABILITY

Increasingly, the American voter is unable to select politicians who will truly represent the middle-class interests. One can only speculate on the reasons, but here are several possibilities.

First, the good life being within reach of many citizens, they are nonetheless pressed for time and resources. As two-earner families, they are spending 80–100 hours a week working, leaving little emotional energy or time to dwell on the political questions of the day. The liberal alternative of the mixed economy, the conservation of natural resources, and income redistribution by nonmarket means is a complex one. It requires great study and politicians who are in touch and accountable. This takes time and effort, and there is increasing evidence that the middle class has neither. They are thus susceptible to the television image, to the two-minute news analysis or "sound bite," and spend little or no time actually analyzing critical issues. The sad fact is that middle-class voters are so busy just hanging onto their economic status that they are prone to being fooled by the television image.

The conservative alternative, on the other hand, is easier and simpler to understand. Make what you can. The market rules. Cut the size of the government. This may work for the upper 10 percent of the income strata, but it doesn't work for the middle class. Yet the middle class seems to be impervious to the social problems closing in on it—which will be *its* problems and the problems of the poor. If the middle class is not voting responsibly, it goes without saying that the poor can't protect themselves in the political arena. With the increasing abandonment of quality education for the poor, they cannot be expected to understand the differences between million- and billion-dollar budgets, save for those entrepreneurial individuals who enter the drug trade.

It has been observed, though, that the highest voter turnouts are now being produced by the conservative upper 20 percent of the population, which is unfailingly Republican and conservatively oriented. Thus, it has been said, the Republican party has become the party of the upper class in America. Further, that class still draws votes from the middle class, due to a weak Democratic party alternative.

A NONREVERSAL THESIS?

Will there be a reversal in this conservative tide that has emasculated the middle class—to say nothing of the poor—in America?

It doesn't seem likely. Those who look for political cycles will today find fundamental changes in the equations for the peaks and valleys. The simple fact exists—and this is the subject of this book—that capital and its capital-enhanced individuals have gained a commanding upper hand over labor and labor-dependent individuals. People are being held hostage to their jobs, which are increasingly threatened not only by automation but by capital mobility and a one-sided free trade argument. The Democrats have a blurred economic message; the Republicans, a clear one.

The claim that Roosevelt's New Deal was simply a routine swing leftward in the political cycle must be rejected upon examination of its accomplishments. It was an aberration—and a phenomenal one—for which the middle class was both lucky and blessed. In the same vein, there is no guarantee that such a sudden reversal of the excesses of capital will occur again. The forces of the capital-enhanced are today smarter, more organized, better financed, and operate on a worldwide scale to protect their interests. To restore the viability of the middle class—that is, the labor-dependent in the society—will be a task of unprecedented magnitude, concerning which our leaders have heretofore shown little in the way of ideas or fortitude.

NOTES

1. Henry S. Farber, "The Recent Decline of Unionization in the United States," Reprint No. 1012, National Bureau of Economic Research, Cambridge, Mass., 1988.

2. Kevin Phillips, *The Politics of Rich and Poor in America* (New York: Random House, 1990).

12

Rescuing the Middle Class:
Some Modest Proposals

Any man who thinks that civilization has advanced is
an egoist.

Will Rogers

The major aim of this book is to show why and to measure the extent
that the American middle class has declined economically, particularly
since 1973. It has been a long process and a complicated one. The
decline accelerated even further in the 1980s. Therefore, the solution
toward restoring both the numbers and the economic viability of the
middle class will likewise take a long time and be complicated. It will
not simply take place with the supposedly periodic leftward swing of
the political cycle. This is because, as the book points out, the decline
of the middle class has been primarily caused by a decline in the power
of labor. And the main reason for the decline in the economic power
of labor has been the ascent of the forces of capital over a *long* period
of time. Individuals whose incomes are enhanced by capital holdings
quite simply have gained the upper hand economically and politically
over those Americans whose incomes are primarily labor-dependent.

THE ROAD BACK

However, all is not lost. Numerically, the number of labor-dependent
voters in the United States far exceeds those whose incomes are

significantly capital-enhanced. Yet the struggle of the labor-dependent to make their views known and to effect political change that can once again widen the economic base of the middle class will be long and bitterly fought. The sheer numbers of the American middle class and the lower classes are not alone sufficient to guarantee a victory. And when I speak of victory, I am not speaking of eliminating or even materially reducing the wealth of those in the upper strata of American society. What I am speaking of as a victory is simply a restoration of that economically secure base of consumers and voters that were relatively predominant in the 1950s and 1960s. It was in that era more than any other that the New Deal achieved its goals for the American people. But the unraveling of the New Deal has been the result of a long, steady chipping away by the forces of capital.

The one quick answer to restoring the American middle class would be to create "another New Deal." However, times have changed. We cannot create another New Deal because the world economy has changed. Further, there is no crisis of Depression proportions. In the absence of such a dramatic realization that much is wrong with the economy, the voters and the thinkers are lulled into believing that things are alright while there continues a slow, steady erosion of the economic power of the middle and lower classes—nothing dramatic, simply a slow, measured, steady, single-minded, and pervasive advance of the forces of capital as they dismantle what is left of the economic protection that the New Deal offered.

So the chances of getting another New Deal are nil. There is no political mandate such as the Great Depression, but simply the complicated issues that face us. These complicated issues will require complicated and piecemeal solutions. But taken in its entirety, the task is not impossible. Those institutions that have failed us of late—namely the unions, the Democratic party, and the economics profession—can change their directions into more progressive stances if they know what their aim is. Were the Congress led by a strong Democratic party and were a strong Democratic president elected, the two working together could reverse the directions that the capital-enhanced forces have so cleverly and so thoroughly set in motion. However, time may be running out. If the power of the conservative and the rightwing capital-enhanced groups increases much more, a weakened middle class and an utterly despairing lower class could shake the very foundations of American democratic society. This could pave the way for a loss of not only economic democracy, but political democracy. If the Democrats cannot deliver to their political constituency in the form of an elevated middle class, then they are really showing that their party is but a kinder, gentler version of the conservative Republican party. Those progressives who really want to do something for the quality of life of the middle and lower classes in the United States would then be well advised to form a third party with the individuals described in this book as essentially labor-dependent as their constituency. Indeed, as time runs out for economic democracy, time is also running out for the Democrats as representatives of the middle and lower classes.

So, what follows is a program of action and change for the four American institutions that I feel have let the middle class down, namely the unions, the Democratic party, the economics profession, and that nebulous sort of institution that I have identified in Chapter 11 as the ability of the American voter to evaluate economic issues critically and to cause meaningful change through his or her vote. I propose this program though I am fully mindful of the screams that will come from the symbolic citadels of the University of Chicago that are scattered throughout the nation, be they the strongholds of business leaders or economists. However, I have faith that a number of other people will listen—maybe even some at the University of Chicago, and hopefully union members along with many of my colleagues in the economics profession. So, let the screams begin.

AN ALL-LABOR UNION MOVEMENT

As detailed earlier, a major failure of the American union has been its inability to convince the average laborer or the public at large of the value of union membership. The numbers tell the story, with the decline in union membership from approximately 32 percent of the workforce in 1962 to 15 percent or perhaps less in 1985. With some of the biggest losses in union membership coming in those sectors that were traditionally union-ized, and in a country where the labor force has grown by leaps and bounds, the unions have certainly missed the boat. It is quite fashionable to criticize the unions—which pleases the emerging financial elite no end. But the plain fact remains that the disaffection with unions has come from the unions' inability to convince the public at large and the labor movement as to the benefits of union membership. Everybody knows that many of the major unions still extract an admirable level of wages and fringe benefits from their employers. Yet many union members are also perceived as bigoted, closed minded, and increasingly to the right politically, particularly where social issues are concerned. The unions are further perceived—and not without cause—as being very protective and very hard to get into. Very little in the way of social responsibility, protection of minority rights, protection of immigrant rights, or the provision of health care for the poor and indigent is ever espoused by the unions to the extent that it reaches the popular media. To put it quite simply, American union leadership has not joined the great social issues of the day.

This is not the case in Europe, however, where the union movement has remained, although slightly weakened, a generally strong and vibrant institution. Unions work hand in hand with politicians in elections and in supporting causes favorable to labor as a whole, not simply to their membership. Many nonunion voters tend to support the social issues that are pushed by the unions. Thus governments are elected that are generally favorable toward union membership and appoint cabinet ministers who are appropriately sympathetic to labor.

The difference in the American labor movement is that it generally advocates and reserves the welfare, the retirement, the medical care, the high wages, and other fringes benefits simply for those in the labor union and says, in essence, "The hell with everyone else." Thus it is no wonder that the nonunionized sectors of the workforce look on our unions with increasing disdain. It is no wonder that these feelings are spread to the new arrivals in the workforce, who therefore have no guilty conscience about strikebreaking or similar activities. The more the unions treat the rest of labor with arrogance, the greater they will weaken the whole labor movement. The more they weaken the whole labor movement, the lower the wage will go for the nonunionized sector of the economy; and the lower the wage goes for the nonunionized sector of the economy, the more pressure there will be for management to break the unionized sector of the economy, and the smaller and poorer will be the middle class.

The point is simple: The leadership of the American unions must be more progressive. It must embark on increased membership drives, and it should actively campaign to draw in more minority members. It must meaningfully support political candidates who advocate for the lifeblood issues of the labor-dependent classes—namely, environmental issues and social issues—and support the nonconservative party, that is, the Democrats.

Union leadership should also become active in community affairs. Look at any community. Who tends to be running for office? Is it a union member? Hardly ever. Who tends to be directing the United Way? Who tends to be actively involved on city planning boards? Always members of the business community—hardly ever union members. True, the business executive has more free time and more latitude. But then too, unions and union finances could be structured to facilitate such activism. Unions should actively promote more community involvement to establish their influence in the community as a countermeasure to the many community activities that are almost wholly business dominated. The point is not that the business domination is abhorrent or unproductive. Much business involvement in the community is progressive. It is, however, out of balance—which is the main point of this book. There must be more balance between the powers of labor and capital, and community involvement today is a business-dominated playing field. It is no wonder that there is so much pressure for tax cuts not for labor, not for homeowner property taxes, but for property taxes on commercial and industrial property. The prospect of more jobs is always waved as the carrot when this pressure is being turned up; but as pointed out earlier, economic studies have shown that local taxes are but a small part of the business location decision. Investors will take all that they can get, however; and if they can convince a local community that the main reason they are locating in the area is because of taxes and if all of the decision makers in the community are primarily representatives of business, then they will get the tax breaks and pass the costs of government on to the middle class. The point must be emphasized again: Labor unions and labor in general must establish a presence in the councils of local government in order to watch over the needs of their constituents. Further, they must become more involved on national political issues.

President Reagan drew much support from labor union members in 1980 and 1984. Yet he fired the Professional Air Traffic Controllers (PATCO) who were on strike. Reagan's Labor Department became the first in the postwar era not to involve itself actively in mediating national disputes between management and labor. Even the Nixon administration tried to expedite the resolution of labor conflicts. Many times a balanced outcome was achieved. However, under Reagan, the hands-off policy swung the balance of power to management. Like it or not, union leadership and union membership will—for its own survival—have to support those candidates who advocate and deliver on progressive stances for all of labor; and like it or not, they must recognize these progressive stances as involving better treatment of minorities, an increased openness to union membership for all labor, a more caring attitude for the poor and the indigent, and support of environmental issues. Failure to change its direction could mean the practical elimination of the American union that has set the standards for labor, whether unionized or not, when it comes to fair wages, protection of pension rights, health care, and occupational health and safety standards. Without a healthy union movement, all labor and all labor benefits are diminished.

THE DEMOCRATS SHOULD BE DEMOCRATS

The first thing the Democratic party should do is stop trying to pass laws that are "good for business" or "job creating." Business, as we have seen, will take care of itself. Yet the Democrats, who eased into such a stance in the early 1960s with early experiments in supply-side economics, have carried the experiment too far. Their message has been diluted. Rather than primarily working to protect the rights of workers, to protect the rights and incomes of consumers, they have been co-opted in many ways by the forces of capital. It is not that they have ignored the small homeowner, the small businessperson, the small farmer, and the consumer. It is that they have increasingly supported the forces antithetical to these groups. Many politicians think they are doing labor a tremendous favor by granting huge tax exemptions to firms when they locate in a particular community. Yet, the bigger picture is that the firm has often left some other locale and, with it, perhaps a rundown tax base and a number of unemployed workers. Tax concessions given by communities in the United States to "create jobs" are a zero-sum game. Jobs are lost in Peoria, Illinois, and jobs are created in Mobile, Alabama. But if Durham, North Carolina, is suddenly cheaper than Mobile, jobs will be lost in Mobile and gained in Durham. Yet the politicians—many of them Democrats in the local area—think they are being progressive and doing something for labor, when in fact they are eroding the tax base on which the services— education, police, fire protection—are based for the labor-dependent individual. It is the middle class that picks up the tab.

The Democrats must return to their traditional constituency. That constituency is still very New Deal-oriented, and it can be described in two words: "labor dependent" for its income. The New Deal coalition that has traditionally supported the Democratic party has been that group of individuals who rely primarily on their own income, on the income of their own labor, to survive—the income of the small homeowner, the small business person, the small farmer, and the newly arrived immigrant.

Let the large businesses push for their tax breaks through their Republican representatives. Then let the Democrats evaluate these tax proposals with the welfare of their labor constituency in mind. A meaningful check and balance will evolve. When both parties push for such business tax breaks, however, the benefits are highly skewed toward capital.

It is thus no accident that the Democrats have had a very difficult time in electing a president. The plain fact is, their message is garbled. They are very good at taking care of local constituencies, and this is only natural. Democrats are traditionally closer to local issues and local causes. They tend to serve the masses very well locally because of the nature of the Democratic party and of its history. Republican candidates for office, as representatives of a monied class, have only so much tolerance or indeed ability to deal with welfare issues, minority rights, problems of the ghettos, and so forth.

True, the Democrats do an excellent job in servicing their constituencies and, as such, do an excellent job in electing congressmen. However, electing a president is a different matter. The message is garbled. "We are good for labor, and we are also good for business." Come on! The *Republicans* are good for business! The *Democrats* should not try to *out-Republican* the *Republicans*. A Democratic presidential candidate must have a clear and unequivocal message as to what and for whom he or she stands. And he or she should stand for those persons in the society who are the traditional inhabitants of the Democratic party, that is, those persons who rely primarily on their own labor for income. Again, let the Republicans protect business.

A Democratic majority in Congress is not sufficient to aid the middle class in this society, because the executive branch is all powerful in interpreting and enforcing the laws made by the Congress. The Reagan administration repeatedly demonstrated an ability not to enforce congressionally passed laws, or to change the emphasis and rewrite the regulations to such a degree that the laws are only minimally enforced. This has happened with occupational health and safety standards stemming from OSHA, as well as in equal opportunity enforcement of (i.e., relaxing the mandate of) the National Labor Relations Board to protect the rights of unionization. Duly elected unions who struck in the 1980s saw the government tolerate the situation when nonunion workers took away their jobs—in violation of workers' rights to collective bargaining. The string of conservative judges appointed to the benches of the federal courts by Republican presidents have had an enormous impact, elevating the power of capital and diminishing the power of the middle class. To the Democratic party, the message should be clear. Merely electing a Democratic

Congress is insufficient. A cohesive national political policy that emphasizes its traditional constituency must be forged. One cannot have two
masters. Either the Democrats will work for the middle and the lower
classes, or they will work for no one and as a party will not survive. The
Republicans are in no danger of being weakened under the current system.

In line with this, the Democrats should work toward a repeal of the law
allowing for political action committees and in the meantime accept no
money whatsoever from PACs. The PAC has been one of the most
disruptive elements in American democratic political history. A new
method of campaign financing must be achieved, and this may well
involve simply the provisions of publicly provided funds for most campaigns, along with small contributions. Again, to repeat, the *Democrats*
should stop trying to *out-Republican* the *Republicans*. Such will buy them,
and the middle class, nothing in the end.

A PROGRESSIVE AGENDA FOR THE
ECONOMICS PROFESSION

An obvious message of this book is the failure of the economics
profession—despite its huge quantity of talent—to enter effectively into
the national political debate where economic issues increasingly dwarf all
others. Any national policy debate on economic issues should embrace
the whole profession and not merely the "traditional" leaders of the
American Economic Association. There are many ways to join the debate
on national policies, and some specific steps must be taken.

One such step would be to change the current procedure for the
presentation of academic papers at the national American Economic
Association meetings. The association should limit the number of invited
papers to 50 percent of the total presented. This would still give the
traditional interests of the American Economic Association a substantial
input. It should then invite contributed papers to form the balance of the
presentations at the meetings. The mechanism for judging the quality of
the contributed papers presented at national meetings should be a slate of
editors elected by the general membership. Likewise, the slate of editors
for the *American Economic Review* and the *Journal of Economic Perspectives*, the two major organs of the American Economic Association,
should be elected. Currently, only invited papers to the annual meetings
are published, and contributed papers are not. How ironic that a profession

so "free-market" oriented in recent years should continue to operate its annual meeting on such a noncompetitive basis.

This change should set the stage for a more all-embracing study and discussion of economic issues within the profession and lessen the over-emphasis on microeconomic issues and "efficiency."

At the educational level, there should be a new emphasis on the policy aspects of economics. Too much emphasis is placed on mathematical models of little relevant use in the economic policy arena. Thus, with the majority of the profession engaged in microeconomic modeling often involving highly complex and abstract issues, the leaders of the profession have become out of touch with national policy issues. Increasingly, the expert in the profession is the microeconomist, while the major problems facing the United States are macroeconomic in nature.

The profession must seek to reward and encourage economic policy debate and analysis by its graduate students and must incorporate these factors into its tenure and promotion decisions at the major universities. The economic analysis of social costs, social benefits, and social welfare is well known and well developed, but increasingly laid aside. Its practice should be encouraged.

A NEW RESEARCH AGENDA FOR ECONOMICS

Economic research resources should be reallocated into several areas.

Income Distribution

There should be an expansion and a new emphasis placed on the theory of income distribution. Throughout the 1980s, with only a few exceptions (such as the authors of the studies cited in Chapter 3), very little attention was paid to the economics of poverty and the economics of income distribution. The profession still places too much emphasis on marginal revenue productivity (MRP) as the theory that determines income distribution. The marginal revenue productivity theory in economics *allocates* to factors of production the products and their value produced. It does not, however, in a sufficient way *determine* who actually gets the fruits of the productivity. It is the controllers of the factors of production who get the fruits of the factors' productivity. The controllers are not necessarily the persons who actually perform the productivity. Factors of production and factors of distribution are most often two different animals. *People* receive income, and people are not necessarily factors of production. Land and capital are two factors of production that are nonhuman but are in fact generative of income. The control and concentration of control over factors of production is a legitimate area of economic inquiry because it has complicated income-distributional implications. Such an investigation into distribution and defining the factors of distribution as either capital-enhanced or labor-dependent could further lead into new areas of taxation theory.

Full Employment: A Faulty Measure of Economic Well-being

Another major area of economic inquiry should be to examine the blind faith in the desirability of full employment as a measure of well-being. Much has been made—perhaps too much—of job creation and the unemployment rate. The American economy recently has been "glorified" for its enormous job creation (although in the 1980s, while the number of new jobs was large, the growth trend was less than that of the 1970s; see Table 9-3). Yet we find that, despite all the job creation, income distribution is slipping away from the middle. The plight of the lower classes grows as the standard of living of the middle class shrinks. This is because the full-employment notion as we judged it in the 1960s is not appropriate to the 1980s and 1990s. In the 1960s, full employment meant an abundance of jobs that were in the primary labor market. The primary labor market as I interpret MIT's Michael Piore's theories is the labor market where, in general, a single wage earner can support a family. In such jobs there is upward mobility, and health and retirement benefits are often provided. The secondary labor market in Piore's definition contains dead-end jobs, minimum wages, casual employment—jobs where two or three members of a family working together might, by pooling their funds, support the family.

In the 1960s, the United States was the dominant world economy, and full employment generally meant an abundance of primary labor market jobs. Today, full employment means a dearth of primary labor market jobs and a plethora of secondary labor market jobs. Yes, today anyone can find a job at the Burger King, the McDonald's, or the temporary employment agency (such as Western Temporary Services or Manpower). Some new measures for employment as an index of well-being should be developed, and they should take into account such factors as the hours worked per family, as well as the hours worked per individual. U.S. employment data should classify and reflect more accurately and descriptively the types of jobs being held and their sufficiency toward supporting individuals and families. The next time a prospective investor in my local community applies for a tax abatement to open a new factory and holds up the banner of "Jobs, Jobs, Jobs!" the city commissioner should immediately snap back, "What kind of jobs?" This will only occur, however, where the current ethos of "jobs of any type" or "a low unemployment rate" has been modified. After all, anybody can find a job—at Burger King.

Economic Impact of Taxation on Investment, Capital Mobility, and Distribution

Taxation theory is a virtually neglected area of public finance when it comes to translation into policy matters. This is particularly so in measuring the benefits flowing from a number of tax incentives supposedly given as a means of stimulating economic activity. Investigations should take place at the local level to determine the actual job-creating results (and the types of jobs created) of giving tax breaks to firms in return for promises to retain or increase employment.

At the national level, extensive investigation needs to be undertaken by the profession on the results of the Reagan tax cuts, particularly through accelerated depreciation, that were given in the early 1980s. These tax breaks apparently did not have the desired effect of stimulating investment, as the data in Chapter 9 show. However, they did have the effect of markedly increasing the cash flow to major corporations in the hopes that there would be an increased amount of productive investment. It appears, however, that these funds were mainly used to acquire competition, to move productive facilities overseas, to threaten local communities with movement (aided by the new tax-break laws) and—most insidious of all—to privatize, that is, firms' buying back their own stock so as further to concentrate private power. Few chronologies have examined these types of corporate abuses as a result of the national taxation policy changes.

A second area of investigation should be to reopen the debate on differential tax rates between earned and unearned income. Earned income in tax law theory is that which is produced by labor. Unearned income is produced by capital or real estate. In fact, earned income is generally income that is generated by labor-dependent individuals. Unearned income is generally money received by individuals whose incomes are capital-enhanced and is in the form of rent, interest, or dividends. In many ways, the basis for differential taxation on these two classes has very sound economic roots. Logically, a person who earns $40,000 by putting in a 40-hour week with simply his or her own labor as an asset should not pay as high a rate of tax as the person who earns $40,000 a week with accumulated income, that is, through interest. One might say that this would discourage people from accumulating capital; and I agree that it would, to a certain extent. Yet this is not a call for a confiscatory tax on unearned income, but merely for a reasonably higher one. It is ridiculous when one realizes that the baseball player who has as his sole capital possessions a bat and a glove and who might earn $5 million in a peak season is taxed in the same personal income tax bracket as the highly paid manufacturing executive also earning $5 million a year who has at his disposal armies of secretaries, clerks, capital equipment, and the like. We should not confiscate the income of the manufacturing executive, but we must indeed realize that his or her income is considerably capital-enhanced. Indeed, even the so-called wage the executive is receiving may have considerable elements of "unearned income" in it when compared with the Japanese auto executive's salary. As such, it should be taxed at a higher rate.

Also in taxation theory there should be an increased investigation into the monopolistic or "rental" value of a corporate charter once the firm reaches a certain size and age. Corporations of long stature, granted unlimited life and limited liability by the state, have often obtained unlimited life in the economic arena of competition. The corporate charter itself may well be a separate factor of production and thus a separate factor of income production and distribution. Much has been made about the so-called double taxation of corporate income. This stems from the fact that dividends to stockholders are not deductible from the profits of a corporation. Thus, the corporation pays taxes on profits to reach net profits. Then a portion of net profits is distributed as dividends to stock-holders—the owners of the corporation—who are again taxed on such profits. However, current attackers of the corporate income tax, because of this double taxation scenario, ignore the benefits that the corporation receives by its unique form of organization granted by the state. The corporate charter grants to the corporation limited liability for its owners, as well as unlimited life. The latter allows it to protect many products, trademarks, and brand names, and to protect markets and channels of distribution that over the long run tend to take on monopoly elements. To tax a corporation for this particular form of business organization is not unreasonable. This assumes that such benefits are separately identifiable factors of production, and that income uniquely accrues to the corporate form of business organization. Such a matter is a worthy one to be investigated by the economics profession. If such benefits do exist, then the argument about double taxation falls by the wayside. If the benefits do not exist, then the arguments for a cut in the corporate income tax take on more meaning. However, these subjects should be elaborated by the economics profession and then the results put forth into a meaningful political discussion among the electorate.

A NEW DOMESTIC ECONOMIC POLICY AGENDA

As detailed in this book, a major reason for the decline of the middle class has been the advance of the economic power and the holders of capital. This has proceeded to such an extent that labor—and particularly middle- and lower-class income—is taxed heavier than upper-class and corporate income. Therefore, the imbalance of power needs to be redressed in national taxation policies. As illustrated in Chapters 5 and 6, the corporate tax as a percentage of total revenues has fallen dramatically in the post–World War II era such that the rate of corporate taxation in America is the lowest of all our trading partners, yet with little results in improving our balance of trade.[1] Further, the task of reducing the huge federal deficits demands that the corporations pay their fair share. Therefore, in the field of taxation, several steps should be taken.

First, the corporate income tax should be raised to a level where the corporation pays a fairer share of the burdens of national government. Second, lower- and middle-income families should have their income tax rates reduced; and concurrent with this, taxes on unearned income such as interest, dividends, and rent should be raised for large-income recipients of such revenues. What is large? This should not be a tax on middle America. My proposal would be to impose a differential tax rate on unearned income for $50,000 or more per year per family. Thus, the retired person living on past savings, who is in essence middle class, would not feel the brunt of the tax.

Corporate abuses of the tax cuts of the 1980s should be redressed. In the absence of any good information and studies that show a meaningful increase in investment from the tax cuts granted then, the accelerated depreciation for tax purposes should be further modified (beyond the 1986 tax act). Assets purchased by businesses should be depreciated more on the basis of their useful life, with a reasonable cap placed on it.

On the personal income tax side, the deduction of consumer interest and the deduction of state and local sales taxes should be restored within middle-income family limits. Not allowing the deduction of state and local taxes against the federal income tax is indeed double taxation with no good explanation for it. The so-called double taxation of corporate income is partly in response to protections granted to the corporation by the state. No such rationale exists for the IRS's taxing of local sales taxation. Consumers' interest should be deductible, as much of this interest goes to pay for necessities—particularly automotive transportation. Since corporations can deduct the cost of all the interest they pay on assets to sustain their economic vitality, the family should logically be allowed that same deduction.

In order to protect the status of middle class and the consumer, the Cabinet of the president of the United States should be represented by a consumer protection department. With the exception of the Department of Labor, most of the other Cabinet-level positions are business oriented, such as Treasury, Commerce, the Interior, and even the Department of State. A Cabinet-level office of consumer protection should be established to protect the middle and lower classes. Such an office should also be able to initiate antitrust activities that relate to price fixing, price gouging, and other activities in restraint of competition where injury to the consumer is the main result.

Finally, in the area of national policy, some curbs should be put on the powers of state and local governments to interfere with interstate commerce—particularly investment. Since the Constitution prohibits states from interfering with interstate commerce, there is a clear mandate to prohibit states from using tax gimmicks and subsidies to lure industry from one state to another. This use of differential tax concessions has been neatly categorized by economists as tax expenditures. Since states are prohibited from distorting economic activity by taxing goods and capital as they cross borders, states should likewise be prohibited from granting tax concessions and subsidies to lure capital relocation. Such activity encourages the frequent movement of industry without any regard for the social and economic disruption of the communities being deserted. Empty buildings are left behind in the ownership of the community, tax bases are lost, and schools are left with children but with no or greatly depleted sources of revenue. A logical extension of this recommendation to curb state and local enticements is to further strengthen the existing federal plant-closing legislation.

A NEW INTERNATIONAL ECONOMIC POLICY

A major reason for the decline in the middle class has been the inroads of foreign manufacturing. The United States has found it extremely difficult to compete with foreign-manufactured goods in what has become a virtually open economy with very little restriction on imports. However, several other countries are not open to American products to the same degree that we are open to theirs. This is anything but free trade. Japan, of course, is the premier example of such a dual standard. For years, the American government has been trying to chip away at Japanese trade policy, with only moderate success. The dollar has depreciated against the Japanese yen, but nowhere near the amount it should have. Given the huge trade surpluses that Japan has amassed with the United States and the huge outflow of dollars to buy these Japanese goods, the dollar should be extremely cheap against the yen, but yet the dollar seems unexplainably strong. The reason the dollar is strong is that the Japanese have been amassing dollars from their huge sales of goods in the United States, but then using these dollars to buy American assets, land, buildings, stocks, and bonds. Japan's reinvestment of these funds in the United States strengthens the dollar, makes American goods more expensive, but at the same time keeps Japanese products relatively cheap. Japan continues to sell products to Americans since the American dollar is overvalued because of Japanese *asset* purchases. They then take these overvalued dollars and again buy more American assets. As long as this process continues, we will never reach a merchandise trade balance with that nation.

Therefore, a limitation should be placed on foreign investment in the United States by any country that has had a long-standing trade surplus with the United States—particularly Japan. Strict limits should be placed on the purchase of office buildings, land, and manufacturing establishments. Further, strict limits should be placed on the purchase of stock in American corporations by such countries with long-standing trade surpluses. The only category that should be allowed without restriction would be investment in U.S. government debt. Further, for those countries with long-standing trade surpluses with the United States, a substantial tariff (10 percent or more) should be imposed on goods of that country until a clear trend toward an elimination of the trade imbalance is established. Once the trade imbalance is eliminated or shows a clear trend toward elimination, then such tariffs can be lifted.

While many will respond that this is an interference with free trade, let me emphasize several points. A major reason that the trade balance between Japan and the United States has not equaled out is because Japan has limited American access to Japanese markets; she has not practiced free trade. Besides, the United States has a very generous policy in allowing the foreign purchase of American property. Many nations, such as Canada and France, impose very definite restrictions on the foreign ownership of property—particularly land—in their countries. The United States is a world power and cannot afford to be damaged economically by its loose policy in this regard. To meet its responsibilities in the world, it should not bear the decimation of its industry and its international competitiveness under a policy that allows the sale of its assets and artificially strengthens the dollar's value. The strengthening of the dollar only makes American exports more expensive and further undermines the middle class by decimating American manufacturing industry and jobs. Our open-door buyout policy, particularly with respect to the Japanese, must be curtailed in the interest of resestablishing a vibrant middle class and, further, in the interest of national security.

Finally, the mobility of American capital abroad should be limited. American corporations were given enormous tax breaks to invest in America and create jobs. Many American corporations are moving their manufacturing bases overseas, importing the products, and further worsening the balance of trade. Just as we should limit the mobility of capital within the United States, steps should be taken to limit the mobility of capital overseas. The generous tax provisions the United States has granted to American corporations should be expected to produce investment in the United States so as to promote domestic economic growth and middle-class jobs. The investment of American capital overseas should obviously not be prohibited, but stricter limits on the mobility of capital out of the United States should be imposed.

A NATIONAL ENERGY POLICY

Such a simple proposal as to advocate establishing a national energy policy may be trite, but nonetheless it needs mentioning again. Policymakers refuse to address the overconsumption of relatively cheap fuel in the United States. As long as this situation continues to exist, America will be held hostage to periodic disruptive bouts of inflation stemming from the interruption of oil supplies. Such inflation hits hardest the middle and lower classes as well as small, chiefly labor-dependent businesses.

With the minimum price of gasoline in western Europe approaching $3.00 per gallon, it would seem there ought to be some room at the federal level to consider enacting measures that would bring about higher gasoline taxes at least.

If a modest federal 50-cent-per-gallon tax on gasoline were levied, a slowing of U.S. oil consumption would surely depress world prices of crude oil. The probable result would be that gasoline prices at the pumps would rise; but since wholesale or crude oil prices would fall, the gasoline price rise would be less than 50 cents. Who would be paying the tax? Partly the producer of oil: OPEC and the other large oil suppliers, such as major petroleum companies. Let us not forget that OPEC consists of a group of governments who own oil companies and that we are paying taxes to them as we consume oil at such a rapid pace. It would be far better to pay the taxes to the revenue-strapped U.S. government.

Thus, for a number of reasons, a higher federal gasoline tax makes sense. First, we would lower our dependence on foreign oil and the economic (and indeed military) disruptions that ensue. Second, the federal government needs the revenue. Third, environmental conditions such as cleaner air and protection of the ozone layer would be partially achieved.

Why has such policy not been enacted? First, it would be a tax increase on an overly taxed consumer. Quite naturally, the middle and lower classes have short-run but very real self-interest in mind when they oppose such a measure. Second, tax increases of any kind are politically unpopular. Third, the producers of oil, both American and foreign, are against it. The documented presence of that interest group in the nation's capital continues to wield excessive power over the American government, over its president, and over the Congress.

A FINAL STATEMENT: THE ECONOMICS OF BALANCE

The ideas in this chapter are primarily my solutions for promoting and increasing the economic health of the American middle class, bringing with it opportunities and economic openings for those in the lower classes who seek upward mobility. Many other concepts have been proposed from a number of different perspectives and in various fashions. Mine do contain elements of economic restriction. They do impede private, unregulated, untrammeled competition. However they also move the pendulum back toward a degree of labor protection, and toward a national protection from the untrammeled and uninhibited flow of capital. Capital today is extremely mobile. Families and people are not. Communities cannot follow capital as it rambles in search of the highest returns. If the ownership of capital were dispersed in any way equivalent to the ownership of labor, there would be a different equation of power between the two. The economics of such an equivalency would call for an equal taxation of capital right alongside other factors of production. But its distribution is concentrated and is becoming more concentrated. And the very act of concentrating wealth feeds on itself. In the United States, this concentration of wealth has proceeded for such a long period that its dominance has become at one and the same time entrenched and inexcusable. Its dominance over labor reduces the size and the quality of the middle class and of the lower classes. With the loss in size of the middle class and its purchasing power comes the downfall of economic democracy, the mass market, and perhaps even political democracy. This cannot be permitted to continue.

The current degree of capital mobility may be economically efficient. Capital and labor are free to seek their highest rewards as dictated by economic efficiency—in theory, at least. But in practice, capital is far more mobile, far more flexible, and thus can amass significantly higher rewards when it capitalizes on these attributes. However, labor (and the survival of labor and communities, including inner cities, through income sustenance) is really what an economy is all about. Many economists speak of factors of production impersonally—as labor and as capital. Economists also speak equally impersonally about the income that these factors produce. Yet *people*—not capital—are the recipients of income because people own capital, just as people are the recipients of labor income because people possess labor. Thus we must start treating the fruits of production as accruing to people, and we must classify people as receiving incomes that are either capital-enhanced or labor-dependent. This could then give us a guide to national economic policy, including tax policy; and it could give us a guide toward restoring an equitable distribution of income and with it a restoration of a viable middle class. The consequence of an economically nonviable American middle class is one big lower class—something that, historically, economic democracy and political democracy have never withstood.

This book is about balance and imbalance among the groups of people who receive income. When the labor–capital economic equation was in a rough sort of balance—as it was in the late 1940s, the 1950s, and the 1960s—and when each group paid its fair share of taxes, the middle class grew and prospered. America's foreign trade and her federal budget were generally balanced, financial markets were stable, and a healthy national political and economic debate took place.

Compare this former era with the start of the 1990s. Capital's power is abusive, labor's income and the middle class are shrinking, capital is undertaxed, the economy and financial markets are unstable, and we are dangerously out of balance in the international-trade and federal-budget arenas.

The lessons should be clear. When capital and labor hold an equal balance of economic power, when they are both economically healthy, the U.S. economy follows suit, both domestically and internationally. A vibrant middle class supports a strong mass market, and this mass market in turn creates many middle-class and professional jobs. The strong middle class also offers upward mobility to workers in the lower classes—which partially alleviates the poverty burden.

However, when the scale is tipped too much toward capital we have America in the early 1990s, weak, unbalanced, unstable, with its citizens frightened economically. To the extent that Japanese capital is an agent of the current imbalance, its powers should be curtailed. Japan should accept this honestly. To the extent that America is healthy, Japan will be healthy. We are her market. In her own interest as well as ours, she must curb her predatory mercantilistic trade policies. She, too, must recognize the economics of balance.

However, Japan is not the major problem. The real problem is internal. The real problem is the need to legislate economic and tax policies that will restore the economic vibrancy of the middle class in America. This book cites the problems and proposes some solutions. What we now need is a political party with the will, the leadership, and the fortitude to carry out the middle-class rebuilding process.

NOTE

1. In 1985, corporate taxes in the United States were substantially lower than in Japan, Australia, Canada, Italy, Britain, and the Netherlands. Organization for Economic Cooperation and Development, *Revenue Statistics of OECD Member Countries* (Paris: OECD, 1987).

Epilogue
Middle-class Issues in the 1992 Presidential Campaign and Beyond

This book has looked at the decline of the American middle class as essentially a long-run phenomenon that began in the early 1970s and continues to the present day. Since this is essentially a long-run decline caused by basic and fundamental changes in the way America does business, the way its government interacts with people, and the way our institutions function, we must recognize in conclusion that any reversal in the fortunes of the middle class—and with it those of the lower class—will take a long time. Chapter 12 proposed some fundamental and long-run solutions for change. This epilogue will expand on these solutions as an outline for middle-class renewal. Then will follow some observations on the right way and the wrong way governments should create jobs. Where to find the money for improving the lot of the middle class is also discussed. Finally, a critique will be made of various proposals offered by candidates during the 1992 primary and general presidential campaigns when the nation's distressed economy was so important an issue, and the major candidates' positions will be evaluated relative to my criteria for restoration or at least improvement of middle-class economic viability.

AN OUTLINE FOR CHANGE

In 1992, during the presidential campaign, there was much rhetoric about improving the lot of the middle class, along with the usual promises politicians make about creating an America that is strong and productive. The question, however, is whether any of the proposals raised in the campaign addressed the three major categories that have weakened the middle class dearly since 1973. These categories are lost middle-class jobs, increased financial burdens on the middle class (particularly due to taxation), and a depressed level of wages for middle-class job holders. In the subsections below, countermeasures proposed are aimed at reversing the unfavorable trends in each of these three categories.

For Restoring Middle-class Jobs

1. *The U.S. government should review its virtually open-door import policy for foreign products.* Such a policy has decimated many American manufacturing jobs in the 1980s. An economics task force or commission should be appointed specifically to study the problem, and it should be so structured as to be as free as possible from partisan politics. All necessary economic expertise and resources should be provided to such a commission, and it should determine the extent to which long-standing deficits with particular countries are due to natural market forces or are due to the restrictive practices of such countries. If the latter condition holds, then import limitations and/or tariffs should be imposed on that country's products.

A second step taken against any such country should be a restriction on the amount of its foreign investments in the United States, excluding federal, state, and local securities. It has been the practice of Japan—while running huge trade surpluses with the United States—to reinvest many of these surpluses in the United States. Such reinvestment has not been particularly productive, however. Little of it has found its way into creating new manufacturing industries and the jobs accompanying them. Rather, such investment has been for the purchase of existing assets such as real estate and the stocks of publicly held companies. Japan's purchase of many of these assets is certainly of no benefit to the United States. But there is a second source of harm to America in this practice. The wholesale purchase of U.S. assets strengthens the dollar and further weakens the Japanese currency, namely, the yen. As Japan continues to buy our assets, her currency falls in world markets and her products continue to be very inexpensive. Thus the prospect of ever reversing our trade deficit with Japan becomes practically nil. Until there is clear evidence of such a reversal, both of the above steps—a limitation on Japan's exports to the

United States, and on its U.S. investment in the United States—should be effected.

2. *There must be a correction of the deteriorating condition of government at all levels in the United States.* The attack on government—orchestrated to portray it as the main source of all problems in the United States—has become a self-fulfilling prophecy. Governmental units have been starved of revenues and resources and have found it increasingly difficult to hold quality employees. Funds should be appropriated to expand meaningful government employment in areas where the government is now operating on a deficient basis. I would suggest, for instance, that expanded employment in the education area, particularly at the elementary and secondary levels, and in the area of antitrust regulation would be greatly beneficial to the middle class. Further, federal aid to the states in the form of grants for educational purposes should be increased. Such funding would create meaningful jobs—ones, moreover, that would have positive spillover effects on the U.S. economy.

3. *The corporate merger mania that occurred in the 1980s and stripped away many middle-class jobs should be curtailed.* While some consolidation of businesses is normal in a capitalist economy, the manic takeover activity of the 1980s was funded by excessively reckless financial practices; and the U.S. government, by allowing the deductibility of interest on loans used to finance corporate takeovers, participated in the process. Therefore, the federal tax code should be restructured to eliminate the deductibility of interest on loans used to finance such corporate takeovers. Additionally, legal expenses involved in such mergers likewise should not be deductible. This would make takeovers subject to much more of a market test. If they were indeed subjected to such a test, without the government subsidies, many takeovers would not be economically feasible and many lost jobs might be saved.

4. *For job creation in the inner-city areas, the federal government should provide tax breaks for business incentives in such areas.* The creation of so-called enterprise zones is certainly consistent with this proposal. However, the state and local governments—already strapped for revenues—should not be responsible for providing such tax breaks. It should be, appropriately, the federal government that, first, determines which areas are eligible for assistance and, second, provides the funds. The problem with enterprise zones and subsidies for businesses within inner-city areas when provided by state or local communities is that these programs then tend to be competitive and self-canceling. It would be better

for the federal government to apply uniform criteria for such investments, and provide the funding.

Relieving Financial Burdens on the Middle Class

This book has shown repeatedly the increased burden of taxation paid by individual taxpayers, and the corporate escape from such taxes. Accordingly, it should be obvious that the time has come to provide tax relief to middle- and lower-income taxpayers.

5. *The deductibility of state and local sales taxes and interest for personal items such as automobiles, credit card purchases, and education should be reinstituted for individuals.* Corporations still continue to enjoy such deductions as they seek to improve the economic health of their business economic units. Many of these purchases take place to improve the economic health of the family economic unit and should likewise be allowed.

6. *The corporate income tax should be increased to levels that are fair and consistent with the way other major countries tax their corporations.* As I pointed out in Chapter 6, America taxes her corporations at approximately one-third the level of Japanese corporations. Such low taxes have apparently not permitted American corporations to be competitive in the world economy. In the face of such evidence, the U.S. government can no longer afford the loss of revenue. Such revenues could be used to finance other desperately needed programs such as aid to education and federal tax incentives for business investment in the blighted inner-city areas.

7. *The process of state and local governments' competing with one another to lure industry from one state to another through the use of property tax breaks should be eliminated by federal law.* A long history of constitutional law in the United States prohibits the states from interfering with interstate commerce, particularly through taxation. Yet we allow differential tax burdens to distort the pattern of interstate commerce. Such property tax relief, which is often given to businesses but not to homeowners, flies in the face of the equal treatment of equals. The net result is that states competing to lure industry by cutting business taxes erodes the property tax base and places a differential burden on the homeowner—many of whom are middle class. Such gimmicks may be "job creating" in the state that is the winner, but they are "job destroying" in the state that is the loser. In both states, they are revenue destroying,

with the burden picked up by the middle and the lower classes. This is indeed a zero-sum game for America as a whole.

8.   *The political action committee (PAC) method of financing electoral campaigns should be eliminated.* Such financing has all too often corrupted elected officials into loading tax breaks on businesses and the wealthy to the disadvantage of the middle class. Democracy in America should return to its one-man (or one-person) one-vote principle, by allowing campaigns to be financed by small contributions up to a reasonable limit (say $200 per person or business) along with additional government funding.

9.   *The United States should enact a meaningful energy policy.* Such a policy might begin with an increased tax on gasoline, but with the majority of the proceeds spent on job-creating activities such as repair of interstate highways and the many roads and bridges that are now deteriorating in this country. Other proceeds of these increased gasoline-tax revenues could be used for research and investment in renewable sources of energy such as wind and solar power. The regressive features of such a tax could be addressed by providing an income tax credit on gasoline purchased by low-income taxpayers.

Proposals to Raise Middle-class Wages

10.   *The United States should review its immigration policy.* As discussed in Chapter 4, immigration rates in the 1980s, on a per-capita basis, were at the highest levels since the 1920s. Between 25 and 35 percent of all new jobs created in the 1980s were filled by immigrant labor. Further, the Bush administration has further upped the level of immigration to a near record level of approximately 800,000 per year. America is a land of opportunity and, indeed, a land of immigrants. However, there is stark evidence—such as the events in Los Angeles in the spring of 1992—that the American economy is not providing adequate jobs for our longtime residents. My calling for a review is not meant to be immigrant bashing or to be anti-immigrant, but simply recommends that we give the matter a sensible look. The current huge influx of immigrant workers can only depress wage levels of lower- and middle-class citizens.

11.   *Companies' hiring of nonunion workers—commonly called "scabs"—during a strike action should be prohibited.* Federal law allows for collective bargaining and a duly elected union to represent the workers at a given company. Allowing that company to hire nonunion workers renders ineffective the protections given to American workers under the

National Labor Relations Act and as such greatly weakens the bargaining position of union membership and of labor as a whole. Unions generally deliver solid middle-class jobs to their constituents. While unions in the past may have overstepped their bounds and exerted too much power, the evidence today is that the pendulum has swung in the other direction. Management, through the use of strike-breaking techniques and other coercive action, is now overstepping *its* bounds.

12. *The U.S.–Mexican free trade treaty should be defeated.* Despite the argument about increased consumer benefits through lower-priced Mexican goods, a greater burden on the middle class will be a further movement of American manufacturing south of the Mexican border—and a further loss of middle-class jobs. Workers in the Midwest or in the Northeast who need a wage of $12 an hour to maintain a middle-class lifestyle will find themselves competing with child labor, with labor that lives in communities with no or few municipal services and that is often paid less than $1 an hour. To subject American workers who must support families, their communities, and their school districts to such untrammeled competition is unconscionable. While the United States has a stake in ensuring the economic survival of Mexico, there are other forms of aid that should be sought, rather than laying the major portion of the aid on the backs of working America.

In my opinion, the above 12 proposals would do the most good toward reversing the trend of a declining American middle class. In fact, if these proposals were enacted, business conditions and American lifestyles would move more toward the model of the mid-1960s, the heyday of the American middle class. Prices were stable then; businesses were more creatively competitive rather than always seeking tax gimmicks to make profits; and government provided good-quality services—particularly schools—at fair tax levels to the middle class.

Before examining the specific proposals of the 1992 presidential candidates and how their programs would improve middle-class America, I would like to turn first to the overall subject of job creation.

HOW TO AND HOW NOT TO CREATE JOBS

Much has been made about the subject of job creation and how governments should participate in the process. In fact, the rhetoric gets rather wearisome at times. The blatant deficiencies in such current talk are numerous. First, it is little different from the supply-side economics of the 1980s. The idea then was to give tax breaks to businesses prior to their investing and creating jobs, with the hope and the faith that the latter would follow from the former. As the data in Chapter 9 demonstrate, investment as a percentage of national income actually fell in the 1980s despite the huge tax cuts given to American corporations. Today the rhetoric is much the same, however: give tax cuts to businesses and they will create jobs.

First of all, there is a fundamental flaw in this line of reasoning. Businesses do not create jobs; they only provide jobs when there is a strong consumer demand for their product—and they do so grudgingly. Businesses find they must provide jobs when their product is being demanded and/or sold.

Second, too little is made of the nature of the job itself. Too much attention is paid to the unemployment *rate* rather than to the quality of the jobs that make up the rate. Recent evidence shows that the American economy has generated a number of new jobs that are increasingly low paid and low skilled. The number of full-time working persons who live in poverty is now at record levels. So, when analyzed in depth, the political rhetoric of "jobs, jobs, jobs" is a rather hollow one. It is, however, a great flag waver. To provide jobs is to be for motherhood, for apple pie, and for the flag. It is one of the new catchphrases of politicians—one that has achieved equal billing with the anti-inflation campaign promises of many American politicians. But in fact, the cry of "jobs, jobs, jobs" is a smoke screen for further business tax cuts.

How then are jobs provided by government? The best way to ensure jobs—and meaningful jobs—is to ensure the economic health of the consumer. If the economic health of the consumers is sound—that is, if they pay a reasonable rate of taxes, if their government provides them with good schools that give them skilled earning power, if their communities are well run—then they will have the income and the purchasing power to demand products from firms. Only then will the jobs be provided. And mind you, they will not be created. The jobs will be *derived* directly from the demand of consumers. Economic theory holds that the demand for labor is a demand derived from the consumer demand for the good itself. Any sensible government policy on employment should keep this fact in mind.

This also should help us solve the dilemma of what to do about providing jobs in the inner city. If federal government investment in inner-city neighborhoods is carried out in an intelligent well-planned fashion, then jobs will follow from the marketplace. Consider rehabilitating neighborhoods such as Watts by providing meaningful police services where the police are not the enemy of the people, by providing meaningful outreach workers, Head Start programs, school lunch programs, and the like. Couple this with good schools and a good system of public transportation. Moreover, bring in vocational training for the citizens. And then what will tend to happen? A stabilized neighborhood, or inner city—with a reduced fear of crime, and with training, hope, and medical services—will provide a more competent population willing to earn money and eventually willing to spend money. Businesses will not have to be enticed by tax gimmicks to open either manufacturing or retailing establishments in such areas. The market will take care of that.

But as the situation stands today, we cannot wave a magic wand over Watts or the south side of Chicago and "create" jobs. Nor will rapid economic growth create jobs in these neighborhoods. They must be stabilized and rehabilitated with the use of government funds before businesses move in. What businessperson in his or her right mind would locate a business today in Watts or in many similar urban neighborhoods?

The point is simple. America must invest in people, in neighborhoods, in education and training—in other words, in human capital. It will then produce people who are willing and able to earn a living, and their demand for products will follow. The 1980s witnessed scores of tax breaks costing the American taxpayer and the American education and training system over a trillion dollars. Such tax breaks to businesses have not worked. Most of the new jobs that have been provided (not created) are mainly low-skilled, low-paying, and low-fringe-benefit positions. It is time for the American government to invest in the individual. When we invest in the individual rather than in business, then we will eventually create a healthy consumer. And that healthy consumer will spark the consumer demand for products that will then provide meaningful jobs.

FINDING THE MONEY FOR MIDDLE-CLASS PROGRAMS

Any serious candidate proposing to help the middle class in 1992 and beyond must find the revenue with which to do it. There are three potential sources of income for new domestic policy programs. Two sources are to raise revenues through increased taxes on individuals and/or corporations. The third source is to cut other programs and use the funds for middle-class projects.

Increasing taxes primarily on individuals and then using the proceeds for middle-class programs is—as we have seen—all but impossible for numerous reasons, and would be self-defeating. I have shown in Chapters 6 and 9 that the personal income tax has for years made up approximately 45 percent of total federal revenues, while corporate income tax has fallen from well over 20 percent of such revenues to approximately 9 percent in the Reagan–Bush years. I have also shown that American corporations pay approximately one-third the taxes that Japanese corporations pay, while American individual taxpayers pay substantially more. There are some who propose an increased income tax on extremely high-income individuals. For example, Bill Clinton has campaigned on a middle-class tax cut made up by a tax on individuals with incomes in excess of $200,000. However, this would only deliver approximately $350 annually in additional after-tax income to each middle-class family. It is my contention that the high-income individuals are not directly the source of the problems of the middle class. And needless to say, increasing the personal income tax that provides the bulk of federal revenues—most of which comes from the middle class—will not be a solution aiding the middle class.

There remain the other two possible sources of revenues: increasing the corporate income tax, and reducing other programs—specifically, defense spending. Either one or some combination of the two would deliver the needed revenues to make a true difference in middle-class economic life in America. Unfortunately, defense spending and the corporate income tax are the two sacred cows of the American economy; they have enjoyed a very privileged status, indeed. Both are an excellent source of revenues for domestic programs, however, and both are needed. Defense spending is no longer required at its current high levels, because of the collapse of worldwide communism. And corporations have for too long been given tax breaks without showing benefits to the nation's economy and an increase in middle-class-paying jobs. However, U.S. corporations nonetheless continue to push (sucessfully) for lower and lower taxes. Their lobbies advocate complete elimination of the corporate income tax or, at least, elimination of the personal tax on dividends and the substitution of a national sales tax or value-added tax (VAT).

The potential for increased revenues via the corporate income tax is substantial. In 1972 at the start of the second term of the Nixon administration, the corporate income tax made up 15.5 percent of total federal revenues (with the personal income tax making up 45.5 percent). In 1991, the corporate income tax made up only 9.1 percent of federal revenues. Suppose we were to return the corporate income tax merely to the levels of 1972 under a very conservative Republican administration. The total corporate income taxes delivered to the federal government by raising such taxes merely to 1972 levels would be (in 1991) $163,410,000 or an increase in such tax revenues of $65 billion. This is a substantial amount of money, which could go a long way toward domestic programs aimed at aiding the middle and lower classes. American corporations will cry, "You can't do this. We can't compete in the world economy. We need additional funds for savings and investment." But as the 1980s have shown, the continued pattern of increased corporate tax breaks has not produced additional investment when viewed as a percentage of GNP. If anything, corporate tax cuts have actually produced less domestic investment in America. The "be nice to corporations" approach has not worked and it has robbed critical tax dollars from the federal, state, and local governments with which to carry out middle- and lower-class programs.

As for reduced defense spending, one can easily demonstrate the source of revenues to be achieved. The 1991 budget estimate for national defense is $307 billion. For 1992 it is estimated to be cut by approximately 5 percent to $291 billion—a savings of approximately $16 billion. However, a 20 percent cut in defense spending would yield approximately $60 billion. The 1993 Bush administration budget calls for defense spending to be reduced from 20.8 percent of total outlays in 1992 to 17.2 percent in 1997. Such protection of the defense-spending budget, along with maintaining low corporate income taxes, will prevent any meaningful programs from being developed to aid the economic status of middle-class America. In 1992 all of the presidential candidates proposing to improve the lot of the middle class have had to face the revenue problem: where are the funds going to come from? There are two obvious choices. Either the corporate income tax must be raised in a measurable way, or defense spending must be aggressively cut. Perhaps a combination of the two is possible; in any case, some action must be taken along these lines. Without this action, an improvement in the lot of the American middle class—no matter what programs are proposed—will not come to fruition.

WHITHER THE MIDDLE CLASS?
THE CAMPAIGN OF 1992

As of this writing in late August 1992, there has been much political debate about the economic status of the middle class in America. Let us examine the middle-class economic proposals of the major presidential contenders in the 1992 campaign.

Jerry Brown's Flat Tax

Reduced defense spending will probably provide a more meaningful source of funds for the improved lot of the middle class, in the long run, than either raising personal income taxes directly (which is impossible, in my view) or raising corporate income taxes, which would meet stiff, well-funded political opposition.

However, this is not to say that taxes on individuals could not be increased by changing the form of personal taxes or by introducing new taxes. The problem is that often new tax proposals are put forth as a panacea for the ills of society when in fact, the basic shortfall of revenues, stemming from low corporate tax revenues, is swept under the rug. Such is the case with the flat tax proposals on which former California governor Jerry Brown campaigned in the 1992 Democratic primaries.

Put simply, first, Brown would lower the federal income tax to 13 percent as a flat rate with few deductions. Corporate income, Social Security, and federal inheritance taxes would all be done away with. Second, he would also impose a value-added tax (VAT) of 13 percent with no exemptions—which, though an excise tax on business, would immediately impact consumers as a national sales tax.

The flat tax proposal has been rightly criticized for several reasons, but most significantly on revenue grounds. Since the employer and employee currently each contribute 7.65 percent of the employee's gross income for Social Security, the U.S. Treasury would lose a 15.3 percent payroll tax with no deductions, and replace it with a 13 percent payroll tax with major deductions such as mortgage interest and rent payments. Further, this does not even begin to account for the revenue loss of corporate, individual, and inheritance taxes.

Enter the VAT, which as I have pointed out in Chapter 5 is a favorite proposal of the conservatives, who hope to substitute it for the current corporate tax. It is indeed interesting that a VAT proposal—a regressive, conservative position—should come from a Democrat. Yet it does illustrate one of the central themes of my book: The Democrats have become largely indistinguishable from the Republicans. And the latter, I have shown, have been very successful in the economic enhancement of the upper classes, at the expense of the middle and lower classes. When middle-class voters are only offered such anti-middle-class solutions as basically no change in current policy by the Republican Bush administration, and a regressive tax structure by a leading Democrat, is it any wonder that an H. Ross Perot would rise to prominence?

The anti-middle-class stance of the Brown proposals is enhanced by the fact that they would not raise the required revenues. They might indeed be sold to the public as a panacea and would succeed in eliminating the corporate income tax and the inheritance tax. But once the revenue shortfalls became evident—as with the Reagan supply-side tax cuts—either taxes would have to be raised or government services cut.

As we saw in Chapter 6, the United States has reduced corporate taxes since 1945, while increasing personal and Social Security taxes. Thus, the odds are that, in reaction to the flat tax's revenue shortfall, income tax on the middle class would rise further, coupled with a new tax: the VAT. One could also easily predict lower Social Security benefit payments, and a further loss of middle-class income tax deductions. All taxes would now fall on labor, and none on capital.

However doomed the flat tax proposals of Jerry Brown in the 1992 campaign, calls for the VAT will certainly recur. Conservatives see it as a way to eliminate the corporate income tax completely. Its burden will fall mostly on the middle and lower classes. The VAT is truly an anti-middle-class measure, and it probably will not go away so long as capital continues to hold its present power over labor.

President George Bush's Continuing Agenda

The Bush administration has basically continued the economic policies of the Reagan administration. As indicated in Chapter 9, this has resulted in an additional national debt in Bush's four years equaling 78 percent of the debt Reagan created in eight years. Bush has maintained the high personal income tax but lowered the corporate tax. His current tax proposals hardly improve the lot of the middle class. In fact, the odds are that they would strongly depress it further. What are these proposals?

First, the president continues to call for a capital-gains tax cut. Studies have repeatedly shown that this would be of primary benefit to upper-income individuals and not to the middle class. While there may be some argument for a capital-gains tax cut to provide an incentive for business investment, such a proposal cannot be seriously entertained given the 1992 federal budget deficit. These record deficit levels, both in terms of dollars and as a percentage of GDP, make such a revenue loss unacceptable. Second, a Bush administration Treasury study has proposed the elimination of the so-called double taxation of corporate income. It calls for eliminating the tax on corporate dividends since they are not deductible from corporate revenues as expenses. Such a proposal would further diminish federal revenues. To those who claim that dividends are being doubly taxed, we have only to respond that state sales taxes paid by individuals are no longer deductible from the federal income tax. Therefore, individuals are suffering double taxation on their everyday purchases in most states of the union. Moreover, the 1990 tax reform bill mandates that deductions for families whose incomes are over $100,000 be reduced gradually. Many of these are in fact middle-income families; they too are suffering double taxation by losing deductions for state income and local property taxes.

A "mild" Bush middle-class proposal is to increase the personal exemption. However, his call for allowing Americans to specify that 10 percent of their income tax payments be used for deficit reduction will in reality force spending cuts, as these funds will no longer be available for existing programs. It is hard to see how such cuts will benefit the middle class since it is already suffering underfinanced middle-class services, because of an underfinanced government.

In the main, the rest of the Bush proposals, coupled with the above, don't even spell out a status quo for the middle class, but rather a continuation of the decline. These include no plans to reduce the current high immigration levels, strong advocacy of a U.S.–Mexican free-trade treaty, no serious energy policy, and only modestly increased spending on education. The president has at times advocated the elimination of PAC financing for campaigns, but has recently vetoed a congressional bill containing such a provision. In sum, Bush's report card on the middle class has to be marked with a letter grade of "D"—for "deteriorating."

H. Ross Perot's Challenge

On balance, the economic proposals of one-time candidate H. Ross Perot were stronger on middle-class issues than those of Democratic primary candidate Jerry Brown and incumbent President George Bush. A major contention of this book is that the decline of the middle class has come about largely as a result of the ascent of the upper class and the forces of capital. Thus, any meaningful proposals for tax fairness must necessarily be in the middle class's favor.

Perot has several proposals that are important in this context. For one thing, he proposed that the top federal income tax bracket be increased from 31 to 33 percent. Further, he would not allow mortgage interest to be deductible for amounts over $250,000. Although these would not be major revenue raisers, they are certainly a step toward addressing the issue of tax fairness.

Other middle-class issues addressed by Perot include a faster reduction in defense spending with cuts some 1.6 percent above those of the Bush administration. Since, presumably, these funds would be fair game for spending on middle-class programs, this is indeed a pro-middle-class position.

Certainly, a major benefit to the middle class would be derived from Perot's proposed tax credit for companies that engage in worker training. The dollar amount of such funds is substantial, at $61 billion over five years. This represents a level of worker retraining that could be significantly beneficial.

Also, consistent with my own criteria for improving the lot of the middle class (as listed earlier in the Epilogue), Perot would eliminate political action committees. PACs have been overly representative of major business interests, to the detriment of middle-class economic positions.

Another major positive in the Perot platform is his energy tax. Seemingly regressive, the proposed 10-cent-per-year hike in the gasoline tax to a maximum of 50 cents per gallon after five years would, of course, place an initial burden on the middle class. However, as I argued in Chapter 12, the lack of an energy policy hurt the middle class substantially in the late 1970s and 1980s. With America still held hostage to a cartel of foreign governments, her citizens are practically powerless when OPEC decides to increase oil prices. The revenues paid for the massive price increases in 1973 and 1979 went directly to foreign producers, refiners, and distributors of petroleum products. Large oil companies, be they foreign or domestic, reaped enormous profits. The middle class paid most of the tab, and the American government has had little to show for in the way of additional revenues from even our own producers' profits.

A reasonable tax on gasoline would accomplish several things. First, it would reduce energy usage, encourage conservation, and quite simply benefit the planet. Second, it would give the government additional revenues, now sorely needed for many middle-class programs. Third, the increased cost would probably be less than 50 cents a gallon to the consumer, since the reduced demand for petroleum products would depress the price of oil in world markets. The price of gasoline, it follows, would fall. In other words, OPEC and the other major oil producers would see the price that they receive per barrel of oil fall, and they would also share in the tax burden. Since European prices on gasoline—largely driven up by governmental excise taxes—are without exception greater than $3.00 a gallon, it would seem that the American consumer could afford to pay $1.60. If gasoline continues to be available here at its currently low tax levels, the odds are strong that more than once in the 1990s we will see substantial oil price hikes by OPEC. Such price hikes will increase revenues directly to the oil producers and not to the American government, which could sorely use these funds for middle-class and other programs.

Again in line with my criteria for rescuing the middle class is Perot's opposition to the U.S.–Mexican free trade treaty. As I've argued above and in Chapter 10, subjecting American workers who need a $10 or $12 an hour wage to raise a family—including paying the mortgage on a house, paying tax bills to their local government, and running an automobile—to the untrammeled competition of labor paid 50 cents to $1.00 an hour in Mexico is quite simply unfair. Though many who argue in favor of the treaty have spoken of its opening up new markets in Mexico, the plain fact remains that the purchasing power of Mexico is far below that of the United States. Perot recognized this problem, the potential job loss, and the economic disruptions that could flow from many displaced American workers' having to default on mortgages, some of which are government insured. Perot's position is a realistic assessment that the so-called fast-track negotiations for the U.S.–Mexican free trade treaty are much *too* fast.

One major negative in the Perot economic proposals is his pledge (a pledge also included in the Clinton campaign) to cut government programs and employment. As I have argued above (and in examining the "denigrative approach" in Chapter 5), a growing major problem in the United States is the lack of good government. This is largely due to an underfinanced government, resulting from losses of tax revenues—particularly corporate tax revenues. Perot apparently does not see this tie-in. Further, he does not see the need for corporate tax reform. As I have shown in Chapter 6, corporate taxes, which averaged some 27 percent of federal tax revenues in 1955, are estimated to drop to 8.3 percent of such revenues in 1992. Personal income taxes, however, which averaged 43.9 percent in 1952, will make up 44.5 percent of all federal revenues in 1992. While Perot made *some* gestures toward tax fairness, cutting government and continuing this extremely low level of corporate taxation would be irresponsible.

Perot's positives are also counterbalanced by another ominous negative for the middle class. He initially proposed that Social Security recipients be "means tested" before being eligible to receive their Social Security payments. Later he modified his stance, advocating instead taxation of 85 percent of Social Security payments for couples with incomes over $32,000 per year. There are several major problems with this proposal. For one thing, most Social Security recipients are middle-class individuals. In most parts of the United States, an income of $32,000—even for a retired couple—is a middle-class income. The danger in any such Social Security proposals is that in reality they play into the increasingly hectic "revenue search" on the part of the federal government, rather than facing the task of either cutting defense spending or increasing corporate taxes.

For evidence of this danger, one has only to look at the revenue and expenditures of the Social Security Fund. In fiscal year 1992, with a federal deficit of $366 billion, the Social Security Fund will show an operating surplus of $26.4 billion and interest income of $23.9 billion— for a total surplus of $50.2 billion! Five years from now in 1997, the Social Security budget will show a greater surplus—$115 billion—while the White House projects the overall federal deficit to be $209 billion. The point is clear. While expenditures of the Social Security Fund are large in terms of absolute dollar amounts, payments *into* the fund are even larger, and these come mostly from middle-income and lower-income Americans. However, in the absence of corporate tax increases and reduced defense spending, the fund is ripe for revenue searchers. Like VAT proposals, any proposals to raid the Social Security Fund or to tax such entitlements are clearly anti-middle-class positions.

On fairness grounds, Americans for years have been required to pay Social Security taxes according to a "fund" concept. Thus there is every right for Americans paying money into this system to be entitled to a return upon retirement; means has nothing to do with it. Since 50 percent of Social Security payments are now taxable, and the individuals' contributions are not tax deductable, the Perot plan would amount to double taxation on Social Security. H. Ross Perot, with a net worth of $3.2 billion, might indeed feel bad about receiving $1,000 per month from Social Security, but the average American—the lower-, middle-, or even slightly upper-class person—would probably have no such pangs of conscience.

All in all, the proposals of H. Ross Perot are far more middle-class oriented than those of President George Bush. They are a start in that direction, and they should be duly considered by the next president, whether Bush or Clinton, or Perot himself.

Bill Clinton's Campaign for "Change"

In a number of areas, the Democratic presidential nominee, Arkansas governor Bill Clinton, has offered middle-class proposals that outreach those of Ross Perot and clearly outreach those of George Bush. These include an even faster reduction in the defense budget than either Bush or Perot, and a higher level of investment in infrastructure and in new environmental technology for recycling, treating toxic waste, and cleaning the air and water. He has also proposed funding community investment projects: direct expenditures on infrastructure; small loans to low-income entrepreneurs; and urban enterprise zones for the stagnant inner cities. Other middle-class pluses are an expansion of the earned income tax credit to make up the difference between a family's earnings and the poverty level, and funding to improve K–12 education. Programs are also proposed for a national apprenticeship for non-college-bound students to be trained in a valuable skill, and a requirement that employers spend 1.5 percent of their payroll for continuing education in the training of all workers, not just executives.

One simple measure Clinton has proposed that would not cost money, but save money—and measurably improve middle-class status—is his call for an end to tax deductions for American companies that move operations overseas and to deductions for companies paying excessive executive salaries. While this would only yield approximately $3 billion in taxes, it would measurably reduce the frequent threats made by American corporations that they will leave the country if they do not get their way in labor contracts, tax concessions, and so on. As seen in Chapter 5, this threat of capital mobility is a major reason for middle-class decline. Elimination of such tax deductions would be a start in eliminating the litigation and other expense deductions claimed by many corporations when they routinely browbeat state and local governments into tax concessions through threats of moving their operations to another state. Such a simple proposal—low on the revenue productivity scale—is nonetheless high on the protecting of middle-class job security. Clinton's proposal to eliminate deductions for excessive executive salaries is not one that will directly aid the middle class, but certainly can be considered on its merits as a fairness issue in taxation.

A major plus for the middle class is Clinton's movement toward a universal health care system. His program would put caps on rising medical costs, hopefully extending the availability of quality affordable health care. It is a proposal that is long overdue.

There are two major negatives for the middle class in the Clinton position, however. First, he is generally in support of the U.S.–Mexican free trade treaty. While his position supposedly will guarantee elements of fairness in whatever form the treaty finally takes, it is in reality— for all the reasons offered in the above discussion of Perot—a very ill advised and distinctly anti-middle-class position. In fact, despite all the funds the Clinton campaign proposes to spend on worker retraining and education and on the promotion of American products in foreign markets, it will be hard pressed to create enough new jobs to make up for the loss of jobs sustained by American workers if the U.S.–Mexican free trade treaty is approved.

Second, another major negative is that, in spite of the fact that Clinton has moved substantially further on tax fairness issues than either Perot or Bush, little has been said about the currently low level of taxation on American corporations. Corporations in general are not paying their fair share of taxes to the U.S. government, nor to state or local governments (see Chapter 6).

As discussed above, there are two major sources of the revenues needed to accomplish middle-class programs, and all others pale in comparison. First, we can make even deeper cuts in defense spending, which Bill Clinton has courageously proposed. Second, we can raise corporate taxes. The American middle class is currently suffering high income taxes because it is largely assuming the tax burden for the corporations. The issue of corporate tax fairness is an essential element in any plan to improve the status of the middle class.

All in all, however, the Clinton economic proposals would benefit the American middle and lower classes vastly more than those of George Bush and moderately more than those of H. Ross Perot. Were the Clinton campaign or presidency to embrace a very cautious or "slow-track" approach to the United States free trade treaty with Mexico, it would clearly enhance American middle-class economic interests. It would also more clearly distinguish itself from the economic programs of President Bush. Further, were Clinton to advocate placing higher taxes on corporate income, with the ensuing funds being spent for middle-class programs or tax cuts, his would truly be a campaign for middle-class Americans.

MIDDLE-CLASS ISSUES THAT WILL NOT GO AWAY

The economic decline of the American middle class has been brought about by a complex set of causes and forces that have been operative since the early 1970s. These will continue to play out in various forms, long past the 1992 presidential election. If the middle class is to be elevated from its reduced economic status, the following issues must be addressed.

1. Communities and individuals must be protected from the rising power of capital and of corporate America. Such protections should include higher taxation of corporate profits, an end to the threats and the browbeating of state and local governments by major business interests (particularly in the property tax arena), and a ban on the hiring of nonunion workers by firms who have duly signed a union contract.

2. The American worker in the middle class must be protected more substantially from the untrammeled international competition of nations with low-wage labor. Trade should rightfully take place in substantial amounts between the United States and the other *developed* nations of the world, but the substitution of low-priced labor in less developed countries such as Mexico and China (where slave or prisoner labor is often an element in exportable products) should only be allowed in moderate amounts.

3. Social Security should be protected for all elderly Americans, regardless of income level. Social Security contributions have been required of workers at all income levels during their working lifetimes. The option to save that money in a bank, or invest in the stock market, bonds, real estate, or similar investments, was therefore closed to them. It's only fair that they be able to draw the money back without double taxation. The taxation or cessation of Social Security benefits for people who have actually "saved" this money in a government fund smacks of the communist expropriation of prior savings that has occurred in dictatorial regimes, including the former Soviet Union.

4. America needs good government and not necessarily less government. The continued drive to cut government employment as a means to save money is ill founded. Government employment should not be cut across the board, but rather in areas where programs are unnecessary or are being reduced, such as defense. Government programs should not be slashed in areas where we are trying to help the middle class, that is, in education, in infrastructure rebuilding, and in health care. So long as the United States has an expressly antigovernment mood, it will be anti-people and anti-middle class. In the end, the government *is* the people, and a weak understaffed government is a poor government. It is better to improve the government's quality and thus improve the lot of the people. And the majority of the people are still the middle class.

Index

Adams, Walter, 87–88, 146
American Economic Association, 82
Anderson, Martin, 155–56

baby boomers' entrance in labor
    force, 61–62
Barnet, Richard, 86
Bartley, Robert, 127
Beard, Charles, 9, 10
Berle, A. A. Jr., 12, 16
Bluestone, Barry, xvn1, 86, 162n9
Bradbury, Katherine, 44–45, 62,
    101, 103, 107, 166
Bouvier, Leon, 62
Brady, Ray, 71
Bretton Woods, collapse of, 56
British coal miners' strike and
    Margaret Thatcher, 67
Brock, James, 87–88, 146
Bush, George, 32, 159–61
Business Council, 11, 26–33

capital-enhanced individuals, theory
    of, 15–17

Carter, Jimmy, 30, 78
Clayton Act of 1914, 87
Clinton, Bill (Arkansas Governor),
    42, 52
consumer protection department,
    cabinet level, 200
corporate federal income tax shares,
    92–94, 111
corporate state and local tax shares,
    94–97, 111–12

Danziger, Sheldon, 46, 103
democracy, loss of: economic, 175;
    political, 175–76
Democratic party decline, 181–82
deregulation, 60
Duke, Paul Jr., 178n12
Duncan, Gregory, 42, 52

Economic Recovery Tax Act of
    1981, 32, 81
economics profession's loss of
    influence, 182–85
Edsall, Thomas, 80, 82

Eisenhower, Dwight D., 28, 32, 41
energy policy, need for, 202–3
energy shocks of 1973 and 1979,
    56–60, 105

factors of distribution, defined, 17
factors of production, 17
Farber, Henry, 60, 66, 67, 107
female labor-force participation,
    61–62
Flanagan, Robert J., 67, 107
Francis, David R., 54n11, 98, 178n6
Freeman, Richard, 107
Friedman, Benjamin, 150
Friedman, Milton, 80
Full Employment Act of 1946, 27
full employment as a faulty welfare
    measure, 196

Galbraith, John Kenneth, 3, 184
Gardiner, Robert, 62
Garn–St. Germain Act of 1982, 158
General Motors, 10; and Comstock,
    Michigan tax dispute, 86–87
Gilder, George, 81
Glass Steagal Act, 25
Goldberg, Fred (former IRS
    Commissioner), on middle-class
    tax audits, 173
Gottschalk, Peter, 46, 103
government employment slowdown
    and middle-class decline, 69–70
Greider, William, 129

Haberler, Gottfried, 178n10
Harrison, Bennett, xxn1, 86, 162n9
Haugen, Steven, 51
Healy, Nigel, 161n6
Heilbroner, Robert, 184
Hoover, Herbert, 165
Horrigan, Michael, 51

immigration, 62–66

Johnson, Lyndon, 28, 34
Jones, Al, 89n9

Kane, Mary, 52
Kennedy, John, 28
Keynes, John Maynard, 3, 18n15;
    and Roosevelt, 14–15
Kuttner, Robert, 50, 52, 82, 104, 184

labor-dependent individuals, theory
    of, 15–17, 22
labor unions' decline in America,
    179–81
Laffer, Arthur, 81, 127
Laffer curve, 127
Langewiesche, William, 64–66
LaRoe, Ross, 165
Lawrence, Robert Z., 61
Lekachman, Robert, 184
Levy, Frank, 103

marginal revenue productivity
    theory, 115–16
McGuire, Therese, 85
McQuaid, Kim, 18n10, 26, 30
Meade, Walter Russell, 162n9
"messiah," rise of, 176–77
middle class: definitions of, 41–44,
    52–53; reasons for decline
    summarized,   113–14
Modigliani, Franco, 116
Monetary Control Act of 1980, 158
Moon, Marilyn, 46, 103
Moore, Barrington Jr., 178n16
Moyers, Bill, 178n11
Muller, Ronald, 85

Nadar, Ralph, 86
New Deal: economic actions of,
    4–7; microeconomic accomplish-
    ments of, 22–26; theories of, 7–13
Niskanen, William, 124, 135,
    145–46, 157

Nixon, Richard, 13, 32–36, 78

personal income tax shares, 93
personal state and local tax shares,
    94–97, 111–12
Phillips, Kevin, 165, 183–84
Pilzer, Paul Zane, 162n26
Piore, Michael, 196
political action committees (PACs),
    79–80
Pool, Charles, 165
Professional Air Traffic Controllers
    (PATCO) strike and Ronald
    Reagan, 67
professional class decline, 167–69

Rauch, Basil, 10
Reagan, Ronald, 25–26, 32, 35, 73,
    91, 109, 123; and PATCO, 191
Reagan economic philosophy, 123–27
Reaganomics, assessment, 159–60
recessions: of 1973–75, 24; of
    1980–82, 24
Regan, Donald, 124
Reich, Robert, xiv, 184
Roberts, Paul Craig, 127, 153
Rockefeller, Nelson, 35
Rogers, Will, 187
Roosevelt, Franklin Delano, 4,
    12–13, 16–17, 21–26, 133, 179

Sawhill, Isabel, 46, 103
Schlesinger, Arthur M. Jr., 10, 13
Schor, Juliet, 162n9
service-sector growth and
    middle-class decline, 70–71
Sherman Antitrust Act of 1890, 87
Simmie, James, 71
Smolensky, Eugene, 46, 103
"spendthrift" American consumer,
    151–53
Steinberg, Bruce, 50, 52, 104
Stockman, David, 81, 125–27

Stolberg, Benjamin, 11
Strobel, Frederick, 72n20, 161n4

Taft–Hartley Act, 28
tax structure of U.S. compared
    internationally, 97–98
Thurow, Lester, 184
Truman, Harry, 28
Tugwell, Rexford, 8–9

underconsumption and the business
    cycle, 170
union membership decline in Lewis
    Harris survey, 66
U.S. economy in the 1980s: business
    savings and investment,
    142–44; business versus personal
    savings, 98–101, 112–13, 141–43;
    disinflation, 139–41; inflation
    comparisons, 148–50; international
    comparisons, 148–50; merger ac-
    tivity, 146; productivity and real
    hourly compensation, 140, 144,
    147; unemployment–real-wage
    link, 137–139

value-added tax (VAT), 83–84
Vinton, Warren Jay, 11
Vobejda, Barba, 53n1
Volker, Paul, 129

Walker, Charls, 83, 183
Wannisky, Jude, 81, 127
Wasylenko, Michael, 85
Weber, Susan, 62
Weidenbaum, Murray, 126, 153–55,
    158
Wills, Garry, analysis of changing
    political thinking in *Nixon
    Agonistes*, 34–37; 88n1, 127
Wilson, Charles, 10
Windt, Ted, 52
Wolfe, Tom, 172

About the Author

Frederick R. Strobel received his B.S. in accounting and M.B.A. from Northeastern University, and his M.A. and Ph.D. in economics from Clark University. In addition to Northeastern and Clark he also has taught at Holy Cross College, Georgia Institute of Technology, and in the winter of 1992, the Russian–American University in Moscow. He served for four years as senior business economist at the Federal Reserve Bank of Atlanta prior to joining Kalamazoo College in Michigan as the Stephen B. Monroe professor of money and banking. His credits include numerous articles in such publications as *Business Week*, *American Banker*, *The Chicago Tribune*, *The Detroit News*, *The Eastern Economic Journal*, *The Journal of Economic Issues*, and a number of various works published by the Federal Reserve Banks of Atlanta and Chicago. He makes his home in Kalamazoo.